IMPERIUM ROMANUM

Scythia

ARAL SEA

Sarmatia

CASPIAN SEA

BLACK SEA

SINOPE

hrace

Pontus

Anatolia

Armenia

Parthia

TROY
ASSOS
PERGAMUM
CHIOS

Asia Minor

HIERAPOLIS Cilicia
TARSUS
SOLI

APAMEA

Babylonia
SELEUCIA
BABYLON

Persia

LINDOS
Rhodes

KITION
CYPRUS

NEAN SEA

TYRE
JERUSALEM

PERSIAN GULF

ALEXANDRIA

Arabia

Egypt

RED SEA

N
NE
NW
W   E
SW   SE
S

LIVES OF THE STOICS

LIVES

❯ OF THE ❮

STOICS

The Art of Living from
Zeno to Marcus Aurelius

RYAN HOLIDAY
AND
STEPHEN HANSELMAN

Authors of *The Daily Stoic*

PORTFOLIO / PENGUIN

PORTFOLIO / PENGUIN
An imprint of Penguin Random House LLC
penguinrandomhouse.com

Most Portfolio books are available at a discount when purchased in quantity for sales
promotions or corporate use. Special editions, which include personalized covers, excerpts,
and corporate imprints, can be created when purchased in large quantities. For more
information, please call (212) 572-2232 or e-mail specialmarkets@penguinrandomhouse
.com. Your local bookstore can also assist with discounted bulk purchases using the Penguin
Random House corporate Business-to-Business program. For assistance in locating a
participating retailer, e-mail B2B@penguinrandomhouse.com.

Illustrations by Rebecca DeField. Used with permission.

LIBRARY OF CONGRESS CATALOGING-IN-PUBLICATION DATA
Names: Holiday, Ryan, author. | Hanselman, Stephen, author.
Title: Lives of the stoics : the art of living from Zeno to Marcus Aurelius /
Ryan Holiday and Stephen Hanselman, authors of The daily stoic.
Description: New York : Portfolio/Penguin, 2020. | Includes index.
Identifiers: LCCN 2020011797 (print) | LCCN 2020011798 (ebook) |
ISBN 9780525541875 (hardcover) | ISBN 9780525541882 (ebook)
Subjects: LCSH: Stoics.
Classification: LCC B528 .H66 2020 (print) |
LCC B528 (ebook) | DDC 188—dc23
LC record available at https://lccn.loc.gov/2020011797
LC ebook record available at https://lccn.loc.gov/2020011798

Printed in the United States of America
1   3   5   7   9   10   8   6   4   2

Book design by Daniel Lagin

CONTENTS

INTRODUCTION

The only reason to study philosophy is to become a better person.

Anything else, as Nietzsche said, is merely a "critique of words by means of other words."

No school of thought believed this—in the power of deeds over ideas—more than Stoicism, an ancient philosophy that dates to Greece in the third century BC.

It was Seneca, a Stoic philosopher of the Roman era, far removed from the academy, who would say quite bluntly that there was no other purpose to reading and study if not to live a happy life.

Yet this is not the role philosophy plays in the modern world. Today it's about what smart people say, what big words they use, what paradoxes and riddles they can baffle us with.

No wonder we dismiss it as impractical. It is!

This book will be about a different and far more accessible type of wisdom, the kind that comes from people like Seneca, a man who served his country at the highest levels, endured exile and loss, struggled with ambition and personal flaws, and ultimately died tragically and heroically trying to make good on his theories. Unlike the so-called "pen-

and-ink philosophers," as the type was derisively known even two thousand years ago, the Stoics were most concerned with how one *lived*. The choices you made, the causes you served, the principles you adhered to in the face of adversity. They cared about what you did, not what you said.

Their philosophy, the one that we need today more than ever, was a philosophy not of ephemeral ideas but of action. Its four virtues are simple and straightforward: Courage. Temperance. Justice. Wisdom.

It should not surprise us then that we can learn just as much from the Stoics' lived experiences (their works) as we can from their philosophical writings (their words). The wisdom offered by Cato the Younger's published works is scant—as a lifelong public servant, he was too busy in office and in battle to write down more than a few sentences. But the story of how he comported himself—with ironclad integrity and selflessness—amid the decline and fall of the Republic teaches more about philosophy than any essay. Along those lines, little survives to us about the theories of Diotimus, an early-first-century BC Stoic, but the legend of his literary fraud shows us how easily even righteous people can go astray. The same goes for the life of Seneca, whose eloquent letters and books survive to us at length, and yet must be contrasted with the compromises required by his job in Nero's administration.

And it's not just the lives of the Stoics that teach volumes but also their deaths—every Stoic was born to die, whether it was by assassination, suicide, or, most uniquely, of laughter, as was the case for Chrysippus. Cicero once said that *to philosophize is to learn how to die*. So the Stoics instruct us wisely not only in how to live, but in how to face the scariest part of life: the end. They teach us, by example, the art of going out well.

The Stoics profiled here are mostly men. This was the curse of the ancients: It was a man's world. Still, they were diverse. The philosophers in this book hailed from the far-flung corners of the known world, from Cyprus, Turkey, Egypt, Libya, Syria, and Iraq. And though their philosophy would take root in Athens, the Stoics saw the whole earth as their country. The founder of Stoicism, Zeno of Kition, a Phoenician, would famously refuse Athenian citizenship because it conflicted with his sincere belief in cosmopolitanism. Stoicism eventually made its way to Rome, where it loomed large in Roman life, directing the course of one of the biggest and most multicultural empires in history.

Across the first five hundred years of Stoic history, its members form an astonishing spectrum of stations in life, ranging from Marcus Aurelius, the all-powerful emperor, to Epictetus, a lowly slave who was crippled in captivity but whose writings and life were an example that inspired many, including Marcus. Some of their names you may already be familiar with, and others (Aristo, Diogenes of Babylon, Porcia, Antipater, Panaetius, Posidonius, Arius, and Musonius Rufus) likely not. But each is worth knowing about, whether they were merchants or generals, writers or athletes, parents or professors, daughters or diplomats.

Each has something important to teach us. Each walked the path of virtue in a way that we must learn from.

The word "stoic" in English means the unemotional endurance of pain. Yet even a cursory look at the stories of these (mostly) men proves an enormous difference between the expectations of that lowercase stoicism and the realities of the philosophy, uppercase Stoicism. Stoicism is a vibrant, expansive philosophy filled with people who loved, who grieved, who strove, who fought bravely at close range in the great battles of history, who raised children, who wrote important works, who stood tall, who believed, and who *lived*. In their own time, these philosophers resisted the stereotype of lowercase stoicism, that they were unfeeling beasts of burden who suffered through life and looked only inward.

The Stoics were never simply resigned to the current state of things, accepting without objection the injustices of the world. Rather, they formed the most ardent "Resistance" to the tyranny of Julius Caesar, Nero, and others in the ancient world, even influencing popular democratic reforms. Just as Stoicism was the "stern nurse of heroes during the first century of the Empire," to borrow historian Richard Gummere's expression, it would play a similar role for many centuries after, including inspiring the leaders of the American Revolution as well as patriots like Thomas Wentworth Higginson, who led a black regiment for the Union cause in the Civil War (and was a translator of Epictetus). The Stoics have always been people who bled and died for change, whether it was appreciated or successful or not.

"I know," Seneca wrote in 55 AD in a book on mercy written for the young emperor Nero, "that the Stoics have a bad reputation among the uninformed for being too callous and therefore unlikely to give good advice to kings and princes: they're blamed for asserting that the wise man does not feel pity and does not forgive. . . . In fact, no philosophical school is kinder and gentler, nor more loving of humankind and more attentive to the common good, to the degree that its very purpose is to be useful, bring assistance and consider the interests not only of itself as a school but of all people, individually and collectively."

The structure and style of these pages are inspired by Plutarch, one of the great biographers of history and, as it happens, both a chronicler and a critic of Stoicism.* We will be presenting to you overlapping but independent biographies of all of the major Stoic figures. The aim is to give you a rich resource you can turn to over and over again—as millions of readers of *The Daily Stoic* and *The Obstacle is the Way* have done for years now.

---

*His grandson, Sextus, would be a philosophy teacher of Marcus Aurelius.

We have presented each of the Stoics through the lens of a defining characteristic or role they played in the history of their philosophy. You'll meet Porcia the Stoic Iron Woman, Diogenes the Diplomat, Antipater the Ethicist, and Zeno the Prophet. We want to leave you not only with some facts about these figures, but with a fuller sense of their essence and the aspects of their lives that teach us the most about the art of living.

Our aim in these pages is not to achieve strict scholarly accuracy—which is impossible after so many centuries—but to elucidate the moral lessons that can be drawn from the lives of these complicated figures. For many of the early Stoics we turn to Diogenes Laërtius—the so-called "night watchman of the history of Greek philosophy." His classic work, *Lives of the Eminent Philosophers*, compiled in the third century AD, is at times contradictory, offering what is clearly a mix of collected facts and fictions. But it is also filled with beautiful insights and stories. Diogenes cared as much about the personal as the philosophical, and that's why his observations resonate in ways that other ancient scribblers and critics do not.

Because of the proximity of the later Stoics to political power in the Roman era, their names appear in the classic histories of Tacitus, Suetonius, and Dio Cassius, often with admiration where they lived up to their ideals (such as Tacitus's accounts of the deaths of Thrasea and Seneca), or with derision where they failed them (such as Dio Cassius's account of Seneca's questionably accumulated wealth). Pliny, Strabo, Athenaeus, Aulus Gellius, and others shed additional light on the lives and teachings of the Stoics. Later, Christian writers such as Justin Martyr, Clement, Origen, Tertullian, Eusebius, Jerome, and Saint Augustine, who all learned so much from many of the Stoics, also help to bring their lives into focus.

In other cases, we rely on the accounts of writers like Cicero or on the Stoics themselves for information. Cicero, who identified as a member of the skeptical Academy and kept busy climbing to the top of Roman politics, nevertheless dedicated a huge chunk of his life to a deep immersion in the history and doctrines of the Stoics who preceded him, and through his effort we have access to many sources long since lost. Seneca is another equally valuable source, as he not only crafted new writings on Stoicism but filled them with a wealth of quotations and anecdotes about his Stoic predecessors we'd otherwise not have. It is these intersections that are most interesting, even if we don't always have other confirming documentation, because they show us how the Stoics influenced each other, and how moral tales—like the one generations of Americans taught their children about George Washington and the cherry tree—can demonstrate important lessons regardless of veracity.

What the Stoics were after, what we remain interested in to this day, were lights to illuminate the path in life. They wanted to know, as we want to know, how to find tranquility, purpose, self-control, and happiness. This journey, whether it begins in ancient Greece or modern America, is timeless. It is essential. It is difficult. Which is why we ask, as the Stoics asked: Who can help me? What is right? Where is true north?

"You've wandered all over," Marcus Aurelius wrote to himself in *Meditations*, "and finally realized that you never found what you were after: how to live. Not in syllogisms, not in money, or fame, or self-indulgence. Nowhere."

If philosophy is anything, it's an answer to that question—how to live. It's what we have been looking for. "Would you really know what philosophy offers to humanity?" Seneca asks in his *Moral Letters*. "Philosophy offers counsel."

It will be your job, after you read these pages, to heed this counsel, and to struggle with what Seneca described as the most important job

The story of Stoicism begins, fittingly, in misfortune.

On a fateful day late in the fourth century BC, the Phoenician merchant Zeno set sail on the Mediterranean with a cargo full of Tyrian purple dye. Prized by the wealthy and by royalty who dressed themselves in clothes colored with it, the rare dye was painstakingly extracted by slaves from the blood of sea snails and dried in the sun until it was, as one ancient historian said, "worth its weight in silver." Zeno's family trade was in one of the most valuable goods in the ancient world, and as it is for many entrepreneurs, their business was on the line every day.

No one knows what caused the wreck. Was it a storm? Pirates? Human error? Does it matter? Zeno lost everything—ship and cargo—in a time before insurance and venture capital. It was an irreplaceable fortune. Yet the unlucky merchant would later rejoice in his loss, claiming, "I made a prosperous voyage when I suffered shipwreck." For it was the shipwreck that sent Zeno to Athens, on the path to creating what would become Stoic philosophy.

There are, like the origin stories of all prophets, some conflicting accounts of Zeno's early life, and his shipwreck is no exception. One account claims that Zeno was in Athens already when he learned of his cargo's demise and said, "Well done, Fortune, to drive me thus to philosophy!" Still others hold that he had already sold the cargo in Athens when he took up the pursuit of philosophy. It's also quite possible that he had been sent to the city by his parents to avoid the terrible war between Alexander the Great's successors that ravaged his homeland. In fact, some ancient sources report that he possessed an estate and maritime investments worth many millions at the time of his arrival in Athens. Yet another source records that Zeno arrived in 312 BC, at the age of twenty-two, the very year that his birthplace was razed and its king was killed by an invader.

Of all the possible origins for a philosophy of resiliency and self-discipline, as well as indifference to suffering and misfortune, an unexpected disaster rings the most true—whether or not it fully wiped out Zeno and his family financially. A shipwreck might just as easily have driven Zeno to an ordinary life as a land-based merchant, or, depriving him of his family, it could have driven him to drink or destitution. Instead, it was something he *used*—it was a call he decided to answer, spurring him to a new life and a new way of being.

This ability to adapt was a survival trait well suited to the times. The world of Zeno's boyhood was one of chaos. In 333 BC, the year after he was born in Kition, a Greek city on the island of Cyprus, Alexander the Great liberated the country from two centuries of Persian rule. From then on, Zeno's home was a valuable chess piece on this shifting board of broken empires, one that changed hands many times.

His father, Mnaeseas, was forced to literally navigate this chaos, as he traveled the seas in the family trade. There would have been blockades to run, bribes to pay, and enemy lines to avoid as he sailed from Cyprus to Sidon, Sidon to Tyre, Tyre to the Piraeus, the great port city outside Athens, and back again. Yet he seems to have been a loving father who made sure to bring home many books to his son, including those about Socrates.

It was likely never a question of whether Zeno would enter the family trade and follow his father to the sea, trading Phoenician dye, dreaming of adventure and riches. We're told he was tall and lean, and that his dark complexion and bearing earned him the epithet "an Egyptian Vine." In his later years, he would be described as thick-legged, flabby, and weak—attributes that caused him some awkwardness and social shyness as he aged and adjusted to life on land.

For all the uncertainty of the conditions of Zeno's arrival in Athens, we know what the city was like when he arrived. Athens was a bustling commercial center with twenty-one thousand citizens, half as many foreign nationals, and a staggeringly large slave population, which numbered in the hundreds of thousands. The entire city was turned toward business, ruled by literate elites whose success and education allowed them time to explore and debate ideas that we are still talking about today. It was fertile ground for the awakening that was to come for Zeno. In fact, we even know exactly where this awakening happened—a surprisingly modern place: a bookstore.

One day, Zeno found himself taking a break from the fray of business, browsing titles in a bookshop, looking for something to read, when he learned that a talk had been scheduled for that day. Taking his seat, he listened to the bookseller read a medley of works about Socrates, the philosopher who had been put to death in Athens a century before and whose ideas Zeno's father had introduced him to as a boy.

On one of his voyages before his shipwreck, perhaps inspired by a similar trek that Socrates had made, Zeno consulted an oracle about what he should do to live the best life. The oracle's response: "To live the best life you should have conversation with the dead." It must have struck him there in that bookstore, possibly the same one his father had shopped in years before, as he listened to the words of Socrates read aloud and brought to life, that he was doing precisely what the oracle had advised.

Because isn't that what books are? A way to gain wisdom from those no longer with us?

As the bookseller read from the second book of Xenophon's *Memorabilia*, Zeno was hearing Socrates's teachings as they had been conducted in those very streets just a few generations before. The passage that struck him most was "The Choice of Heracles," itself a story of a hero at a crossroads. In this myth, Heracles is forced to choose between two maidens, one representing virtue and the other vice—one a life of virtuous hard work, the other of laziness. "You must," Zeno would have heard the character Virtue say, "accustom your body to be the servant of your mind, and train it with toil and sweat." And then he heard Vice offer a very different choice. "Wait a minute!" she cries. "Don't you see what a long and hard road to the joy she describes? Come the easy way with me!"

Two roads diverge in the wood, or, rather, in a bookstore in Athens. The Stoic chooses the hard one.

Approaching the bookseller, Zeno asked the question that would change his life: "Where can I find a man like that?" That is: Where can I find my own Socrates? Where can I find someone to study under, as Xenophon had under that wise philosopher? *Who can help me with my choice?*

If Zeno's misfortune had been to suffer that terrible shipwreck, his luck was more than made right for having walked into that bookshop, and made doubly good when in that moment, Crates, a well-known Athenian philosopher, happened to be passing by. The bookseller simply extended his hand and pointed.

You could say it was fated. The Stoics of later years certainly would have. The hero had suffered a great loss, and because of it crossed a threshold to find his true teacher. At the same time, it was the *choice* that Zeno made—to go into the bookstore after his terrible loss, to sit and listen to the bookseller, and, most important, to not be content to leave the words he had heard there at that. No, he wanted more. He *demanded* more answers, demanded to be taught more, and it's from that impulse that Stoicism would be formed.

Crates of Thebes, like Zeno, was the son of a wealthy family and heir to a large fortune. From Diogenes Laërtius we learn that after Crates watched a performance of the *Tragedy of Telephus*—the story of King Telephus, son of Heracles, wounded by Achilles—he gave his money away and moved to Athens to study philosophy. There he became known as the "door-opener," Diogenes wrote, "the caller to whom all doors fly open" of those eager to learn from the great philosopher.

When the student is ready, the old Zen saying goes, the teacher appears. Crates was exactly what Zeno needed.

One of Crates's first lessons was intended to cure Zeno of his self-consciousness about his appearance. Sensing that his new pupil was too worried about his social status, Crates assigned him the task of carrying a heavy pot of lentil soup across town. Zeno tried to sneak the pot through town, taking back streets to avoid being seen doing such a humiliating task.* Tracking him down, Crates cracked the pot open with his staff, spilling the soup all over him. Zeno trembled with embarrassment and tried to flee. "Why run away, my little Phoenician?" Crates laughed. "Nothing terrible has befallen you."

Just because someone has anxieties or self-doubts or was taught the wrong things early in life doesn't mean they can't become something

---

*Lentils were then seen as a food eaten only by poor people. Undoubtedly, Crates was attempting to challenge the snobbish identity of Zeno's upper-class upbringing.

great, provided they have the courage (and the mentors) to help them change. With Crates's tough love, Zeno overcame his self-consciousness to become who he was called to be.

As Zeno left his trading days behind him, he chose a new way of living that balanced study and thought with the needs of a world driven by commerce, conquest, and technology. To Zeno, the purpose of philosophy, of virtue, was to find "a smooth flow of life," to get to a place where everything we do is in "harmonious accord with each man's guiding spirit and the will of the one who governs the universe." To the Greeks, each of us had a *daimon,* an inner genius or guiding purpose that is connected to the universal nature. Those who live by keeping the individual and universal natures in agreement are happy, Zeno said, and those who don't are not.

In an effort to reach this harmony, Zeno lived a simple life, not all that different from that of his rival Epicurus, who began his school just a few years before Zeno struck out on his own. His diet mostly consisted of bread and honey and the occasional glass of wine. He lived with roommates and rarely hired servants. Even when he was sick, he refused attempts to spoil him or change his meager diet. "He thought," a later Stoic would say, "that someone who once experiences gourmet cuisine would want it all the time, inasmuch as the pleasure associated with drinking and eating creates in us a desire for more food and drink."

As part of the simple life, Zeno kept to himself, preferring a close circle of friends to large social gatherings, and would later famously slip away from a party thrown by King Antigonus (and rebuff invitations to visit the king's court). He made his points quickly and shook his head at needless rhetorical flourishes. He was also clever and funny, making a habit to ask strangers for money, so as to deter others from asking *him* the same question. There is no indication that his early life of ease and wealth in any way spoiled him or inflated his baseline sense of comfort. If anything, losing it had proved to him that money was not to be prized and mattered very little. It became almost a proverb in Athens, when someone was describing a sober, frugal, and disciplined person, to say, "He is more temperate than Zeno the philosopher!"

After his studies with Crates and the Megarian philosopher Stilpo, Zeno began to teach as well—fittingly for a former merchant, in the *agora* itself. There, amid the shops where people bought and sold their wares, Zeno discussed with them the true value of things. In this literal marketplace of ideas, he offered to them something he believed vital— an engaged philosophy of life that could help people find peace in an often turbulent world. "Of the three kinds of life, the contemplative, the active, and the rational," Diogenes would write, the Stoics "declare that we should choose the latter, because a rational being is expressly produced by nature for contemplation and action."

Zeno learned to be a creative kind of instructor, pitching his wares, as it were, alongside so many other merchants. At a dinner with a man who was known for eating so much so quickly that there was little left for his guests, Zeno grabbed an entire tray of fish and made as if he was going to eat it all himself. Catching his host's surprised eye, he said, "What then, think you, must those who live with you suffer, if you can't endure my gluttony for a single day?"

When one young student attracted too many admirers, Zeno ordered him to shave his head to keep them away. When a different rich and handsome student from Rhodes begged Zeno for instruction—no doubt reminding him of himself at that age—he assigned him a seat on a dusty bench, knowing it would dirty the boy's clothes. Later, he sent him to rub shoulders with the city's beggars, much the way Crates had sent him through the city carrying soup. But unlike Zeno, who had endured his humiliations and learned from them, this student simply left. Zeno believed that conceitedness was the primary obstacle to learning, and in this instance he was proven correct.

Zeno would eventually move to what became known as the Stoa Poikilē, literally "painted porch." Erected in the fifth century BC (the ruins are still visible some twenty-five hundred years later), the painted porch was where Zeno and his disciples gathered for discussion. While his followers were briefly called Zenonians, it is the final credit to Zeno's humility and the universality of his teachings that the philosophical school he founded didn't ultimately carry his name. Instead, we know it today as *Stoicism*, an homage to its unique origins.

Is it not also fitting that the ancient Stoics chose a *porch* as their namesake and their home? It was not a bell tower or a stage, nor a windowless lecture hall. It was an inviting, accessible structure, a place for contemplation, reflection, and, most of all, friendship and discussion.

It was said that Zeno had little patience for idlers or big egos on his porch. He wanted his students to be attentive and aware. And those who came to him with an inflated sense of their own self-worth either quickly lost it or were sent away. But for those who were ready and willing, the porch was a place to learn and be taught.

Sadly, none of his works survive to us, not even his most important work, *Republic*, which masterfully rebutted the arguments of Plato's book of the same name. What we know of it comes via summaries from people who read it. From them, we learn that the early Stoics were remarkably utopian. Much of that would be discarded by later, more pragmatic Stoics, but still Zeno's early thinking set a tone that rings true today, namely that we "should consider all men to be of one community and one polity, and that we should have a common life and an order common to us all, even as a herd that feeds together and shares the pasturage of a common field."

Zeno also wrote well-known essays on education, on human nature, on duty, on emotions, on law, on the *logos,* and even one tantalizingly titled *Homeric Problems.* What could *Of the Whole World* be about? How wonderful would it be to read Zeno's *Recollections of Crates*? Alas, all we have of these writings is the occasional fragment or quote.

Even these scraps are enough to teach plenty. "The goal of life is to live in harmony with nature," we are told he wrote in *On Human Nature,* "which means to live according to virtue, because nature leads us to virtue." Zeno is also credited with originating the expression that man was given two ears and only one mouth for a reason. He supposedly said that there was nothing more unbecoming for a person than to put on airs, and that doing so was even less tolerable for the young. "Better to trip with the feet," he once said, "than with the tongue."

He was also the first to express the four virtues of Stoicism: courage, temperance, justice, and wisdom. He held these traits "to be inseparable but yet distinct and different from one another." We don't know where or when Zeno first put this "Big Four" in writing, but we can feel its impact—for they appear in the works and the decisions of nearly every Stoic that came after him.

Unlike many prophets, Zeno was respected and admired in his own time. There was no persecution. No angering of the authorities. He was given the keys to the city walls of Athens, awarded a golden crown and a bronze statue in his own lifetime.

Yet for all the adoration Athens heaped on him and the adoration he gave in return, Zeno knew that *home* mattered. After donating money for the restoration of some important baths in Athens, he specifically requested that "of Kition" be inscribed on the building next to his name. He may have been a citizen of the world, an expat who loved his adopted Athens where he would live for half a century, but he didn't want anyone to forget where he came from.

For all his clever quips, the only thing Zeno really cared about, what he tried to teach about, was truth. "Perception," he said, stretching out his fingers, "is a thing like this," meaning expansive and large. Closing his fingers together a bit, he would say, "Assent"—meaning to begin to form a conception about something—"is like this." Now closing his hand into a fist, he called that "comprehension." Finally, wrapping one hand around the other, he called this combination "knowledge." This full combination, he said, was possessed only by the wise.

In his studies with living teachers like Crates, and his conversations with the dead—that chance encounter with Socrates's teachings that the oracle had predicted—Zeno danced with wisdom. He explored it in the *agora* with his students; he had thought deeply about it on long walks and tested it in debates. His own journey toward wisdom was a long one, some fifty years from that shipwreck until his death. It was defined not by some single epiphany or discovery but instead by hard work. He *inched* his way there, through years of study and training, as we all must. "Well-being is realized by small steps," he would say, looking back, "but is truly no small thing."

As with many philosophers, accounts of Zeno's death stretch our credulity but teach a lesson nonetheless. At age seventy-two, leaving the porch one day, he tripped and quite painfully broke his finger. Sprawled on the ground, he seems to have decided the incident was a sign and that his number was up. Punching the ground, he quoted a line from Timotheus, a musician and poet from the century before him:

I come of my own accord; why then call me?

Then Zeno held his breath until he passed from this life.

CLEANTHES
THE APOSTLE

(Clee-AN-theez)

B. 330 BC

D. 230 BC

ORIGIN: ASSOS

C leanthes may have entered Athens under circumstances equally desperate as those of Zeno, the founder of the philosophy to which he would dedicate himself, but their early lives could not have been more different. While Zeno was born into wealth and conflict and was groomed for the life of a trader, Cleanthes came from a small city on the Aegean coast—what is today northwestern Turkey—with nothing but a burgeoning scholarly tradition thanks to Aristotle's decision to found his first school there less than twenty years before Cleanthes's birth.

Cleanthes experienced no sudden disaster, no reversal of fortune like the one that brought Zeno to philosophy. He instead arrived in Athens dead broke, with only his reputation as a boxer preceding him. What brought him there we cannot say for certain, but one suspects it was what has always brought poor but bright boys to the big city: opportunity.

With only a few days' wages in his pocket, Cleanthes began his journey to study and work, but mostly, at the beginning, it seems, to work.

To support himself, he toiled in a number of odd jobs, including as a water-carrier for the many gardens of the city that needed to be watered by hand. He was so commonly seen at night carrying large jugs of water that he earned the nickname "water-boy," or Phreantles. In Greek, it means "one who draws from the well," and also conveniently happens to be a pun on the name Cleanthes.

We don't know how or when he met Zeno, but it seems likely that it was through Crates, under whom Cleanthes also studied. What is interesting is that long after Cleanthes had made a name for himself as a budding philosopher, he kept at his manual labors, studying hard during the day and working harder at night.

When suspicious citizens of Athens thought the middle-aged Cleanthes looked in too fine a condition to be burning the candle at both ends, they hauled him before the court to give an account of how he made a living. Quite readily, he brought forth a gardener for whom he drew water and a woman whose grain he crushed to testify in his defense. Not only would the resourceful Cleanthes be acquitted, but he would also be awarded a hundred *drachmas*—many times what he had in his pocket on coming to Athens.

The large settlement was a message from the city elders: We could use more folks like this. Centuries later, we still don't have enough people like him.

There is an unmistakable earnestness in Cleanthes's work ethic. And why shouldn't there have been? Philosophy, like life, requires work. And suffers for pretensions.

This event also says something about the outsized role that philosophy had begun to play in Athens. Few care today how Harvard professors can afford the car they drive or what their personal life is like. But in Athens in the third century BC these radical thinkers were more than just public intellectuals. They were stars. Their movements were observed with rapt attention. Their quips passed from person to person the way we might pass along memes in our time.

Even with this fame, Cleanthes not o ontinued his
actively turned down large financial gifts fr patrons, incl
Macedonian king Antigonus II Gonatas, who hed to help h
to his studies.

To Cleanthes, labor and philosophy were not vals. They
sides of the same coin, pursuits that furthered and nabled ea
In John Steinbeck's *East of Eden*, Lee, a brilliant mind, well v
Stoic philosophy, is asked why he demeans himself with the lo
fession of being a servant. He retorts that being a servant is actu
perfect profession for a philosopher: It's quiet. It's easy. It lets hir
people. It gives him time to think. It is an opportunity, like any otl
for excellence and mastery.

In the elapsing centuries, this idea has fallen out of favor, bu
mains a good one. Anything you do well is noble, no matter how hu
And possibly even more admirable if you deliberately forgo status
pursuit of what you really love.

So it was for Cleanthes. A king once asked him why he still
water. His answer follows along the same lines:

> Is drawing water all I do? What? Do I not dig? What? Do I not
> water the garden? Or undertake any other labor for the love of
> philosophy?

Cleanthes loved work and philosophy the same. Indeed, that's
word the ancients used to describe his industriousness: *philoponia*
love of work. Literally, a marrow-deep dedication to honest labor.
just for money, of course, but also to improve himself.

Arius Didymus, writing at the time of Augustus, the first Rom
emperor, explains what Cleanthes believed was at stake in our effo
toward self-improvement: "All human beings have from nature init

g like a half-formed iambic verse according
s while half-complete, but worthy once com-

this hardworking man to philosophy in the first
Had he known about it from birth, growing up not
id one of his wealthy clients hand him a book? As
start to want something more out of life? Was it a
on the street or in the same bookstore as Zeno?
d a deeper meaning in life, to figure out how to live, can
at any time. Saint Paul received his awakening on the
us; where Cleanthes's came from we cannot say. What
whether we respond to the call in the first place—
sue that question until we find its answer, or at least until
wer.

e was prompted, we know that after Cleanthes met Zeno,
student and remained so for nineteen years. If he was
t until the man's death in 262 BC, that would mean Cle-
t begin his philosophical studies until he was nearly fifty
at's a long, hard life as a water-carrier, a long time to toil in
fore pursuing spiritual and mental greatness.

Cleanthes started when he was younger and "graduated"
en years, before moving on to another role inside the bur-
hool that Zeno was building. In any case, he likely got his
ilosophy at a later age than Zeno (who was only four years

egaard would later make the distinction between a genius and
e. The genius brings new light and work into the world. The
the prophet. The creator. The apostle comes next—a mere man
an) who communicates and spreads this message. Given Cle-

anthes's dedication to Zeno, it seems likely that the two were never contemporaries or peers, but always master and student. Zeno, the prophet. Cleanthes, the apostle of Stoicism.

Certainly, Cleanthes was the kind of student who warms a teacher's heart. The one who sits and listens. Who isn't afraid of asking "dumb" questions. Who puts in the work. Who never gets discouraged, even if they pick things up slower than other students.

Over the course of nearly twenty years, Cleanthes must have sat at the Stoa Poikilē for thousands of hours, not only listening to debates and discussions, but with a front-row seat as the early principles of Stoicism were established. He was there as Zeno divided the curriculum of Stoicism into three parts: physics, ethics, and logic. He would have heard Zeno riff on the choice Heracles made between living a life dedicated to pleasure or one according to virtue, the passage in Xenophon's *Memorabilia* that Zeno had first heard in the bookshop and had been so transformed by. Cleanthes, like a sponge, soaked in all of this, believing the whole while that he had much to learn, clearly, for no one with a large ego can remain a student for two decades.

Because of his age, and his methodical, workmanlike approach to things, Cleanthes was sometimes ridiculed as a slow learner and referred to by other students as "the donkey." When so insulted, he liked to reply that being likened to an ass didn't bother him because, like the pack animal, he was strong enough to carry the intellectual load Zeno saddled his students with. Zeno, on the other hand, picked a more generous analogy: Cleanthes was like a hard waxen tablet that, being difficult to write upon, nevertheless retains well what's recorded on it.

Slowly, Cleanthes began to make a name for himself—though it's impossible to know when he first began writing and publishing for himself.

Some of the first attention he got was not positive. The satirical poet Timon of Phlius parodied him as a simpleton poring over lines of written text like a general reviewing his soldiers:

Who is this, who like a ram ranges over the ranks of warriors? A masticator of words, the stone of Assos, a sluggish slab.

In fact, Assos was famed for its rock quarries and its hard white stone that was used to fashion ancient coffins. When a satirist takes aim at you and finds only your love of language to criticize, it probably says something positive about your character.

So it was for Cleanthes. Quiet. Sober. Hardworking. One with his philosophy. And his money.

Money earned with hard labor is not to be spent frivolously, and Cleanthes did not easily part with his wages or the security they provided. Plutarch marveled at Cleanthes's frugality and his desire to maintain his financial independence. *I continue to carry water,* he has Cleanthes say, *in order not to be a deserter of Zeno's instruction, nor from philosophy either.* It was said that Cleanthes was supporting his teacher, and that Zeno took a portion of his wages as Athenian law prescribed for masters and their slaves. And even with this payment, Zeno joked that Cleanthes was so disciplined that there was enough left over for him "to maintain a second Cleanthes, if he liked."

It is clear that Cleanthes abhorred debt and luxury, preferring the freedom of a humble life to the slavery of extravagance. The saying in Athens was that no one was more temperate than Zeno, but Cleanthes did more to establish the Stoic image of indifference to pain or discomfort as well as distaste for luxury. His cloak was once blown open by the cold wind to reveal not even a shirt underneath, a feat of asceticism that passersby spontaneously applauded. Cleanthes was said to be so frugal that he recorded Zeno's teachings on oyster shells and the blade bones of oxen to save on the cost of papyrus. The latter claim is doubtless an exaggeration, for Diogenes records that Cleanthes wrote fifty books, many in multiple volumes, and we know of another seven from other authors. Though one could speculate that he saved on buying papyrus until he could put it to the best of all possible uses—recording wisdom for the generations.

A young Spartan, raised in a culture of hard living and soldiering, once asked Cleanthes if pain was something to be avoided or whether, with the right training and under the right circumstances, it might be considered a *good*. This was music to Cleanthes's ear. Quoting the *Odyssey*, he responded:

> You are of good blood, dear child, because of the kind of words
> you say.

To Cleanthes, suffering—if in pursuit of virtue—was a good and not an evil. And we can see that in his life. He did not shirk from hardship or discomfort. In fact, he almost seems to have sought them out, to the admiration but also the bafflement of his fellow citizens. What mattered, of course, was where this strength of will was directed. To Cleanthes, we should be striving to become strong in those four virtues Zeno had talked about:

> Now this force and strength, when it is in things apparent and to
> be persisted in, is wisdom; when in things to be endured, it is
> fortitude; when about worthiness, it is justice; and when about
> choosing or refusing, it is temperance.

In short: Courage. Justice. Moderation. Wisdom.

Cleanthes, the middle-aged "water-boy," "the donkey," the slab of Assos rock, a virtual slave to his master Zeno, would slowly come to acquire a reputation as a kind of new Heracles among his fellow citizens. But as the poet Timon was only the first to illustrate, the fate of any exemplary figure is mockery by parasites, just as the great bull is beset by flies.

With this newfound respect came more criticism as well, particularly as the philosophy became more popular. Zeno and Cleanthes and their students were living differently, thinking differently, holding themselves to vastly different standards not just to the population of Athens but even to their fellow seekers of wisdom. While other schools debated behind closed walls or doors, the Stoics had taken philosophy to the streets. This gave them greater impact and almost made them targets.

Cleanthes dealt with his critics like he dealt with all adversity—as an opportunity to practice what he preached. Once while he sat in a theater, the playwright Sositheus attacked him from the stage by declaiming about those "driven by Cleanthes' folly like dumb herds." Cleanthes sat stone-faced, and the audience was so astounded by his calmness that they erupted in applause for his self-discipline and drove the playwright from the stage in response. When Sositheus apologized after the show, Cleanthes readily accepted, saying that greater figures than he had suffered worse abuse by poets and that it would be crazy for him to take offense at such a minor slight.

This came as no surprise to those who knew Cleanthes, as he was a man who held himself to the highest of standards. What some called cowardice or overcautiousness, he better defined as *conscientiousness*, and believed it was the reason he made so few mistakes. It was not uncommon to find him examining the slightest faults with himself or scolding himself out loud as he walked the streets of Athens. When another of

Zeno's students, Aristo of Chios (see "Aristo the Challenger"), heard him do this, he asked who he was talking to, and Cleanthes laughed, saying, "An old man with grey hair and no wits."

This kind of self-talk was a core practice for Stoics, and it wasn't always negative. Once Cleanthes overheard a solitary man talking to himself and kindly told him, "You aren't talking to a bad man." That is to say that one's self-talk must be strict, but never abusive. It appears his frugality and work ethic followed along similar lines. He was tough. He was firm. But he hardly relished self-punishment.

The Stoics are underrated for their wit. It was certainly a critical tool for Cleanthes, both in responding to criticism and in disarming those he needed to deliver it to. Speaking to a young man who could not seem to grasp his point, he asked, "Do you see?" Yes, of course, replied the youth. "Why, then," Cleanthes asked, "don't I see that you see?" When Cleanthes heard his fellow Stoics complaining about a prominent critic of Stoicism, Arcesilaus, who disagreed with their teachings on the role of duty (*kathekon*), Cleanthes jumped to his defense, saying that by all accounts Arcesilaus appeared to live a dutiful life. When Arcesilaus heard of Cleanthes's defense of him, he said, "I'm not easily won by flattery," to which Cleanthes quipped, "True, but my flattery consists in alleging that your theory is incompatible with your practice."

Throughout their history, Stoics used this kind of good humor as a way to avoid complaining or blaming and to shine a light on how our everyday actions should be aligned with our words. Plutarch, in his essay *How to Tell a Flatterer*, tells us that Arcesilaus paid back the respect Cleanthes showed him by banishing a student named Baton from his classroom for composing a put-down rhyme about Cleanthes, and not letting Baton back into his school until he had apologized to its subject. We can imagine that forgiveness came easy to Cleanthes and that he probably read the poem with some delight.

Like his master Zeno, Cleanthes was a man who preferred listening to talking and expected students to do the same. Whereas Zeno said that we were given two ears and one mouth for a reason, Cleanthes preferred to quote from *Electra:*

Silence, silence, light be thy step.

Indeed, his criticism of the Peripatetics (the followers of Aristotle) was that they were no different from a musical instrument like the lyre, producing beautiful sounds but never able to hear for themselves.

While Cleanthes was a listener and often slow and cautious in his thinking, that doesn't mean he wasn't a *communicator.* More and more, Zeno began to rely on his hardworking apostle, especially as the Stoics suffered attacks from rival schools. However difficult it may have been for this penny pincher to splurge on writing materials, we know that several of the prolific Cleanthes's fifty-some books articulated and explained the Stoic approach to all sorts of topics. Diogenes lists many of his books, but a few stand out:

On Time
On Zeno's Natural Philosophy (two volumes)
Interpretations of Heraclitus (four volumes)
On Sensation
On Marriage
On Gratitude
On Friendship
On the Thesis That Virtue Is the Same in a Man and a Woman
On Pleasure
On Personal Traits

It is a tragedy of history that all these books are lost.

From the titles alone, we can tell that this man was no stubborn donkey, that his interests were varied and active, and that he had a mind that loved to challenge itself. When he found a topic he liked, he attacked it with vigor, writing multiple volumes on physics, Heraclitus, impulse control, duty, and logic. Nothing interested Cleanthes more than ethics—this man who refused gifts from kings—so it should not surprise us that roughly half of his known works deal specifically with how we should act in the world.

Curiously, what survive directly from Cleanthes's writings are largely his poetical fragments.* They are filled with beautiful lines that give us glimpses into his unique combination of determination and acceptance. "Fate guides the man who's willing," he writes in one short fragment, "drags the unwilling."

In another, preserved more than three centuries later by Epictetus (and before that by Seneca):

Lead on God and Destiny,
To that Goal fixed for me long ago.
I will follow and not stumble; even if my will
Is weak I will soldier on.

Cleanthes loved the challenge of poetry, believing that the "fettering rules" of the medium allowed him to reach people in a deep and moving way. He offered the analogy of the way that a trumpet focuses our breath into a brilliant sound. This too would be a metaphorical in-

---

*One thirty-nine-line poem from Cleanthes survives in its entirety. You can see it at https://dailystoic.com/cleanthespoem/.

sight that remains central to Stoicism: that obstacles and limitations—if responded to properly—create opportunities for beauty and excellence.

In one short poem, he gives us a powerful definition of what "good" is and should look like:

If you ask what is the nature of the good, listen:
That which is regular, just, holy, pious,
Self-governing, useful, fair, fitting,
Grave, independent, always beneficial,
That feels no fear or grief, profitable, painless,
Helpful, pleasant, safe, friendly,
Held in esteem, agreeing with itself: honourable,
Humble, careful, meek, zealous,
Perennial, blameless, ever-during.

As beautiful as the language there is, what matters more is that these words were a perfect self-portrait of the man. They were words that he lived by . . . and that we must strive to as well.

It was said by Seneca that while we each have the power to live, none possess the power to live long. Cleanthes, the second head of the Stoic school, then must have been blessed by fortune. For he not only lived well, but lived to be exactly one hundred years old, likely the oldest of all the Stoics.

To the end he maintained his humor. When someone mocked him as an old man, he joked that he was ready to go at any time, but considering his good health and the fact that he could still write and read, he might as well wait it out. As he neared his centennial, however, his body began to fail him. At the advice of doctors who were attempting to treat his severely inflamed gums, Cleanthes fasted for two days.

The treatment worked, but that final act of deprivation had clearly shown him something—mostly that it was time to go. When the doctors told him he could resume his normal diet, he replied that he'd gone too far down the road to turn back. And so he died a few days later, fasting into the world beyond.

It would be Diogenes who wrote the best eulogy of the man:

I praise Cleanthes, but praise Hades more,
Who could not bear to see him grown so old.
So gave him rest among the dead,
Who'd drawn such a load of water while alive.

ARISTO THE CHALLENGER

(Ah-RIST-oh)

B. 306 BC

D. 240 BC

ORIGIN: CHIOS

I t can be easy, in retrospect, to see "the Stoics" as a unified voice. To view the early days of philosophy with Zeno and Cleanthes and their first students as salad days of teamwork and friendship. It was, after all, a school, with a straightforward claim: that virtue was the path to happiness and from virtue came a better flow of life.

We must live in harmony with nature, the Stoics had taught since the beginning, so where could the conflict possibly be?

The answer, of course, is *everywhere*. For instance, what exactly do "nature" and "virtue" entail? Whose definition is correct? Whose pre-scriptions are best? And who is the true heir to Zeno's legacy both as the founder of the Stoic school and as the promoter of virtue above all else?

History gives a clear answer—Cleanthes and then Chrysippus (whom you will meet in the next chapter)—though it was never so clean. Written history obscures the also-rans and the contrarians who did not carry the day. There is no such thing as a movement without disagree-ment, after all, and nothing that involves people does not also involve differing opinions. Stoicism is no exception.

There should be little surprise that knives flashed among the ancient philosophers, as they have and always will flash in academia. A school that venerates reason and grit, courage, and a keen sense of right and wrong above all things is naturally going to attract strong-minded students who don't like to concede or compromise. The rising popularity of the school only raised the stakes of this conflict.

No one embodied that more than Aristo, the contentious rival son who could have very nearly changed the entire course of Stoic philosophy.

While Cleanthes was Zeno's favored student and chosen successor in 262 BC, Aristo was an equally promising philosopher, who was far less passive and far less reserved than the hardworking water-carrier who would inherit Zeno's mantle. Aristo the Bald, of Chios, son of Miltiades, was nicknamed "the Siren" for the persuasive power of his eloquence that wooed audiences, and allegedly led them astray.

A better name would have been Aristo the Challenger, because he was constantly questioning, undermining, and disputing much of the early Stoic doctrine, including their practical rules for daily living.

Some three centuries after the debate with Aristo last ran hot, Seneca would rehearse in great detail the disagreement between Aristo and Cleanthes in a letter to his friend Lucilius, almost in the way a historian might lay out the differences between the American Founding Fathers on the separation of powers.

The dispute? It was over the role of precepts, or practical rules, to guide us in everyday decision making. Rules about how to act in a marriage or how to raise children or how masters ought to treat their slaves. Rules like what to do when your brother makes you angry, or how to respond to the insults of a friend, and what to do when an enemy is spreading lies about you.

These might seem like relatively harmless (and actually helpful) hints, but to Aristo they were crutches that sent people down the path to memorizing a script for the challenges of life. "Advice from old women," he called it. Aristo argued that the expertise of a javelin thrower in the Olympic Games comes from training and practice, not from studying the target or memorizing rules. You get better by practicing with your javelin. "One who has trained himself for life as a whole," he said, "does not need to be advised on specifics. He has been taught comprehensively, not how to live with his wife or his son but how to live well, and that includes how to live with members of his family."

An athlete isn't *thinking* on the court or the field; their movements come from the muscle memory of their training, guided by their intuition. It's from this flow state, rather than from conscious deliberation, that excellence—moral or physical—emerges.

So what Aristo wanted people to focus on were big, clear principles, things that could be internalized by the wise from their training. He wanted the Ten Commandments, not books about what order the sacraments go in. He wanted to give students a North Star to look to—virtue—and believed every caveat and explanation beyond that would lead to confusion.

Virtue was the sole good, Aristo was saying. Everything else was not worth caring about.

This put him at odds with Zeno, who believed there was plenty of gray area in between virtue and vice. Zeno had held that certain things in life, like wealth and health, which have no moral value per se, do tend to approximate the nature of truly good things. Having lots of money isn't virtuous, but certainly there are virtuous rich people—and like all other fates, financial success presents its own opportunities for moving toward virtue as well as temptations for turning to vice. Zeno's somewhat ingenious argument was to call these things—being healthy, being handsome, possessing an illustrious last name—"preferred indifferents." It's not morally better to be rich than poor, tall than short, but probably nicer to be the former than the latter.

Right?

To Zeno, it was not controversial to say that one could lean toward virtue and still desire wealth or fame or preeminence, for those were tools to employ in the building of an even more virtuous life. In this way, the early Stoics argued that we can and should pursue preferred indifferents as part of the good, virtuous life. It's a classic middle ground, practical realism to be expected from someone like Zeno who was a merchant before he was a philosopher, as well as precisely the kind of thing that his student Aristo could not stand.

Aristo strongly argued that the goal of life is to live in a state of indifference to *everything* that is in between virtue and vice, making absolutely no distinction between those tricky things that can be nice to have but dangerous in excess. He didn't want some complicated list of categories. He didn't want to rank things in order of their goodness or badness. He didn't want to consider gray areas or consult a rulebook. He wanted black and white. He wanted to rely on his training and his intuition to immediately *know* what to do in a given situation.

It's like the story of a general who, in taking over an important command, was given a thick book of the practices established by the generals who had preceded him. "Burn them," the general said. "Anytime a problem comes up, I'll make the decision at once—immediately."

It certainly sounds impressive: *I make no equivocation. There is only good and evil. There can be no in between. A wise man simply* knows!

It's also a pretty ridiculous belief for someone as smart as Aristo, as Cicero would point out. With the refusal to rank or prefer, "the whole of life would be thrown into chaos." Surely some things are better than others, surely there are general rules that can guide us as we live. We need precedents, because situations are complicated and fast-moving. Because sometimes the people who preceded us were actually wiser, and figured things out by painful experience.

Still, Aristo knew how to argue brilliantly. Disputing Zeno's notion that health was one of these preferred indifferents, he said that "if a healthy man had to serve a tyrant and be destroyed for this reason, while the sick had to be released from the service and, therewith, from destruction, the wise man would rather choose sickness." It's an argument that could be applied to so many of the preferred indifferents. Is it really better to be rich if your wealth makes you the target of those same tyrants? Aren't there situations where height has disadvantages?

We can easily imagine young students nodding their heads at these disruptive critiques and Zeno struggling to explain himself, despite his relatively commonsense position. (Is it really up for discussion that it's generally preferable *not* to be sick?) These questions are also seductively fun to discuss—for in disputing Zeno's gray area, Aristo was introducing endless amounts of gray himself. He was saying that circumstances *always* and *uniquely* alter the value of things.

Aristo's point in pressing on all these soft spots in the philosophy is that, like the general dispensing with precedents, a skilled pilot doesn't go to a ship's manual when he's hit by a wave—no, he uses his deep grounding in the principles of seamanship and his training and experience to make the right call. There is a part of this argument that appeals to the ego: We want to see ourselves as wise, with flawless intuition. We want to believe that all an athlete is doing is going with the flow. But the best athletes also stick to a strict game plan, they *submit* to a coach. What tattoos the walls of most locker rooms? Inspirational sayings, reminders, and codes of conduct. There are rules that each athlete is following, that they have to be aware of for their performance to count. It's less sexy to count those other factors, but it's the truth. It's this role—the coach—

that Zeno and Cleanthes had attempted to stake out for the philosophy teacher.

Sources tell us that Aristo added to this contrarian approach a rather forceful style, and that he spoke much more than he listened, flouting quite deliberately Zeno's dictum about the natural ratio between ears and mouths. Diogenes reports that Aristo would discourse at great length, and with little grace, overwhelming weaker minds in the process. At times, Zeno had no choice but to interrupt and cut him off. *You're a babbler,* he once shouted at him, *and I suspect your father was drunk when he sired you.*

It wasn't a Stoic response, but one every frustrated and exhausted teacher can sympathize with. Still, has yelling ever deterred a contrarian? It didn't stop Aristo's questioning or contradictions either. Indeed, his antipathy to Stoic orthodoxy extended into writing, where he attacked his fellow Stoics aggressively, even publishing an argumentative book on Zeno's doctrines and a book titled *Against Cleanthes.*

These written attacks were answered, Cicero tells us, by Chrysippus, who returned fire with a book against Aristo, and also had a direct personal confrontation with him about the dangers of his commitment to total indifference. "We might ask," Chrysippus pressed, "how could we live a life if it didn't matter to us whether we were well or sick, at ease or racked with pain, whether we could keep off cold or hunger or not."

Indeed, how could we? Life would be chaos.

Aristo was undeterred, answering with confidence and a smile, "You'll live, splendidly, wonderfully. You will act as seems right to you, you will never sorrow, never desire, never fear."

It's as tempting—and empty—a call as any Siren has ever made. And a little beyond the reach of most, however enticing it sounded. Yes, the true sage firmly grounded in the right principles will intuitively know just what to do in every situation and won't need a rulebook. But what about the rest of us?

Is that even possible—a world where everyone, as Aristo claimed, should simply do "whatever may enter one's head"? Is that a world anyone would want to live in?

We can imagine these great Stoics pulling their hair out in frustration. We can see their desperation in their tricks and lost tempers. *This guy is giving Stoicism a bad name. I thought we were on the same team here.* Aristo presents to us the conundrum that John the Baptist presents to Christians and that contrarian figures have always presented to incipient movements. Is this person a rival or a follower? A saint or a heretic? A friend or a foe? Aristo was all these things, then and now.

Shunned by the Stoics, while perhaps still considering himself in their camp, sharing many of the ideas of the Cynics, influenced by the skeptical Academy, locking horns with the Peripatetics, Aristo by his independence earned himself a spot outside the walls of Athens, away from the Stoa Poikilē, in a Cynic gymnasium called, appropriately, the *Cynosarges.* As with the Sirens for whom he was nicknamed, men flocked to him. Aristo taught there with other radicals like Antisthenes, one of the founders of the Cynics. Aristo earned fame and was soon regarded as the founder of his own school, as Diogenes tells us: the Aristonians, who were known for persuasiveness and decency.

But as a challenger he had his enemies. He would say that "when people build up their reputations little by little, other people attack from all sides," which is true, though one suspects his contrarianism and challenging demeanor had something to do with the antagonisms he faced more than anything else. Could a more conciliatory and respectful Aristo have accomplished more? Almost certainly, and it would be left to the later Stoics to prove that working within the system was a more effective way of changing minds than challenging everyone and everything.

Aristo taught that beyond following virtue or excellence, when dealing with indifferents, the wise man will simply do whatever pops into his head. He was the first Stoic we know to push the argument that the wise person is like an actor who willingly takes on the roles assigned by fate. We'll hear this very same argument from Epictetus centuries later, who himself would reprimand his students for asking for rule-books, as if they could run their whole life by a script. Aristo and Epicte-tus both felt that when it came to playing our role in life, the script was already written and we shouldn't be trying to come up with our own. We should work hard at living up to our given roles. But unlike Aristo, that didn't stop Epictetus from giving lots of good advice.

Diogenes also tells us that Aristo was fond of the idea that he, being a wise man and having true knowledge, would therefore not be misled by mere opinions. This so alarmed the Stoics that they sent Zeno's scribe to prove him wrong. The prank was simple: He had one twin deposit a sum with Aristo for safekeeping and then the other brother, pretending to be the one who had deposited the money, come and reclaim it. Aristo, who had so arrogantly claimed that he could make a wise decision in any circumstance, stupidly gave the money to the wrong brother.

It was a simple case where a rule—like checking for identification—was vastly superior than relying on your gut. When Aristo discovered that he had given the money to the wrong brother, he was dumbfounded and embarrassed that his wisdom had been so refuted.

Once again, was it Stoic for them to play such a trick? To do so with the intention of humiliating a fellow Stoic over such a minor difference of opinion? The rift was bigger than that, however.

Aristo's school, in a kind of deliberate hard fork that deviated from Zeno and Cleanthes, had abolished the topics of physics and logic. The former is beyond us and the latter not worthy of concern, was Aristo's position. Only ethics mattered, only virtue.

With little irony, this master of clever arguments held that the arguments of a logician were like a spider's web—clearly a product of expertise, but completely useless (though quite useful to spiders!).

Aristo's questions encouraged other heterodox and renegade thinkers, which must have created the sense inside third-century BC Athens that Stoicism was a school tearing itself apart.

It should humble and shame us a little to see, in retrospect, how insignificant these intensely—and violently—argued debates were. To the early Stoics who fought them, however, the distinctions of "preferred indifferents" were a matter of life and death. Power and influence and ego played a part in this. Only Cleanthes had kept his day job, which meant that these philosophical debates were *everything* to a Zeno or a Chrysippus or an Aristo. They were like cloistered monks arguing over how many angels could fit on the head of a pin.

It was the narcissism of wanting to be right—to be the one who settled the debate. With the future of the school up for grabs after Zeno and Cleanthes, who could afford to concede? Being remembered by history does very little for you after you're dead . . . but it's hard to be indifferent about your legacy.

All understandable, but hardly philosophical, let alone Stoic. It would have been far more impressive if these men could have prevented antagonisms from dominating their relationships with people with whom they mostly agreed. They should have focused on *their* work, *their* self-improvement.

As should we.

In any case, the passing of history sorted it all out. Aristo's work, and his questions, though quickly stamped out by the Stoics who came after him, would make a great impression on the young Marcus Aurelius. At age twenty-five, a generation or two after Seneca, Marcus found himself reading Aristo and was so shaken by the challenge of Aristo's questions that he couldn't sleep and had to step away from them. Instead of seeing a heretic, all he saw was someone urging him not to memorize but to practice and train until virtue became second nature. As he wrote to his rhetoric teacher, Fronto:

> Just now Aristo's writings are delighting and tormenting me at the same time. When they teach virtue, of course they delight me; but when they show how far my own character falls short of those models of virtue, your pupil blushes sadly often, and is angry with himself because, at twenty-five, he has absorbed in his heart nothing as yet of good opinion and pure reason. And so I pay the penalty, I am angry and sad, I envy other men, I fast. The prisoner at present of these cares, every day I put off the task of writing till the next.

In short, forget the precepts. Don't pore over rules. *Just do it.*

Marcus knew the history of his school quite well. And he knew that all dogmatic disputes come to naught in the end. It all disappears. It becomes dust or legend, or less than that. Quotations of quotations from books that were lost to time.

All that remains, Aristo would have said, is how we lived our lives, how close we came to virtue in the moments that mattered.

CHRYSIPPUS
THE FIGHTER

(Cry-SIP-us)

B. 279 BC
D. 206 BC

Origin: Soli

I t was early in life that Chrysippus, the man who would go on to be the third leader of the Stoic school, was introduced to running, a sport that would change his life. Running in the ancient world, as now, is not like other sports. Wrestling is a test of strength and strategy between two evenly matched fighters who are entangled body-to-body. The tossing of a ball or a javelin is a feat of technique and coordination, measured by distance.

But running, particularly endurance running, with its length predetermined and competitors separated by lanes, is as much a battle of one's mind and body *against themselves* as it is a competition against anyone or any*thing* else.

What is the connection between philosophy and running? There is none. But between Stoicism, a philosophy of endurance and inner strength—of transcending one's limits and of measuring oneself against a high internal standard—and distance running?

Here the overlap is profound, particularly for a young man like Chrysippus, born in the port city of Soli, Cilicia, competing for the first time in an Olympic distance race like the *dolichos*, a three-mile race for which there is no modern equivalent. The *dolichos* was not a three-mile loop like a modern cross-country course or even a track event like the 5,000 meters, but instead consisted of approximately twenty-four stadium lengths, done almost like wind sprints on a basketball court.

It's not hard to imagine this Stoic mind forming as its molder, Chrysippus, ran as hard as he could *back and forth, back and forth,* not only trying to beat the other racers, but trying to convince himself to keep going as he heaved for air and his brain told him to stop. As he jostled for the lead in a pack of runners, he was unconsciously developing the ethical framework that would direct his life and the future of the Stoic school.

"Runners in a race ought to compete and strive to win as hard as they can," Chrysippus would later say, "but by no means should they trip their competitors or give them a shove. So too in life; it is not wrong to seek after the things useful in life; but to do so while depriving someone else is not just."

But mostly it would have been on the long training runs by himself through the coastal plains of his homeland of Cilicia, in what is today southern Turkey, that Chrysippus prepared himself for the challenges that life had in store for him and for the feats of intellectual and physical endurance that philosophy would demand.

Indeed, like the other Stoics living in the chaos of a post-Alexandrian world, Chrysippus experienced little peace in his early years. Cilicia was a frequent target of deadly raids. His family had relocated to Soli from nearby Tarsus in response, only to experience a raid of a different kind, when the family's significant property was confiscated to swell the coffers of one of Alexander's former generals. As with Zeno, the loss of a fortune became a piece of good fortune, because it drove Chrysippus to philosophy.

It also drove him to Athens. With little in the way of options at home, and likely fearing what a tyrannical regime might come to take next, Chrysippus, like Cleanthes before him, left home in search of something better. For generations, Athens attracted not only the best and the brightest of the Hellenistic world in the pursuit of philosophy, but also the disenfranchised, the bankrupt, and the lost. Chrysippus, like Zeno and Cleanthes before him, was a mix of all of these.

We don't know exactly when he arrived in the shining city of learning and commerce, but by the time he did, the legacy of Zeno and Cleanthes had been firmly established. Their philosophy and fame had spread throughout the Greek world, and whether Zeno himself was still alive by the time the seventeen- or eighteen-year-old Chrysippus arrived in Athens, students would have felt their presence in every conversation, every book and idea they studied.

It is clear that Chrysippus—his name literally means "Golden Horse"—brought with him the energy and attitude of a fresh generation. This energy was packed in a tight package, for we also know that he was of slight stature, based on a statue of him erected by his nephew Aristocreon that once stood just northwest of the Athenian *agora* near the Stoa Poikilē. Diogenes reports that the statue was small enough to be completely obscured by a horse statue next to it, which led to one later philosopher to make the pun that Chrysippus was "horse-hidden."

The statue, which stood long enough for Plutarch to write about it in 100 AD, tells us about more than his size. Its inscription read: "Aristocreon dedicates this to his uncle Chrysippus, the cleaver to the Academy's knots."

What knots? The criticism that Cleanthes had received from poets and satirists was not because he was not well liked. Stoicism, with its growing popularity, had become a target for critics and skeptics. We can imagine the philosophical schools of Athens at this time—Epicureans,

Platonists, and Aristotelians—battling it out like religions, each one claiming to have access to the true god.

Cleanthes had been content to respond with quips or stone-faced silence. When Stoicism was merely the thoughts of Zeno or the teachings of Cleanthes, perhaps this was sufficient. But at some point the school would need to be defended. Its theories would need to be shored up, its doctrines defined and codified. Contradictions—even within the writings of those two first thinkers—would need to be clarified.

And there were also Aristo's challenges—and the challengers he encouraged—which loomed heavily over the future of Stoicism. There was Dionysius the Renegade, who began as a Stoic and joined a rival school that said life should be about pleasure. There was Herillus, who had studied under Zeno but believed, in opposition to Zeno, that knowledge was more important than virtue. There were all these voices, fighting, questioning, contradicting.

What was Stoicism to be? What kind of instruction and guidance would it offer? Who would its leaders be?

Thus fell to Chrysippus the thankless but essential role of fighting to protect this ascendant but still fledgling school. When Aristo published his book *Against Cleanthes*, it was Chrysippus who felt compelled to write a reply. When a philosopher attempted to debate Cleanthes on some minor logical point, it was Chrysippus who jumped in to shout at the man to stop distracting his teacher and that if he wanted to take up the quibble, Chrysippus was ready for it. Not just ready, but ready to win, it seems.

Let no one think that ideas that change the world do so on their own. They must, as a wise scientist would later say, be shoved down people's throats. Or at least defended and fought for.

Cicero would render a verdict years later of one such conflict, involving the lesser-known but controversial Stoic Herillus. He "has been dismissed for a long time," Cicero wrote. "No one has directly disputed him since Chrysippus."

The fighter had settled the matter and sent another early challenger to the dustbin of history.

Seneca would later speak of the importance of reading and studying other philosophies like a spy in the enemy camp. Indeed, we find that the early years of Chrysippus's career were spent not at the elbow of the living Stoic masters but at the side of Arcesilaus and Lacydes, both of whom headed Plato's Academy. It's not that he had conflicting loyalties; it's that he knew that if Stoicism was to survive, it would have to learn from its more established rivals.

We can picture Chrysippus—the competitor, the racer—wanting desperately to win. He studied the arguments of rival schools, even taking classes in the Platonists' school so that he could identify weak points in their arguments. He studied the weaknesses of his own arguments to see where Stoicism had to improve.

There is sometimes no better way to strengthen your defense than to learn your opponent's offense, and this is precisely what a good philosopher does. Today we called this "steel-manning"—you don't need to cheat by assuming the worst about the ideas you're arguing against. Instead, you can engage with them seriously and earnestly, winning by merit, not by mischaracterization. And as a fighter, Chrysippus enjoyed the challenge.

We are told that Chrysippus was so confident in his ability to break down competing arguments that he once told Cleanthes he only needed to know what a person's doctrines were and he would discover the proofs (or, presumably, the refutations) himself.

Where Cleanthes was slow and methodical, and always charitable in his assessment of rivals, Chrysippus was proud and loved intellectual combat. His competitiveness honed in the *stadia*, it turns out, had transferred right over to the world of philosophy. He would never stoop to cheap tricks—a line that, unfortunately, not all the later Stoics would toe—but he was in it to win.* Because to Chrysippus, philosophy, like life, was a battle. But should be fought fairly.

It's strange, in that way, to consider the personalities and respective athletic pursuits of teacher and student, master and protégé. Cleanthes, the boxer, was the plodding, enduring one, while Chrysippus, who had excelled in a more solitary sport, was the explosive, aggressive one.

He added to this temperament real skill too. There was a saying popular in his time that if the gods were to take up the science of argument, they would use Chrysippus as their model. Stoicism was lucky to have such a brilliant thinker in its camp. Where Aristo was using his mind to question the orthodoxy in a way that left very little standing, Chrysippus, in defining philosophy as "the cultivation of rightness of reason," was systematizing all of Stoic teaching.

It's a timeless but unsung role in the history of countless philosophies, businesses, and even countries: The founding generations have the courage and the brilliance to create something new. It is left to the generations that follow—usually younger, better prepared, and far more pragmatic—to clean up the messes and excesses and contradictions that those founders created in the process.

This job is hardly as glamorous as the founder's work, or as recognized. It's not even as rewarding as the work of the apostle, who gets to spread the gospel. But it is in many ways the most important. The history of Stoicism quietly recognizes this and, in fact, immortalizes the truth of it in the most famous line we have from antiquity about Chrysippus: "If there had been no Chrysippus, there would be no Stoa."

Or rather, we'd likely not be talking about it the same way today.

---

*We can imagine he did not approve of Zeno's trick on Aristo.

When Cleanthes died in 230 BC, the forty-nine-year-old Chrysippus became the third leader of the Stoics. His first order of business was not only to clarify the teachings of his predecessors but to popularize them. Whereas Zeno and Cleanthes taught only on the Stoa Poikilē, Chrysippus sought out the larger stage of the Odeon (a concert hall) as well. He was apparently also the first to deliver open-air lectures in the grove of the Lyceum, the school of Aristotle's followers, the Peripatetics. We can imagine that as a cleaver and a fighter, he enjoyed bringing his message directly into the enemy's camp.

Where Cleanthes had preferred the power of poetry and often used analogy, metaphor, and meter to convey his truths, Chrysippus insisted in both his teaching and his prose on the precision of logical argument and formal proof. Though renowned for his passion for and acumen in argumentation—it was rare for Chrysippus to simply leave a point to speak for itself, for instance, as he was fond of arguing repeatedly on the same topics—he was equally known for his innovations in the field of logic and for his prodigious literary output. He boasts a body of writings exceeding 705 volumes, some 300 of them tackling the topic of logic. From the titles Diogenes details, we can see nearly two dozen books on the infamous Liar Argument alone. (We won't believe anything a liar says is true, but can we believe a complete liar when he says that what he's saying is false? If he's always lying, it's not false, but true . . . but then he wouldn't always be lying.) One of his works, *Logical Questions*, was even discovered among the entombed papyri at Herculaneum (in a library of the rival Epicurean school that belonged to Philodemus). As Homer was to poetry, one ancient writer said, Chrysippus was to logic.

He also had a passion for literature and poetry in a way that belies his reputation for logic. In one essay, Chrysippus supposedly referenced so many lines from Euripides's tragic play *Medea* that people joked he had included every word of it. It was the "*Medea* of Chrysippus," they said. In fact, he was so fond of quoting other writers that their voices overshadowed his own in some of his writings. Critics of his books called these quotations "extraneous," but a better reading is that Chrysippus truly loved sharing and sampling from the great thinkers and playwrights of history, and he would become notorious as a result for his diligent citation of them and other sources whenever they supported his points.

But was he really that different from Cleanthes or the other Stoics? Chrysippus too was humble, a hard worker, and unimpressed with finery. It seems he kept a simple house with only a single servant. According to her, his intellectual marathon meant he kept a steady pace of writing at least five hundred lines per day. He declined invitations, even from kings, because it would have kept him from his work. He rarely left home unless it was to deliver a lecture.

He was reported to shy away from social gatherings and would often remain quiet at the ones he did attend. His servant reported that at drinking parties only his legs would get tipsy, presumably meaning they were the only sign he was enjoying himself. He was once criticized for not joining a throng that attended Aristo's lectures, to which he simply replied that "if I had cared about the mob, I would not have studied philosophy."

It's not that Chrysippus forsook all pleasures and all money; it's that he was suspicious of *wanting, lusting* for anything. A wise man can make use of whatever comes his way, he said, but is in want of nothing. "On the other hand," he said, "nothing is needed by the fool for he does not understand how to use anything but he is in want of everything."

There is no better definition of a Stoic: to have but not want, to enjoy without *needing*.

From this belief came freedom and independence for Chrysippus. He never sold his work or charged for his advice, out of a wish not to cheapen philosophy. He didn't borrow or lend money. Diogenes notes that not a single one of Chrysippus's books was dedicated to a king. Some contemporaries saw this as arrogant, but it was actually evidence of his self-sufficiency. Unlike Zeno and Cleanthes, who had taken money from kings, Chrysippus was not interested in patronage. If you accept money from a king, he said, then you must humor him.

He didn't take the money . . . which meant nobody could tell him what to do.

Chrysippus's independence of thought, his love of high-minded principles, and his intellectual zeal were clearly virtues, but like anything, they can be taken to excess. The smarter we are, the easier it is to fall in love with our own voice, and our own thoughts. The cost of this is not just pride, but the quality of our message. Epictetus, whose students struggled to make sense of Chrysippus's writings some three centuries later, would say, "When someone puts on airs about their ability to understand and interpret the works of Chrysippus, tell yourself that if Chrysippus hadn't written so obscurely they'd have nothing to brag about."

Since most of Chrysippus's legendary output is lost to us, except for about five hundred small excerpts gleaned from other writers, it's hard to know how bad a writer he really was. It says something that despite these purported faults, his insights have endured—and remained widespread even after his death.

As dedicated as he was to his work, Chrysippus was also a loving family man. He sent for his sister's sons, Aristocreon and Philocrates, and took them into his home and oversaw their education. He was particularly close to Aristocreon, to whom he dedicated at least three dozen of his books. Aristocreon returned the favor not only with the statue and inscription over his burial site, but also by writing a book commemorating him.

Yet even as a father figure, Chrysippus's competitive nature was evident. A mother once asked him who she ought to entrust her son's education to. He answered that there was obviously no better teacher than himself . . . because if there were, he'd be studying with them himself.

For all his disputes with Aristo (who believed that only ethics mattered), they were in more agreement than they thought. Plutarch tells us that everything Chrysippus wrote was for "no other purpose than the differentiation of good and bad things." Virtuous living was the end-all, be-all for them both.

As mentioned earlier, as a runner, Chrysippus had developed a philosophy of good sportsmanship. He knew that even as athletes are competing with each other, and want desperately to triumph over the rest, there remains an essential brotherhood between everyone participating—from the best to the worst. Tad Brennan, the classics scholar, calls it, appropriately, Chrysippus's "no-shoving model" of behavior, a model rooted in our relatedness to each other. It was not his only contribution in this regard. Another of Chrysippus's ethical breakthroughs was to develop the Stoic idea of *sympatheia*, built on Zeno's belief that we all belong to one common community, which encourages us to meditate on the interconnectedness of all persons and our shared citizenship in the cosmos.

If only the jostling rivalries of the early Stoics could have reflected this idea a little better. If they could have realized that there was no "winning" since they were already on the same team, since they already agreed on the big things, imagine how much trouble they would have spared themselves. What a better example they would have set for us today.

Ironically, it was only from the skeptical Platonist Carneades, who, as you will see, would become the greatest thorn in the side of the Stoics long after his death, that Chrysippus received one of his best compliments, for not only did Carneades believe that without Chrysippus there would be no Stoa, he also claimed that "had Chrysippus not existed, *I* would not have existed." The truest words are often spoken in jest.

While Chrysippus's work might endure eternally—and his face would even be minted on coins in his native land decades after his death—the man knew that he himself could not.

It was after a lecture one night at the Odeon that a bunch of his students invited Chrysippus out for a drink. After drinking some un-diluted sweet wine, he was struck by a dizzy spell and died five days later at the age of seventy-three.

If this is how Chrysippus truly died, it would confirm the image of him as a man who took himself and his work seriously, and in the end died after taking the rare evening off from writing and thinking. It may be true, and if so, rather uninteresting.

The other reports of Chrysippus's death are more tantalizing, for they add another dimension to the man and to the image of the sup-posedly joyless Stoic stereotype. In one recounting, Chrysippus was sit-ting on his porch when a lonely donkey wandered by and began to eat from his garden. Chrysippus found the sight inexplicably funny and began to laugh and laugh. "Give the ass some wine to wash down the figs," he cried out to the owner, and then laughed even harder, until he literally died.

And so, if true, it would be Stoicism's second founder who passed away not in the heat of debate or in a sprint of writing—which he had spent so much of his life doing—but from good humor and the enjoy-ment of a simple pleasure.

Not a bad way to go.

ZENO THE MAINTAINER

(ZEE-No)

B. Unknown

D. 190–180 BC?

Origin: Tarsus

At the turn of the second century BC, Stoicism was a hundred years old. Zeno's teachings had passed to Cleanthes and then Chrysippus. They had survived the provocations and doubters and attacks from other schools.

But now what? Who would be next?

One of the central beliefs of Stoicism is the idea that history is cyclical. That the same thing happens again and again and again. We are not so special, they would say. We are interchangeable pieces, role players in a play that has been playing since the beginning of time.

Very little makes this clearer than the fact that the next leader of Stoicism, starting a new century, would in a way be starting us back at the beginning. For he too was named Zeno.

After Chrysippus's successful consolidation of the school, the choice of who would take up the mantle after him was his to make. As Chrysippus's family had originated in Tarsus and he had risen to such acclaim, he must have drawn the interest of many fellow Tarsians. One of these Tarsian students, Dioscurides, about whom little is known except that Chrysippus had dedicated at least six works to him that spanned twenty-one volumes, was the presumptive heir. But Dioscurides was likely too old or infirm, or perhaps he died.

He did, however, have a son, and that son was Zeno of Tarsus. We hear from the Christian writer Eusebius that this second Zeno didn't put too much stock in the idea of reincarnation:

> It is held by the Stoic philosophers that the universal substance changes into fire, as into a seed, and coming back again, from this completes its organization, such as it was before. And this is the doctrine which was accepted by the first and oldest leaders of the sect, Zeno, and Cleanthes, and Chrysippus. For the Zeno who was the disciple and successor of Chrysippus in the School is said to have doubted about the conflagration of the universe.

Perhaps it was too on the nose for him. But we should not draw from this doubt or disagreement that he was another Aristo. He was, most likely, not a revolutionary or a disruptor. He was not even an ardent defender. But he may have been exactly what the philosophy needed at that time—a *maintainer*, an administrator, just agreeable enough to calm things down and then become established. Sometimes history—just like life—calls for a fighter, then sometimes it calls for someone with a steady bearing, an even hand, and a calming presence. Sometimes a moment calls for a star; sometimes it calls for something humbler.

Courage isn't always rushing into the fray. Sometimes it's endurance. Sometimes it's looking inward. We have each of these abilities inside us, the Stoics believed, and it was a matter of matching the right virtue to the right moment. We must do our duty, whatever it is.

So it went with the second Zeno. When he quibbled with doctrine, they were minor cavils. In some places he sided with Cleanthes, in others with Chrysippus. But he does not seem to have had an ego. He didn't thrive on conflict, though we can assume that when trouble knocked on his door it found him home (he published a book titled *Against Hierony-mus of Rhodes*). He did not need the limelight, he did not need to write hundreds of books or hold big lectures. Zeno of Tarsus was a man who was boring enough—and wrote just little enough—to smooth over the ripples and conflicts of his day and pass the philosophy on to the next generation.

The first Zeno carved out new territory. Chrysippus threw punches and blocked some too. The second Zeno didn't need to do any of that. Stoicism was well established, and had been now for decades. It was a boat that floated, a philosophy with thousands of practitioners spread across Greece. What the second Zeno needed to do was stabilize and carry on.

The timing could not have been more critical.

Greece was on the decline. Rome was on the rise. And Stoicism would be leaving the cradle of democracy and standing to meet the needs of a growing power. We don't know when Zeno of Tarsus died, but he was succeeded by Diogenes of Babylon, another student of Chrysippus, a transition that would be marked by the rise of Roman power.

It would also usher in the golden age of Stoicism, when the Republic and philosophy met and merged, and then the Republic would become *empire*.

That Zeno of Tarsus would be mostly forgotten—remembered like so many important people as, at best, a transitional figure? Well, that's something a Stoic can't care about. What mattered is that he did his job when it needed to be done.

DIOGENES
THE DIPLOMAT

(Die-AHHJ-en-eez)

B. 230 BC

D. 142 BC

ORIGIN: BABYLON

In 155 BC, Diogenes of Babylon, the fifth leader of the Stoa, was sent on a diplomatic mission from Athens to Rome. There, he, along with the heads of the other great philosophical schools of Greece, would give a series of lectures about their teachings. This might seem like a minor event, yet it would change not only Rome but the world.

As a form of diplomacy, the idea of sending a group of old philosophers of rival schools to a city notoriously hostile to philosophy seems crazy. Just a few years earlier, the Roman Senate had decreed an outright ban on philosophers, and here Athens went, sending precisely these undesirables to argue and perform on its behalf. It was not sending soldiers. Or professional diplomats. Or lawyers. Or even gifts and bribes. It was sending philosophers. Why?

Desperate times required desperate measures.

The years since Alexander the Great's death had been an endless series of raids and counterraids in Greece and Italy. The period was marked by the rise and fall of countless kings and principalities. Athens had been under garrison for much of the preceding century and a half as the Macedonian kings fought rivals to hold on to power. Into this breach,

Rome slowly gained power, growing from a small city on the Tiber to an international hegemon with colonial ambitions. Supervising a dispute between Athens and a neighbor, Roman-controlled magistrates had decided against Athens and handed down a massive five-hundred-talent fine. It was an amount the city could scarcely afford to pay, so Athens fought back with one of the few weapons it had: its philosophers.

The leader of neither city knew it, but Athens's decision to dispatch its towering intellectual minds to Rome to appeal the judgment was the first salvo in what would be a century-long battle for cultural supremacy. It was also Stoicism's first major step out of the classroom and into the halls of power.

So it came to be that Diogenes of Babylon, born the year of Cleanthes's death, was the first man the Athenians turned to in their hour of need. Hailing from the city of Seleucia in what today is metropolitan Baghdad, Diogenes had studied in Athens under Chrysippus. He was still a young man when Zeno of Tarsus inherited the mantle, and unlike his own more famous predecessor and namesake Diogenes the Cynic, this Diogenes was not some antisocial rebel. He was far too pragmatic for that.

This Diogenes, unlike the famous Diogenes the Cynic, some two centuries before, did not sleep in a barrel. He did not masturbate in public. As far as we know, he wore perfectly reasonable clothes and was capable of civil debate and discussion. He was not a challenger like Aristo or a fighter like Chrysippus. He wasn't notably funny or clever, but he was a brilliant thinker able to communicate his ideas credibly as a *normal functioning citizen of Athens*, a respectable leader and not just some clever mind. Diogenes was a rising star in philosophy, making important contributions in the early days of Stoic thinking, including in areas as diverse as linguistics, music, psychology, rhetoric, ethics, and political philosophy.

What brought Diogenes to Stoic philosophy? Plutarch tells us he was inspired by what he'd read of the founder Zeno's character. It's a reminder all these years later for everyone considering their legacy. It's not what you say that lives on after your time; it's not what you write or even what you build. It's the example that you set. It's the things that you live by.

We don't know when Zeno of Tarsus died and Diogenes succeeded him, but we know that Diogenes was an able teacher who attracted many students. One of them, an abrasive contrarian named Carneades, would go on to lead the skeptical Academy. He had been drawn to Diogenes through the study of the works of Chrysippus, and ended up serving as one of his counterparts in Athens's diplomatic embassy to Rome.

Again, it says something about the power of philosophy—or at least how far it has fallen since—that these thinkers would be entrusted with such an important mission. But in the ancient world, philosophers occupied a different place than do our professors today.

The diplomatic mission began in a series of public lectures, followed by addresses to the Senate itself, all intended to show off the extreme culture and learning of these heads of the great schools of Athens, thereby softening the sentiment surrounding Rome's indictment and sentence.

The mission did not begin well. Carneades spoke first, arguing eloquently on the theme of justice to a large, spellbound audience. But the next day he returned, and to a now larger crowd began to argue *against* justice just as vehemently as he had spoken hours before. One witness, Cato the Elder, one of Rome's most sober and politically influential citizens, was horrified. What kind of nonsense was this? Where men argue one point and then refute it? He demanded that the brash Carneades be sent home before he could corrupt any more of Rome's youth.

We don't know exactly what Diogenes said to the Senate, but it was clearly a calming message, one that presented Athens as a better ally than enemy. Each of the speakers had likely been assigned to talk about the power of justice, to show the Romans that the Greeks were deserving of it. Carneades, in his ego, had threatened to undermine this message, but thankfully Diogenes and Critolaus, the third speaker, were polished and persuasive enough. A gifted and strategic thinker, Diogenes might have argued that harsh punishments would have been less beneficial to Rome than mercy. We are told that the Romans were awed by Diogenes's "restraint and sobriety," which was likely heightened by the contrast of his showboating and tone-deaf compatriot.

This was part of Diogenes's brilliance, and what made him such a great *real-world* philosopher. Carneades had referred to Rome in one of his speeches as "a city of fools"—not exactly a prudent remark from a man sent to plead for leniency. Worse still, when the insult offended his hosts, he blamed Diogenes, as the Stoics since Zeno believed only a sage was fit to rule. Instead of being abrasive, Diogenes was diplomatic in every sense of the word. He did not rise to provocations or get sucked into conflict.

We can imagine him responding to Carneades's self-destructive antics and the jeers or criticism of his Roman audience with the same aplomb that he had once dealt with being spit on and heckled by a teenager in Rome. "I'm not angry," he had replied with a twinkle, "but I'm not sure whether I should be." So too did he shrug off everything that distracted from this mission from Athens. Too much was at stake.

For all the hoopla about these visiting ambassadors, their learning and eloquence, and the heated arguments over Carneades's contradictory lectures, this historic political mission was a resounding success. The fine was lowered from five hundred talents to one hundred, and the reputations of the three, especially Diogenes, were established firmly in the Roman mind. Cato the Elder, as appalled as he was by what he witnessed, would unknowingly be proof of the wisdom of the mission. His great-grandson, Cato the Younger (see our subsequent chapter on Rome's Iron Man), would not only not escape the "corruption" of philosophy, but would become one of the greatest students of Stoicism and win eternal glory through it.

But it was actually Greece and the Stoics themselves who gained the most from this exchange—or rather by the *process* through which the exchange occurred. Philosophy for the previous several centuries had been primarily a classroom exercise. It had been about the pursuit of the good life—about truth and meaning—but for the student first and foremost. Almost all the philosophical schools—Cynic, Platonist, Aristotelian, Epicurean, even Stoicism—had tuned out the real world of social and political life.

Instead, they argued among themselves about the definition of "virtue." What need did they have for anything else? Athens may have been the cradle of democracy, but it was like life in a small town. Insular. Sheltered. Self-absorbed. While Zeno had maintained that Stoics must participate in public life unless they are unable—and a few of his students had done so—most, to this point, did not.

The rise of Rome, the call to public service in a crisis like the one that Diogenes had answered, changed that. Cicero, "whose knowledge of previous political philosophy was extensive," Dirk Obbink writes in his "Diogenes of Babylon: The Stoic Sage in the City of Fools," "is aware of no Stoic writings concerned with practical political questions before Diogenes." Sure, there had been some lesser-known Stoics who had served as generals and even died in battle, and others who had advised and consulted with kings, but the teachers of the philosophy had remained largely out of the fray by dealing with politics only in the abstract.

Early Stoic political thought had structured itself largely in opposition to Plato's *Republic* and *Laws* beginning with Zeno's own quite radical *Republic*, and continuing in Chrysippus's work in *Against Plato* on *Justice* and in his *Exhortations*. These debates were little more than arguments about different types of utopia. Before Diogenes of Babylon, Stoic thinking on politics up to this point was best expressed by Chrysippus, who presumably got it from Zeno, *that only the sage is truly fit for political leadership.**

It's an appealing notion, but hardly one that scales. How possible would it be to find enough sages to fill the Senate, let alone to rule an empire? If Carneades is any indication, Athens seemed to have trouble finding enough wise men to fill its embassy to Rome! Exactly why Diogenes would suddenly prioritize a more practical political philosophy makes sense when you understand the shift of power that took place during his lifetime, when the tiny world of Greece fell under the enormous shadow of the rising monolith of Rome.

While it was ultimately successful in the mission to Rome, we know that Athens decided not to pay even the reduced fine that Rome's magistrates had levied. Was Rome going to go to war over it? Over a fine for Athens's raid on a neighboring city? After Athens had so masterfully distracted and dazzled the Romans with its philosophy and talk of justice? It was unlikely. And it seems Athens got away with its bluff.

For Diogenes, it must have been an illustrative political moment. While a few centuries later Marcus Aurelius would remind himself that life was not "Plato's Republic," Diogenes saw that it wasn't Zeno's Republic either. Instead, he saw a world filled with confused and flawed people. Diogenes had seen the truth of this firsthand—and perhaps first of all the Stoics—as he entered Rome and the diplomatic arena. What came from it was a crucial sense of pragmatism that the philosophy desperately needed.

Aristo had seemed to think that philosophy was for the wise man

---

* This is the idea Carneades used to insult the Romans with.

exclusively, for the individual's self-actualization. His Stoicism worked well in the classroom, and raised interesting debates, but it would not work in the *world*. Diogenes saw Stoicism differently. It was a way of thinking—as well as a set of rules—for serving the common good, for serving one's country.

No longer was it sufficient for the philosopher to fantasize about populating a small city exclusively with wise people in order to form the best social order. Nor were the quips and provocations of Diogenes the Cynic—the man who had treated Alexander the Great with disdain—sufficient either. Urgently, the skills of the philosopher—reason, virtue, logic, ethics—were needed outside the Stoa, even outside the *agora*. To solve problems. To build frameworks and write laws. To guide magistrates. To forge compromises. To persuade and to hold back the passions of the mob. To settle disputes between cities.

Diogenes of Babylon was certainly crafty and had a mind well suited to politics. Cicero tells us about a debate he had with his student Antipater over the ethics of selling a piece of land or a shipment of grain. His student believed that the seller was obligated to fully disclose all information—that several other shipments of grain were coming, likely to drive the price down, or that the asking price for the land was likely higher than its market value. It was only fair and just, he said. But Diogenes argued that nothing would ever sell if every fact was disclosed. How could a market work without the pursuit of mutual self-interest? Besides, sellers have multiple competing obligations, for instance to get the best return for their investors and to provide for their families. Cicero records his direct words of defense: "The seller should declare any defects in his wares, in so far as such a course is prescribed by the common law of the land; but for the rest, since he has goods to sell, he may try to sell them to the best possible advantage, provided he is guilty of no misrepresentation."

As for everything else, *Caveat emptor* was his argument. Buyer beware.

"Even if I am not telling you everything," Diogenes explained, "I am not concealing from you the nature of the gods, or the highest good; yet to know these things would benefit you more than to know that the cheap price of wheat was down." Is there no better encapsulation of the pragmatic philosophy of this diplomat who had gone to Rome to argue for a reduction of a fine his city likely never intended to pay? Who with one hand dazzled the Romans with speeches while picking their pocket with the other, perhaps telling himself he was preventing Rome from doing the same to Athens? There were competing interests at stake: Athens versus Rome, commercial versus colonial power, paying one's debts versus fighting an unjust sentence.

Somehow he made it work. He struck a balance of interests and competing loyalties—exactly the role of a diplomat and a political advisor.

He played a similar role settling, in practice, some of the more complicated debates in Stoicism. Aristo had tried to say that we should be indifferent to all things. Diogenes knew that was unrealistic as well. Wealth, he said, was "not merely conducive to achieving pleasure and good health, but essential." It wasn't *more* important than virtue, but it was important—if you could get it. And virtue, according to Cicero's paraphrasing of his views, "demands life-long steadiness, firmness of purpose and consistency."

Money made life easier. Virtue, on the other hand, was the work of our life.

Unfortunately, little to none of Diogenes's writing survives to us, a sad fact given that he was, at least according to the texts that have been discovered entombed in the town destroyed by the eruption of Mount Vesuvius, one of the most cited authors in the ancient world, even more than Plato and Aristotle.

As Diogenes's works are lost to us, so too was he lost to the world. We not only don't know how he died, we're not even sure when. Cicero says that by 150 BC—only a few years after his mission to Rome—Diogenes was dead. Lucian states that he lived to be eighty. But other sources have him living for another decade or until his student Antipater inherited the mantle.

In any case, this prince of philosophy did not live forever, but his legacy—Stoicism as a political force, and the character he exemplified—was only just beginning. In fact, it would soon conquer the world.

ANTIPATER
THE ETHICIST

(An-TIP-uh-ter)

B. UNKNOWN

D. 129 BC

ORIGIN: TARSUS

I f Diogenes was the pragmatic politician, then his student Antipater, the next leader of the Stoa, was the real-world ethicist. Practical, yes, but intent on establishing clear principles from which every action must descend.

We don't know when Antipater of Tarsus was born, or really any details of his early life in Tarsus, only that he succeeded Diogenes of Babylon as head of the Stoa after Diogenes's death sometime around 142 BC. What is obvious is that Antipater's worldview was very much defined by the influence of Diogenes and a reaction against his master's former student, the seductive but amorphous Carneades.

Where Carneades was content to argue contradictory positions on alternating days as he had in Rome, relishing the opportunity his new-found fame offered him to mislead his Athenian audiences at every turn, Antipater became a stickler for truth and honesty. Where Diogenes had brought politics to the realm of philosophy—or philosophy to the realm of real-world politics—Antipater sought to bring the practice of everyday ethics to all facets of life. And as ambitious as his aims were, he brought a humility back to Stoicism too.

No one would find Antipater fighting for the spotlight. He was too busy, as a good philosopher should be, *working.*

Even the medium through which he made his arguments was relatable and ordinary. Previous Stoics had held forth at the Stoa and in theaters, but Antipater opted out. Instead, he invited friends over for dinner to have long discussions about philosophy. Athenaeus tells us in his book called *The Learned Banqueters,* written just after the time of Marcus Aurelius, that Antipater was a wonderful storyteller at these gatherings, illustrating his points with powerful anecdotes. While supporters urged him to challenge Carneades's oratory with bombast of his own, and Carneades attempted to goad him into public debates, Antipater channeled his energy into this dinner-table diplomacy as well as into written works aimed not at triumph over current rivals but to help with the timeless trials of everyday life.

Antipater's quiet arguments were befitting a man with a fine-tuned sense for ethics, because on the page he could better articulate his views. In these small gatherings he could really connect with an individual, he could get specific, and he could be kind. It also allowed him to see up close the needs, the wants, and the struggles of real people—not just faces beneath the rostrum. Had he been born a couple thousand years later, one could easily imagine him having made a great advice columnist. If Diogenes had been the diplomat and statesman, then we might picture Antipater playing the political ground game, developing relationships, persuading in person, focusing on the individual and improving their lives.

For instance, Antipater was the first Stoic to make strong arguments for marriage and family life, something that had been strangely neglected by earlier philosophers. Zeno had left no natural heirs. Cleanthes had no room in his frugal existence for a wife. Chrysippus tried to be a single parent to his nephews when the need arose, yet he ultimately lived for his work. But Antipater broke new ground for Stoics by speaking passionately on the importance of choosing the right spouse and of raising good children. Try to learn from Socrates's mistakes, he warned the young men he taught, as he told them another story about Socrates's wife, who had a disagreeable reputation and a bad temper. If you don't choose whom to marry wisely, your wisdom—and your happiness—will surely be tested.

To Antipater, a successful city and a successful world could only be built around the keystone of family. Marriage, he said to his students, was "among the primary and most necessary of appropriate actions." Did Antipater get married himself? Was he a better husband and father than Socrates? The records are scant, but this sentence from his book on marriage sure makes it sound that way: "Moreover, it is the case that he who hasn't experienced a wedded wife and children has not tasted the truest and genuine goodwill."

Stoics can love and be loved? Absolutely. Not only can they, but they *should*, as Antipater clearly did.

Michel Foucault, the twentieth-century French philosopher and social theorist, would credit Antipater for pioneering a new concept of marriage, where two individuals blend their souls and become better for joining together, as opposed to some legal or economic transaction. As Foucault notes, the Stoic *oikos*, home, is perfected in marriage, creating a "conjugal unit" that can withstand the blows of fate and create a good life.

It was an important and humanizing shift for a philosophy that was previously focused on maintaining the boundaries of *indifference* when it came to everyday life. As Diogenes Laërtius wrote, the Stoics came to approve "also of honoring parents and brothers in the second place next after the gods. They further maintain that parental affection for children is natural to the good, but not to the bad." It was thinking that would not only transform Stoic philosophy and then Roman life but be absorbed into Christianity and the very world we live in today.

Is that not the job of an ethicist? And far more important than winning debates?

Many early Stoics had held that all sins and wrongs were equal. To be away from home, went the argument, is to be absent—whether you're one mile or a hundred miles distant. But of course this is ridiculous. Being outside is not the same as being gone, just as murder is not the same as a lie, even if both are far from ethical. Similarly, the lie of omission that Antipater's teacher Diogenes argued for in his *Caveat emptor,* or the misdirection of a diplomat trying to shore up peaceful relations, is not the same as a tyrant who manufactures a pretense for war at the cost of many lives.

Antipater was the major force in moving the Stoics in this commonsense direction. He loosened the absolutism of being either all virtuous or vicious. He stopped minimizing the "indifferent" things of daily life—whom we marry, how we dress, what we eat—and brought ethics to the forefront of the philosopher's concern, so that philosophy could be a productive life practice. A guide to living. An operating system.

And again, we can imagine him *modeling* these very things at his dinner parties and in his daily life, just as Zeno had first modeled the way of the sage to Cleanthes long before.

Not that Antipater was the first Stoic to care about practical ethics. Chrysippus had used his experience in sports to suggest a "no shoving" principle—the idea that we should never cheat or resort to foul play in order to win. Antipater not only took it further, but proposed that ethical behavior—or even sportsmanship—was itself a kind of craft that required real work and effort. For him, the human being in action is better understood as an archer. We train and practice. We draw back the arrow and aim it to the best of our abilities. But we know full well that despite our training and our aim, many factors outside our control will influence where the arrow hits the target—or if it falls short entirely.

This is what the pursuit of virtue is in real life. We study. We train until things become second nature. The moment arrives. We commit. We hold up what's right as our target. We take action. But much happens after that—much of it not remotely up to us. Which is why we know that our true worth doesn't reside in whether or not we get a bull's-eye.

In the real world, we miss. Sometimes by a lot. But we have to keep trying. The more we work on it the better we get. The more shots we take, the more times we'll hit the target and the more good we'll do.

It's hard to overstate, again, just what a big breakthrough this ethical model is. Just as Diogenes realized that philosophy would have to enter public life, Antipater made sure to bring it into private life too. He tried to help solve for the real situations that humans face: Who should we marry? Is work or family more important? What rules should govern a transaction between two people where the law is not clear? Should we be honest even if it will cost us money? How do we treat those less fortunate than us? Does society owe anything to the poor or the unlucky?

Monks would later argue about how many angels could fit on the head of a pin. Today, philosophers debate whether we're living in a computer simulation or how to respond to the so-called "trolley problem." But the truth is that you will never have to pull a lever to stop a trolley from running over one person or five. You have no way of knowing whether this life is real or an illusion. We do have, however, just as the citizens of Athens had, real concerns and decisions to make on a daily basis. And how these decisions are made in the *polis* affects the larger *cosmopolis*.

That Stoic idea of *oikeiosis*—that we share something and our interests are naturally connected to those of our fellow humans—was as pressing in the ancient world as it is today. Should we donate some of our income to charity? Is it fair for some people to have more money and resources than others? Doesn't everyone have the right to be happy and to live with dignity?

Let us go back to that debate between Diogenes and Antipater about selling grain or a piece of property. Diogenes is right that the demands of commerce make full transparency unrealistic. But Antipater's concern is nuanced and important—finding the balance between acting justly and crippling, self-defeating moralism. There is obviously a tension between self-interest and the interests of others, but are we not, at least in a way, all on the same team? As fellow citizens? As fellow believers in justice? The man who fails to disclose faulty sanitation in a home he is selling may be helping his family's fortune, but it might come at the direct expense of another family's health and well-being. How is that fair? And doesn't the suffering of that family come at the cost of the success of the city, of the state of which you are also a part?

What's bad for the hive is bad for the bee and vice versa, Marcus Aurelius would later say. It was an insight he drew straight from the life and work of Antipater.

Antipater believed that our affinity for the common good was our primary obligation. Cicero preserved his argument: "It is your duty to consider the interests of your fellow-men and to serve society; you were brought into the world under these conditions and have these inborn principles which you are in duty bound to obey and follow, that your interest shall be the interest of the community and conversely that the interest of the community shall be your interest." Diogenes—who had no problem stiffing the Romans—believed that the individual's good came first, arguing, as we saw, that knowing everything about your own moral state means more than protecting what others should find out on their own. Diogenes said, sure, stay within the bounds of what the law requires, but you don't have to do any more than that for others when it comes to business. Professor Malcolm Schofield explained Antipater's views in this way—that just as we shouldn't commit violence against one another, we shouldn't commit injustice against one another, and that we should treat others' interests as not alien from our own.

How far was Antipater willing to take these arguments? How radically did they affect his politics? It is interesting to see that one of Antipater's students and a prominent Roman teacher, Gaius Blossius, would become involved in the Gracchus affair, a controversial plot that sought to redistribute some of Rome's land to its poorest citizens. Tiberius Gracchus would be assassinated for this revolutionary idea, and Blossius, questioned by the Senate for being Gracchus's teacher and mentor, barely escaped with his life. Antipater was a very old man by this point, but one suspects he might have smiled at the thought of his student looking after the interests of the have-nots. Certainly he would have agreed that vast income inequality was an issue a Stoic in political service would need to address. Perhaps he even raised a toast to Blossius at one of his quiet dinner parties after hearing he survived the inquiry of the consuls. Even Diogenes, had he still been around, would have at least admired the political brilliance of Gracchus's populism.

What's interesting is that Antipater thought that most of these ethical questions were pretty straightforward. His formula for virtue was "in choosing continually and unswervingly the things which are according to nature, and rejecting those contrary to nature." It was about making sure that our self-interest didn't override the inner compass each of us is born with.

You gotta do the right thing. Whoever you are, whatever you're doing. Whether you're Panaetius, whom we'll meet next, on the world stage or the ordinary citizen in the privacy of your own home.

Antipater died in 129 BC. The fear is that a highly ethical person living in an unethical world or an ardent dogmatist, as Antipater was once described by Cicero, would become bitter in old age. It's hard to protect this kind of spirit, and over a long enough life, it often does break, and the wound it leaves quite easily becomes infected.

Not so with Antipater. Plutarch records that his last words were of gratitude. "They say," he writes, "that Antipater of Tarsus, when he was in like manner near his end and was enumerating the blessings of his life, did not forget to mention his prosperous voyage from home [in Cilicia] to Athens, just as though he thought that every gift of a benevolent Fortune called for great gratitude, and kept it to the last in his memory, which is the most secure storehouse of blessings for a man."

And so the generations marched forward, a little better armed in the pursuit of virtue than they were before Antipater walked the earth for his brief allotment of time.

PANAETIUS
THE CONNECTOR

(Pan-EYE-tee-us)

B. 185 BC
D. 109 BC

ORIGIN: RHODES

S toicism was born in Athens, but it came of age and to power in Rome, a story that mirrors the life of Panaetius of Rhodes, who would become one of Stoicism's great ambassadors to the world. We know that in 155 BC, Diogenes and his diplomatic mission had successfully introduced Stoicism to the growing empire, which would absorb the philosophy into its DNA. But it actually may have made a brief appearance thirteen years earlier when Crates of Mallus, a Stoic philosopher from Pergamum, was sent on his own mission to Rome to protect his country's interests in the Macedonian Wars.

Breaking his leg in a fall, Crates spent months recuperating and discoursing on philosophy with small audiences of Romans. As it happens, Panaetius's father was in Rome on his own diplomatic mission at the same time as Crates's convalescence. Did he attend his lectures? Bring home copies of the discourses that had spread through Rome in the form of poems and commentaries? Or did he bring his son with him on one trip and send him to see Crates directly?

Soon enough, the young Panaetius was a student of Crates back in

Pergamum, the future diplomat and connector having been introduced to philosophy through a fortuitous diplomatic connection.

We don't know much about Panaetius's studies under this early Stoic, but clearly they were designed to prepare him to follow in his father's footsteps and into the track that Diogenes and Antipater had set for future Stoics: serving the public good. In 155 BC, Panaetius was appointed to the position of sacrificial priest at Poseidon Hippios in Lindos. It would be the first of the many public roles he would serve in his active life.

Whatever he learned on this job, it became clear to Panaetius that he needed more formal education as well. He eventually made his way to Athens to study under Diogenes, now world-famous after his own diplomatic mission to Rome, and Diogenes's protégé, Antipater. It's as if Panaetius returned to get his PhD in philosophy—this second phase of education in Athens would last roughly five years—and then went right back to the real world once more, where he got to work applying what he'd learned at the highest levels of influence and power in Rome.

Learn. Apply. Learn. Apply. Learn. Apply. This is the Stoic way.

During his time in Athens with Diogenes, Panaetius met a fellow student of Diogenes named Gaius Laelius, with whom he would continue to study. Through Laelius and then later, on a naval contingent, Panaetius met and served with Scipio Aemilianus, one of Rome's great generals, an adopted son of one of its most powerful families and a lover of Greek thought and literature.

Back in Rome, these three men then formed a kind of philosophical club—known to historians today as the Scipionic Circle—that would meet in Scipio's enormous houses to discuss and debate the Stoic philosophy they all pursued. Scipio footed the bill, Panaetius provided the intellectual nourishment. Many others joined them in these discussions and were shaped by them. Not unlike the way that the expat scene in

France after the First World War nurtured the careers of Hemingway, Stein, and Fitzgerald, or how a company like PayPal would give the world Peter Thiel and Reid Hoffman and Elon Musk, the Scipionic Circle became a kind of breeding ground for influential Stoics and a generation of leaders. Publius Rutilius Rufus, who defied Rome's culture of corruption and who you will meet in the next chapter, was often present. The historian Polybius was too.

It was a form of influence and access that neither Panaetius's father, nor his teachers, Crates and Diogenes, could have imagined possible. Scipio, with time and with Rome's growth, became the most powerful man in the Greek world. The kings of Greece now answered to him and to Rome as vassals, while Panaetius served as a kind of translator and advisor and confidant.

Some historians today debate just how often the Scipionic Circle met and how direct its influence was. But there was little of this doubt about its significance in the ancient world. Velleius Paterculus records in his *History of Rome* that Scipio "kept constantly with him, at home and in the field, two men of eminent genius, Polybius and Panaetius." He describes Scipio as being deeply devoted to the art of war and peace, saying that he was constantly "engaged in the pursuit of arms or his studies, he was either training his body by exposing it to dangers or his mind by learning."

Cicero, who was fascinated by stories of Panaetius, sprinkled his dialogues with scenes and anecdotes from these meetings. Later writers like Plutarch not only had no doubts about the Circle, but tell us of the kind of quiet political influence Panaetius managed to exert. In *Moralia: Precepts of Statecraft*, Plutarch writes that "it is a fine thing also, when we gain advantage from the friendship of great men, to turn it to the welfare of our community, as Polybius and Panaetius, through Scipio's goodwill towards them, conferred great benefits upon their native States."

This is what Panaetius had trained for—directing policy and shaping powerful decisions that affected millions of people.

Where Zeno was a founding genius and Chrysippus was the cleaver to the Academy's knots, while Aristo favored absolutism over pragmatic direction and Antipater moved in the opposite direction of trying to lay out rules for everyday life, Panaetius was a kind of weaver—tying Stoic and Roman ethical perspectives together, introducing philosophical consideration to Rome's elite with one hand, subtly directing them to protect and service the interests of his distant homeland with the other. Effectively, the Stoa had a supremely well-placed and practical ambassador in Rome.

The timing could not have been more essential.

It's not hard to detect a provincialism in the early Stoics. Zeno insisted on his hometown being inscribed next to his name on a building he had paid to restore. Cleanthes's frugal lifestyle had little room for travel, let alone concern for international affairs. Even Diogenes had quickly returned to Athens after his trip to Rome. These were not attitudes well fitted to a global empire.

Panaetius was, unlike his predecessors, a born globalist. His life began in Rhodes but expanded when he studied abroad in both Pergamum and Rome. He traveled across most of the Mediterranean. He fell in with Romans fascinated by the East. Panaetius was able to manage and integrate all these diverse and conflicting ties in a surprisingly modern way. Marcus Aurelius would, in *Meditations*, describe himself as a "citizen of the world," and in so doing was following the new course for the philosophy that Panaetius had first set.

Yet even with this international mindset, Panaetius never lost his connection to where he came from. When Athens offered him citizenship, he politely declined, saying that "one city was enough for a sensible man."

All were aware that Panaetius had a moderating effect on the fre-
netic yet practical Scipio, balancing out his ambition with mildness and
principles. But he was clearly no wet blanket, or he would not have been
able to cultivate such a vivacious and diverse social circle. Scipio got
enough out of Panaetius's company that in the spring of 140 BC he asked
him to accompany him on an ambitious embassy to the East. This mission was recorded in many sources and logged stops across Egypt, Cyprus, Syria, Rhodes, and various places in Greece and Asia Minor.
Plutarch writes that Scipio summoned Panaetius directly, and another
source explains that the Senate sent them to "to view the violence and
lawlessness of men." Today we might call this a "fact-finding mission."

We like to think that the world has changed a great deal since Panaetius's time, but the truth is that senates are still sending men to the
same regions to make the same kinds of observations that this soldier
and philosopher were dispatched to make more than twenty-one hundred years ago—just as we are still struggling to strike the right balance,
as Panaetius did, between nationalism and globalism, the concerns of
the many and the concerns of ourselves.

In the way that Zeno followed in his father's trade, so too did Panaetius, the son of a diplomat and the student of two philosopher diplomats, continue the family business—and continue Stoicism's transition
from the Stoa to the levers of power, from the provincialism of the Athenian *agora* to the world stage. In a time when many still believed that the
gods played an active role in human affairs and when sacrifices and ritual
were designed to placate them, Panaetius was a freethinker. He rejected
the silly theories of soothsayers and astrologers, and it was likely on his
advice around this time that Scipio banned them from his regiments.

Plutarch tells a colorful story from this nearly two-year fact-finding
mission in his *Moralia: Roman Sayings* that, when Scipio arrived in Alexandria, traveling in a retinue which included Panaetius and five servants,

the people were in such a frenzy that they yelled for Scipio to take his toga off his head so they could get a good look, and when he did the masses burst into applause. He writes that the Egyptian king Ptolemy "the Fat" VIII "could hardly keep up with them in walking because of his inactive life and his pampering of his body, and Scipio whispered softly to Panaetius, 'Already the Alexandrians have received some benefit from our visit. For it is owing to us that they have seen their king walk.'"

Fat and lazy heads of state are another recurring character of history.

In 138 BC, Panaetius and Scipio returned to Rome. Panaetius was now forty-seven years old and had gained a wide life experience. His schooling long finished in Pergamum and Athens, an interim public career in Rhodes behind him, including time spent in the navy, he now found himself ensconced in the inner workings of Rome. It was again timeless and modern that he would, as so many men do at that age, begin to turn some of his attention to writing.

His most important book, *Concerning Appropriate Actions*, which is an extended meditation on ethical behavior in public life, was not merely theoretical. As he was finishing it, Scipio, who still depended on Panaetius for advice and guidance, began prosecuting a series of major corruption cases against Roman politicians. One against Lucius Cotta was an extortion case. Another involved the Gracchus affair and Scipio's brother-in-law, Tiberius Gracchus. Antipater's ethical teachings partly encouraged this populist revolt (his student Blossius was a ringleader), which sought to distribute lands to the poor, but Panaetius found himself on the other side of it. It was the role of the ruling class to defend and maintain order—and Scipio's aggressive prosecution of the Gracchus affair is interesting in that it essentially pitted two Stoic leaders against each other. We have the Stoic revolutionary in Blossius and the Stoic conservative in Panaetius, both fulfilling what they believed to be their duty to the state. It's not so much a strange coincidence of history as rather a natural outgrowth of Stoicism's increasing integration into the political world. Of course, Panaetius would find himself in the middle of a fierce conflict where he knew all the parties involved—that's what happens when you're connected.

Cicero would write that *Concerning Appropriate Actions* "has given us what is unquestionably the most thorough discussion of moral duties that we have," no small statement given that a hundred years later, Cicero would find himself navigating political revolution as Caesar overthrew the Republic. The previous Stoics had sometimes actively flouted social convention, but Panaetius saw each human being as having a unique *prosopon*, Greek for "character" or "role," that must be fulfilled with honor and courage and commitment, however humble or impressive.

Panaetius argues that if we are to live an ethical life and choose appropriate actions, we must find a way to balance:

1) the roles and duties common to us all as human beings;
2) the roles and duties unique to our individual *daimon*, or personal genius/calling;
3) the roles and duties assigned to us by the chance of our social station (family and profession);
4) the roles and duties that arise from decisions and commitments we have made.

Each of these layers is an essential part of living virtuously in the real world. A soldier has to manage their obligations as a human, as a warrior, as a member of a family (or as an immigrant or as a wealthy heir), and as a person who has made promises and commitments (to friends, to families, to business partners). The pieces of the equation are different for a head of state or a beggar, but the complicated balance—and the need for guidance—is the same.

When we say that Panaetius was a connector, then, we don't just mean that he connected people like some kind of master networker—though he was one. More than just searching for obscure ideas in books, he was connecting timeless principles with real people for use in their real lives.

It's not just the fate of the modern man and woman to ask: Who am I? What should I do with my life? How can I make my life count? The ancients struggled with this too, and Panaetius's formula helped them as it can help us.

Panaetius believed that each person had an inborn desire for leadership, and that we are obligated to fulfill this potential in our own unique way. We may not all be able to be Scipio on the battlefield, or even Panaetius with an elite education and diplomatic connections, but we can serve the public good in many other ways with equal courage. That's really what the Scipionic Circle was—a diverse collection of men of vastly different talents, stations, and interests all trying to find a way to contribute and thrive in the world.

Everyone can have a life of meaning and purpose. Everyone can do what they do *like a good Stoic.*

Panaetius, we can imagine, was the one friends often turned to for advice about how best to do so, and it was *aphormai* (our inborn resources) that Panaetius pointed them to. It would be a theme, in fact, carried forward by Stoics through to the writings of Marcus Aurelius. Humanity is given these instincts toward virtue by nature, and we can thrive and live nobly if we learn to live consistently with our own nature and our duties, while making the most of the resources we have been given. Panaetius, while born to privilege, chose not to settle into that comfortable life of ease. Instead, he openly embraced duty and the responsibility of a much broader stage. He took the resources he was given and leveraged them, becoming the best version of himself and contributing as much as he could to the big projects of his time.

Each of us, he believed, is obligated to do the same.

Unlike the all-or-nothing race of a runner like Chrysippus trying not to shove his way to victory, Panaetius took the model of a different kind of athlete when reflecting on how best to fulfill our social duties. He thought the *pankratist* (the practitioner of *pankration*, a Greek form of boxing) was a supreme model for capturing the tensions and essence of living a virtuous life. His *pankratist* is one of the most powerful and illustrative sports metaphors, not just in Stoicism, but in all of philosophy.

As Aulus Gellius records:

> Of an opinion of the philosopher Panaetius, which he expressed in his second book *On Duties,* where he urges men to be alert and prepared to guard against injuries on all occasions. "The life of men," he says, "who pass their time in the midst of affairs, and who wish to be helpful to themselves and to others, is exposed to constant and almost daily troubles and sudden dangers. To guard against and avoid these one needs a mind that is always ready and alert, such as the athletes have who are called 'pancratists.' For just as they, when called to the contest, stand with their arms raised and stretched out, and protect their head and face by opposing their hands as a rampart; and as all their limbs, before the battle has begun, are ready to avoid or to deal blows—so the spirit and mind of the wise man, on the watch everywhere and at all times against violence and wanton injuries, ought to be alert, ready, strongly protected, prepared in time of trouble, never flagging in attention, never relaxing its watchfulness, opposing judgment and forethought like arms and hands to the strokes

of fortune and the snares of the wicked, lest in any way a hostile and sudden onslaught be made upon us when we are unprepared and unprotected."

It's a metaphor of Panaetius's creation that would appear, uncredited, in the works of Marcus Aurelius and Epictetus—two philosophers who battled their way through life. Unlike Antipater's archer, who captured the reality of the many things out of our control as we seek to choose well among life's challenges, or Aristo's javelin thrower, Panaetius saw life as less theoretical and much more violent and forceful. It wasn't just a contest with oneself, but actual combat—with opponents and fate. He believed we need to be prepared for the blows that will inevitably fall upon us.

Ultimately, Panaetius would not finish the book, for reasons unknown. But what he had captured in writing was an incredible achievement and was recognized as such in his own time. One of his most politically active students, Publius Rutilius Rufus, who also served Scipio in the Numantine War in 134 BC and was involved in reforms of military training, taxation, and bankruptcy, explained that even this partial work towered over the philosophical and political world: "As no painter had been found to complete that part of the Venus of Cos which Apelles had left unfinished (for the beauty of her face made hopeless any attempt adequately to represent the rest of the figure)," he said, "so no one, because of the surpassing excellence of what Panaetius did complete, would venture to supply what he had left undone."

For all that he left unsaid, so much was said and established that allowed Stoicism to thrive in Roman political life for the next three hundred years. Cicero claimed, for instance, that Panaetius argued it was possible for a good lawyer to defend a guilty client—provided they were not egregiously depraved or wicked. Not only is it a position that makes sense given Panaetius's deep belief in each individual's duty and role in life, but it is also a practical innovation that has been a pillar of the legal system over the last two thousand years: If no one steps up to defend undesirable clients, how can we be sure that justice is being done?

Panaetius was a simple and direct writer as well as speaker who helped rid the philosophy of arcane terminology and its unappealing style—undoubtedly the result of his Stoic teachers' early influence. More importantly, he made the philosophy itself more practical and accessible for people. As Cicero explained, "Panaetius strove to avoid [the] uncouth and repellant development of Stoicism, censuring alike the harshness of its doctrines and the crabbedness of its logic. In doctrine he was mellower, and in style more lucid."

He was one of the first Stoics who seems to be less a *philosopher* and more like a great man. Stoics like Zeno had said that virtue alone was sufficient for happiness, which is simple and true enough but light on instruction. According to Diogenes Laërtius, Panaetius was the first Stoic to believe that virtue was not self-sufficient, "claiming that strength, health, and material resources are also needed."

Panaetius knew that none of this philosophizing existed in a silo; it is interconnected with other important things. It is in the balance, the integrating of competing obligations and interests and talents that the good life is found and lived.

In 129 BC, Scipio would die, a dear loss to both the Republic and to his friends. We can imagine Panaetius grieving this loss, but also relying on an exercise he had taught his students. Suppose your son dies, he said. You must remind yourself that you knew he was mortal when you brought him into the world. The same is true for friends, he would have had to reassure himself. The same is true for careers.

All things end. Philosophy is there to remind us of that fact and to prepare us for the blows of life.

After the death of Scipio, Panaetius understood that a chapter of his life had ended—all that was left was for him to write the next (and possibly the final) one. He returned to Athens that same year after another great loss—this time the death of Antipater—to take over as head of the school. There he served the Stoa another twenty years, continuing to teach and write. Perhaps, like retired political figures today, he returned occasionally to Rome to lecture, consult with magistrates, or promote his books.

And then he too, in 109 BC, passed from the earth.

PUBLIUS RUTILIUS RUFUS
THE LAST HONEST MAN

(POOB-lee-us
Roo-TILL-ee-us ROOF-us)

B. 158 BC

D. 78 BC

ORIGIN: ROME

Politics is a dirty business. It is now and it was then. In Rome, as in the modern world, power attracts ego. It corrupts. It rewards vanity. It disincentivizes responsibility. It is filled, and always will be filled, with liars, cheats, demagogues, and cowards.

Which is why Mark Twain was quite right when he said that "an honest man in politics shines more than he would elsewhere." It's a matter of contrast. Of all the political Stoics, perhaps none shone brighter or stood out more than Publius Rutilius Rufus, who stared down Rome's corruption with a fierce but quiet honesty that was as rare among his peers as it is today.

His career began as illustriously as one could imagine. He studied philosophy under Panaetius, who had returned to Rome in 138 BC when Rutilius was about twenty. A roving and beloved member of the Scipionic Circle, Rutilius served on Scipio Aemilianus's staff as a military tribune in the brutal Numantine War in north-central Spain. He was a promising young man in a rapidly growing empire that offered nearly limitless advancement to promising men of his ilk.

While others may have had more glittering personalities, come from better families, or displayed greater ambitions than the somber and severe Rutilius, his presence and conviction were obvious to anyone who saw him. He was well read, well trained, and, as a speaker, according to one witness, "acute and systematic," though Cicero would disparage his eloquence. His Stoicism was without dispute, with Cicero observing in the same book about Rutilius that the self-sufficiency of his philosophy "was exemplified in him in its firmest and most unswerving form."

The first hint that Rutilius operated by a different code came in 115 BC when he was defeated for consul by Marcus Aemilius Scaurus, who, like many others before him, had bribed his way into office. It would have been easy, perhaps expected, for Rutilius to have done the same, but he conspicuously declined even though it ensured his defeat. Instead he brought Scaurus up on charges of *ambitus*—political corruption. Scaurus himself—the corrupt one—would bring the same charges against Rutilius.

Neither trial was conclusive, but it presaged the fight to come.

It was during the Jugurthine War in 109 BC that Rutilius would find himself caught in the crossfire of even more ambitious and unscrupulous political types who had begun to emerge in the struggle for control of Rome's enormous Republic. One of these was Sulla, a conservative strongman who would come to power through raw force and cruelty. Another was Gaius Marius, who began his military service under Scipio Aemilianus at the same time as Rutilius Rufus. Marius, a *novus homo* (new man) of equestrian rank, had a brilliant military career that would lead to his holding a record seven consulships, a feat Marius claimed had been foretold by an omen in which an eagle's nest containing seven young eagles fell into his lap. It was a sign, the seers had said, that he was destined for greatness and to hold power seven times.

For a time, Rutilius and Marius were allies. During this time of army expansion and overhaul, Rufus came to head Rome's training and deployment strategy for these newly diverse troops. It was said that Marius preferred to fight only with troops trained by Rutilius, because they were the best trained, the most disciplined, and the bravest.

If you want the job done right, there's no one better to do it than a Stoic. If you want someone to aid you in your crimes and corruption, there's nobody worse.

Marius, who lived and ate with his troops, and who dropped the property requirement that had previously limited who could serve in the army, was enormously popular with the masses. He was also brutal and merciless. In 101 BC, following his fourth consulship, Marius achieved a dramatic victory over the Germanic Cimbri, in which 120,000 of their fierce troops were slaughtered. Marius was thus heralded as "the third founder of Rome," but like any figure whose career rested on the whims of the crowd, he was deeply feared by the Roman elite, who wondered what his intentions were.

Rutilius's first conflict with Marius was simpler: He believed Marius had bribed his way to one of his electoral victories by paying down debts and purchasing votes. Having been on the wrong end of this kind of cheating himself, Rutilius was not the type to take it lightly, even if Marius had done an admirable job keeping the peace. Besides, what was the point of having elections if they were going to be fraudulent? So when Rutilius saw something, he said something—and in the process made an enemy who was not likely to forget this betrayal.

For a time, Rutilius was safe, if only because Marius's command over the mob was starting to look shaky. A group of angry aristocrats proved too much for even Marius to control. They attacked and murdered one of his former allies, literally ripping the roof off his prison cell, despite Marius's attempts to protect him. Tensions on all sides now exploded, and since the Senate had never quite trusted Marius, it was time for him to leave town for a while.

Plutarch says it was during his exile that Marius incited Mithridates, king of Pontus and Armenia Minor, to start a war against Rome, which he was certain would ease the Senate's fears of him and force them to call Rome's "third founder" back into service once again. It was a time of intrigue and political violence and outright corruption—swinging abruptly from reactionary to deeply conservative political figures—as all times of revolution and unrest are.

Even if he hadn't tangled with Marius, it was probably inevitable, then, that Rutilius, meticulously honest and ruled by his sense of Stoic duty, would eventually find himself a target. Not only had he gained acclaim for his well-disciplined troops, but he had also begun making reforms to bankruptcy law in the face of rising indebtedness, spearheading an initiative to protect Greeks in Asia Minor from the tax gouging of the *publicani*, members of the Roman equites.

It's a populist irony—the strongman comes to power by making impossible and destructive promises to the disenfranchised. Do they actually have any intention of helping these people? Of course not. In fact, they'll actively stymie any reforms that will actually make the system more fair. All that matters is their iron grip on their ignorant base and the power that comes from it.

We can see Rutilius simply doing his job, following his sense of how, in our self-interest, we must never lose sight of the interests of others. His own practice of Stoic *oikeiosis*, in service of the public good, put him on a fast track to a major conflict much bigger than himself. Did Rutilius know who he was crossing by deciding to advocate for reforms that came at the expense of the rich? Did it matter that he was earnestly attempting to stop a gross injustice? No. What happened next is a very old trick, the same one that Scaurus used: Accuse the honest man of precisely the opposite of what they're doing, of the sin you yourself are committing. Use their reputation against them. Muddy the waters. Stain them with lies. Run them out of town by holding them to a standard that if equally applied would mean the corrupt but entrenched interests would never survive.

So it was that Rutilius, who had instigated and presided over the prosecution of various cases of corruption charges himself, was brought up on false charges, accused of extorting the people he was protecting... by the people who were actually doing the extorting. It didn't help that some of his writings had been critical of the people he was accused of stealing from. Still, he seemed almost stunned by the animus of his enemies and the lengths to which they were willing to go. The jury was stacked. Marius operated behind the scenes, pushing the prosecution. How could he not have been involved? The historian Dio Cassius tells us that a man of Rutilius's "excellence and good repute had been an annoyance" to Marius. Annoyance? He was a mirror. A walking condemnation of everything the corrupt and selfish stood for.

Knowing in his heart that he was innocent, Rutilius declined to defend himself, refusing to call on his own political allies or even utter a word in his defense. Did he think his reputation would save him? Was he trapped by his own dignity? In his work *On Oratory*, Cicero remarks on how it wasn't only Rutilius's silence that condemned him, but in fact none of his defense team raised a voice in opposition to the kangaroo court. At such a staggering failure, Cicero joked that Rutilius's defense team must have been afraid that if they had gotten worked up and made a spirited defense, they'd get reported to the Stoics. It was Socrates's strategy: I refuse to dignify the charges. It was Martin Luther: I will not repent. Here I stand. I can do no other.

It was a noble stance, but it allowed his enemies to make quick work of him. The enormous verdict was more than Rutilius—or anyone but the most corrupt officials—could ever pay. His property was seized and he was exiled. No longer could this stickler get in the way of Marius's looting of Rome, nor could the existence of this ethical man embarrass or show up the rising criminal class.

As he no doubt learned from his teacher, Panaetius, like the *pankratist*, you must be prepared at all times for the unexpected blows of life—if not to block them, at least to absorb and endure them without whining.

Rutilius's enemies, in dealing this blow, offered this noble civil servant and military hero one small dignity, and in so doing, all but proved to history his perfect innocence. The false accusers offered their sacrificial victim the opportunity to choose the place of his exile.

Rutilius, with a twinkle in his eye, perhaps, or at least the stone-hard determination of a man who knows he did nothing wrong, chose Smyrna—the very city he had allegedly defrauded. Smyrna, grateful for the reforms and scrupulous honesty of the man who had once governed them, welcomed Rutilius with open arms. They even offered him citizenship. Suetonius tells us that he settled in Smyrna with Opilius Aurelius, "a freedman of an Epicurean, [who] first taught philosophy, afterwards rhetoric, and finally grammar . . . where he lived with him until old age." Cicero would visit with Rutilius there in 78 BC and call him "a pattern of virtue, of old-time honor, and of wisdom."

Was Rutilius bitter? It doesn't appear so. Reports are that he got on with life, and that his fortune grew despite his removal from the circles of power. Gifts from admirers poured in. We are told that a consoling friend attempted to reassure Rutilius that with civil war likely in Rome, in due time all exiles would be allowed back. "What sin have I committed that you should wish me a more unhappy return than departure?" Rutilius replied. "I should much prefer to have my country blush for my exile than weep at my return!"

Better to be missed than to overstay your welcome.

When the state is beyond redemption and helplessly corrupt, the

Stoics believed, the wise man will stay away. Confucius, himself a philosopher and an advisor to princes, had said something similar several centuries before. What we know is that Rutilius stayed in Smyrna and wrote his *History of Rome* in Greek. Hardly broken by the ignominy of what was done to him, he just kept working.

When Rutilius was eventually invited back to Rome by Sulla, who triumphed over Marius and became dictator, the "honor" was politely declined.

Rutilius's fellow Stoics were livid at the treatment of this honorable man, but in a way it was an important lesson. *Doing the right thing could cost a person everything.* This was not Plato's Republic—philosopher kings were not only not desired, they were the enemy of those trying to get rich through the empire. Disgraces had become commonplace. Every major figure of this period would be accused of either electoral or financial corruption.

Unlike Rutilius, almost all of them were guilty.

Why did it seem that the good were punished while the evil got away scot free? It is the way of the world, then and now, sadly. "When good men come to bad ends," Seneca would write, "when Socrates is forced to die in prison, Rutilius to live in exile, Pompey and Cicero to offer their necks to their own clients, and great Cato, the living image of all the virtues, by falling upon his sword to show that the end had come for himself and for the state at the same time, one cannot help being grieved that Fortune pays her rewards so unjustly."

Still, who would you rather be? Because there is a cost to cheating, to stealing, to doing the wrong thing—even if society rewards it. Would you rather go out like Rutilius with your head high or live in denial of your own undeniable shame?

As bad as it was, the Stoics of Rutilius's time had little idea of what the future had in store for them. They could not have known that as bad as what they were witnessing was, it was only, as the writer and pod-caster Mike Duncan would describe it two thousand years later, "the storm *before* the storm." The Roman Republic's institutions had been greatly weakened and all that remained was valiant resistance from great and honorable men. How much longer could they hold back the tides? How much longer could they preserve the ethics and political in-stitutions that Greece had brought to Rome?

With Julius Caesar coming, the answer, sadly, was not much longer.

But for a time, Rutilius Rufus had let his light shine. He had been a force for good in the world and had suffered for it. But never, it seems, did he question whether it was worth it. Nor did he harbor any bitterness about his fate. He had looked at himself and the corruption around him and decided that no matter what other people said or did, his job was to be good. He knew, as Marcus Aurelius would remind himself over and over, that all he controlled was his character and his ability to let his true colors shine undiminished. You can lay violent hands on me, Zeno had said, but my mind will remain committed to philosophy.

But Zeno only had to say it. Marcus was never wrongly convicted. He never lost his home. Rutilius believed it, spoke it, and lived it.

It was he who had to stand there as they brought him up on trumped-up charges, as they soiled his reputation, stole his possessions, and sent him far from the country he loved. And yet, under all this pres-sure, he did not crack. He did not compromise. He did not bend the knee. He refused what must have been the implicit carrot that went along with the legal stick: Drop these pesky objections and we can make you rich and important.

Publius Rutilius Rufus was, uncompromisingly, the last honest man in Rome. It's an example that calls down to us today, as it did to the brave Stoics of his time and every one of them who came after.

POSIDONIUS
THE GENIUS

(Po-si-DOUGH-knee-us)

B. 135 BC

D. 51 BC

ORIGIN: APAMEA, SYRIA

P osidonius of Apamea was yet another Stoic born into a prominent family in a time of anxious abundance. The year of his birth, 135 BC, in what is now Syria, marked the beginning of political turmoil that in a sense continues to this day. But for Posidonius, it was the same kind of formative incubation in uncertainty that had created Zeno and Cleanthes before him.

Perhaps these are the ideal conditions in which Stoicism emerges: a homeland lacking strong leadership and buffeted by powerful outside forces; a ringside seat to the perils of excess and greed. It was all an early lesson that in an unpredictable world, the only thing we can really manage is ourselves—and that the space between our ears is the only territory we can conquer in any kind of certain and enduring way.

In any case, Posidonius would later recall with disapproval that the abundance of Syria in those days made its people "free from the bother of the necessities of life, and so were forever meeting for a continual life of feasting and their gymnasia turned into baths." He wrote of the "drunken ambition" of the local tyrants. Things were good, but good times rarely make for great people, or great governments.

Ultimately, he voted with his feet as many of the other early Stoics did, leaving his birthplace at eighteen or twenty years old for Athens.

When Posidonius arrived in Athens sometime between 117 and 115 BC, he found the Stoa Poikilē firmly in the hands of Panaetius, who was by then an old man and a towering figure, not only in the Stoic school but also in the empire. Fathers from across the Roman ruling class—from senators to generals and even kings of distant provinces—had begun to have their children educated by philosophers. Where Panaetius had taught Rutilius a generation earlier in Rome, many of Rome's richest and most powerful were now sending their most promising children to him in Athens to prepare them for entry into Roman life.

And yet even amid these star pupils from the Eternal City, the young Posidonius must have stood out for his brilliance. Sources portray him as a polymath with diverse interests in natural history, astronomy, meteorology, oceanography, geography, geology, seismology, ethnography, mathematics, geometry, logic, history, and ethics. Perhaps it was Panaetius, who had traveled widely on his fact-finding mission, who encouraged his young student to take his studies on the road. What we know is that after his time in Athens, the next large chunk of Posidonius's life was spent studying in far-flung places from Italy, Sicily, Greece, and Dalmatia to North Africa and the Near East.

It cannot be said that the Stoics, like some philosophers, were interested only in their proofs or debates. Posidonius perfectly illustrates the curiosity, the fascination with the beautiful and complex world that surrounds us which defined Stoicism in the ancient world and continues today. You can and should be interested in everything, the Stoics taught, because you can and should learn wisdom from everything. The more you experience, the more you learn, and, paradoxically, the more humbled you are by the endless amounts of knowledge that remain in front of you.

As Posidonius traveled, his reputation grew as the greatest polymath since Aristotle. He measured tides in Spain and conducted ethnographic research on the Celts in Gaul. He was a keen observer and a lover of data—regardless of the discipline—and a diligent recorder of it all. He measured the circumference of the earth, the size and distance of the sun and the moon, created models of both the globe and the known solar system. The only constraint on his brilliance was the crude measuring tools of his age, which often skewed his calculations. Still, his ceaseless travel and unmatched curiosity dramatically increased the understanding of the known universe at that time.

It also got him outside, down in the dirt and out on the water. His classroom was the sky and the stars and the bustling marketplace, as it had been for Zeno, as it is for the child who can be fascinated even by an ordinary patch of grass. Posidonius lived, as Seneca would later write, as if the whole world was a temple of the gods.

Some geniuses are content to live entirely in their own heads. Many philosophies—filled with philosophers who no doubt see themselves as geniuses—subtly encourage this tendency. Epicureanism, for instance, which was resurgent in Posidonius's time, encouraged its followers to turn away from the world, to ignore politics and the noise around them. Posidonius, thanks to the influence of Stoics like Diogenes and Panaetius, resisted the pull of this bubble and, like a good Stoic, also turned his intellect to politics and governance.

Indeed, his far-flung travels brought him in constant contact with Roman legions, legions that had been trained for Marius by his fellow Stoic and student of Panaetius, Rutilius Rufus. We see evidence from the fragments of his writings that Posidonius studied troop movements, the history of warfare, and the customs of local people, and even gathered intelligence about foreign powers, which he not only provided to generals but later used in his many books. He even wrote a manual on military tactics, a kind of *Art of War*, that was so detailed that it was considered too advanced for anyone but a general. In addition to becoming a repository of military tactics, he also had deep ethnographic insights gathered from the foreign territories, which generals like Pompey would seek from him for many years.

He was the complete man. An explorer. Strategist. Scientist. Politician. He was, then, a *real* philosopher.

At some point, though, every traveler must come home, which for Posidonius became Rhodes. Putting his study of politics into practice, he rose in the leadership ranks there to the highest civil position of prytany, presiding over the governing council in Rhodes while building up his philosophical school.

His political duties would bring him to Rome in 86 BC on embassy, but it was likely his curiosity and desire to study human beings that brought him to the deathbed of one of Rome's worst strongmen, Marius. Marius was elected to his seventh consulship in late 87 BC, and seemed to think that his political power made him immortal. He could not have imagined that Posidonius would be one of the last faces he would ever see.

Delusional, tortured by dark dreams, wearied by a life of endless ambition and the creeping fear that it had all been for naught, Marius received Posidonius, a keen observer, who was repulsed by what he saw. A few days after the meeting, Marius died, convinced until the end that he would once again be leading troops in battle and expanding his conquests. As a Stoic, Posidonius must have noted—as Plutarch would—what a far cry this was from the peaceful passing of a philosopher like Antipater, who had spent his final moments counting the blessings of his voyage through life.

It's a timeless question: If you actually knew what "success" and "power" looked like—what it did to the people who got it—would you still want it?

Posidonius's later writings are filled with firsthand observations about the costs of ambition and insatiable appetites. In one of his histories, he writes of a philosopher named Athenion, who had designs on becoming a tyrant in Athens. It must have struck Posidonius how easily people can be corrupted and cut off from virtue, for here was a man with similar training who had abandoned his genius to marry a prostitute and depended on the mob for his own political advancement.

In another account of a revolt in Sicily, he spoke of a Damophilus, "a slave of luxury and malpractice, driven through the country in four-wheeled chariots at the head of horses, luscious attendants, and a concourse of bumsuckers and soldier-slaves." Almost with a sense of satisfaction, Posidonius tells us how Damophilus came to a violent and painful end at the hands of his slaves. We can imagine Posidonius expecting a similar comeuppance for Apicius, the gluttonous and greedy monster who was responsible for bringing his friend Rutilius Rufus up on a false charge.

What linked all these historical cases together in Posidonius's mind was a deficiency of character. "Robbers, perverts, killers, and tyrants," Marcus Aurelius would later write, "gather for your inspection their so-called pleasures!" Posidonius had actually done that, been in the room with Marius, inspected would-be tyrants and killers up close just as he had observed the tides and the movements of the planets.

From this he was able to pass along insights that were just as valuable as his scientific ones: Be wary of ambition. Avoid the mob. Luxury, as much as power, rots. From Seneca, we get Posidonius's final judgment on Marius: "Marius commanded armies, but ambition commanded Marius." Seneca paraphrased, "When such men as these were disturbing the world, they were themselves disturbed."

After Panaetius's death in 109 BC, Posidonius would leave Athens for the last time, convinced that the people had become simply "a mindless mob" (*ochloi anoetoi*). Posidonius probably didn't think much better of the Romans, after what he had seen firsthand.

Rhodes, at once both isolated and still central to the flow of goods and ideas across the Mediterranean, was a perfect perch for this independent thinker. Posidonius worked on his histories and his theory of the human personality during this time, and they both reflect a more realistic and disillusioned appraisal of his fellow man—an assessment often shared by geniuses. But just as this view was settling in, Posidonius was visited by a bright light. In 79 BC, a young Cicero, then twenty-seven years old, and a kind of once-in-a-generation talent (like Posidonius), would make his way to Rhodes to study under the great man. Panaetius had his Posidonius and now Posidonius would have his own brilliant pupil, who in turn would lovingly refer to his teacher in his writings as "our Posidonius."

The rest of his years would be spent writing and philosophizing, and of course teaching. It's clear that his travels and his real-world experience in politics at the highest level informed all three of these domains. Posidonius, like his teacher Panaetius before him, held aristocratic views—today we'd call him one of the "elites." Except unlike today's elites, who are often out of touch and surrounded by a bubble of their own like minds, Posidonius had formed his suspicions of the mob and populism from firsthand experience.

He had seen the world, he had seen war, which formed a philosophy—grounded in natural sciences, history, and human psychology—that was sought after by the most important people of his time. This is undoubtedly what drew Pompey, the great general just then rising to power, to Rhodes to attend Posidonius's lectures.

In 66 BC, before his campaign against Cilician pirates, Pompey visited Posidonius and in a private audience asked him if he had any advice for him. Posidonius, quoting Homer, told him to "be the best and always superior to others." It was subtle moral advice whose meaning Pompey, with what Posidonius would later call "his insane love of a false glory," ultimately missed.

"Best," to the Stoics, did not meaning winning battles. Superior did not mean accumulating the most honors. It meant, as it still does today, *virtue*. It meant excellence not in accomplishing external things—though that was always nice if fate allowed—but excellence in the areas that you controlled: Your thoughts. Your actions. Your choices.

Even so, the glory-seeking general remained a respectful student. At the height of his powers, following his great victories in the East during the Third Mithridatic War, Pompey made a return visit to Posidonius in 62 BC, and bowed with his army standards lowered at the philosopher's door. Perhaps Pompey did, in his own way, grasp what Posidonius meant by "best," even if he could not live it.

Despite being stricken by a severe case of arthritis and gout during this visit, Posidonius gave Pompey a private lecture from bed on why only the honorable is good, in which, through cries of pain, he had to stress that he would still not admit that pain was an evil.

This triumph over pain—over oneself—that's the "best" Posidonius was talking about. More impressive, he did live it.

In his writings, Posidonius held that the mind seeks wisdom and what is truly good, whereas the lower parts of the soul seek power and the glory of victory (like Pompey), as well as bodily pleasure. Good habits and lifestyle—set in place by the mind—are checks against these irrational parts of the soul. This idea that part of us is rational and part of us is not was a fairly radical departure for the Stoics, who had long held that the whole self was rational.

But this inner battle—as Martin Luther King Jr. would later call the Civil War between the "North" and "South" of our souls—rings true to any person with a shred of self-awareness. We have competing parts within us, and what matters in life is which side we choose to turn ourselves over to. One must design one's life, Posidonius said, "to live contemplating the truth and order of the universe and promoting it as much as possible, being led in no respect by the irrational part of the soul." This was a feat that Marius and Sulla, Athenion and, sadly, even Pompey could not seem to achieve, despite all their cunning or military might.

That's because it's really, really hard to do—whether you're a genius or a conqueror. If you can do it, though, the Stoics believed, you will produce something far more impressive than brilliant writing or splendid victories.

Earlier Stoics had attempted to divide the philosophy into three parts, using the analogy of a farm or an orchard, with a field (physics), fruit (ethics), and fence (logic). Sextus Empiricus tells us that Posidonius differed: "Since the parts of philosophy are inseparable from each other, yet plants are distinct from fruit and walls are separate from plants, he claimed the simile for philosophy should rather be a living being, where physics is blood and flesh, logic the bones and sinews, and ethics the soul." It's the perfect metaphor for the Stoics too, because philosophy is meant to be *lived* as a human being.

Building from Chrysippus and Zeno, Posidonius took this idea even further. He saw the entire cosmos as a sentient, living being in which all things are interconnected (*sympatheia*). The study of science can sometimes lead a person to atheism, but in Posidonius's case his experiments with the tides and his observations of the stars had given him a strong sense of a creator—that there was a providential fate governing the universe. Pushing beyond Chrysippus's "no shoving" rule, he believed every human being was quite literally on the same team. We are all tied together in cosmic sympathy, Posidonius believed, and none of us are entirely self-sufficient or autonomous. Each of us has been given a role in this large body—one of us is a finger, another a skin cell, another a liver—and we exist in collaboration and tension with each other. It was God, he thought, that ran through this organism as *pneuma*—a kind of soul of the universe.

In his later years Posidonius dedicated himself almost entirely to

completing his great histories. Spanning fifty-two volumes and representing a full third of his entire literary output, his histories picked up
at Carthage in 146 BC with Scipio Aemilianus and continued up to
Sulla's sack of Athens in 86 BC. Strabo says that he was even writing a
separate work dedicated entirely to Pompey. His known works ranged
from those on fate and ethics to others dealing with emotions and the
ever-present enemy for the Stoics: anger. He also wrote on grief and
duty, and of course many scientific books based on his early explora-
tions on the oceans, weather, and circumnavigation of the earth.

Although only fragments of these great works survive and Posidonius is mostly unknown today, he was a towering figure in his own time
and for long after. Centuries later, Saint Augustine, in his famous *City of
God*, took the time to call him out by name and respond to the most scientific of the Stoics, if only to criticize his use of astrology. Posidonius
may not be a household name today, but what author wouldn't have been
satisfied to still be cited some five hundred years after his death? And by
a saint no less?

Posidonius worked and lived in many places in his long life—Syria,
Athens, Rome, and Rhodes—and he traveled almost the entirety of the
known world. He wrote many books. He advised many powerful men.
He was one of the smartest men of the ancient world—a small part of a
cosmic universe, by his own admission, but an impressive contributor
nonetheless.

And yet even geniuses are eventually forgotten, and ultimately all
of them are mortal. No Stoic would dispute or fight this, Posidonius
least of all.

In 51 BC, he died peacefully at age eighty-four, and though we don't
have any record of it, we can imagine him having learned to depart from
the world a happier and more grateful man than what he had seen of
Marius's haunting and ignoble end.

DIOTIMUS THE VICIOUS

(Die-oh-TEEM-us)

B. Unknown
D. Unknown (100 BC?)   Origin: Unknown

I t was Shakespeare, the great observer of the Stoics, who would say—in his most Stoic play no less—that the good we do in life is easily forgotten, but the evil we do lives on and on.

Perhaps no Stoic philosopher illustrates this principle more than Diotimus, of whom so little is known. We don't know when he was born. We're not sure when or how he died. We know only of a few of his beliefs: for instance, that the chief end in life was well-being, and that the pursuit of virtue was how we got it.

Who did he study under? We're not sure about that either. Sources suggest that he knew Posidonius, but that's it. How was he introduced to philosophy? Who were his parents? Who were his students? How did he help them? How did he live? What acts of kindness did he perform? What honors did he decline?

Again, we know nothing of any of this. He is a cipher to us.

All we really know about him is from a single act of indisputable malice, one that has baffled historians and students of Stoicism for more than two thousand years. It's an act that seems so pointless, so petty, and so comically at odds with the teachings of the philosophy that Diotimus claimed to adhere to, that it almost sounds made up.

Sometime around the turn of the first century BC, as the philosophies of Epicurus enjoyed a resurgence in Athens amid the rising splendor and power of Rome, Diotimus sat down and forged more than fifty "licentious letters" intended to slander the reputation of the founder of that rival school. Indeed, he went much further than that. Diotimus portrayed Epicurus as some kind of depraved maniac—a reputation that Epicurus has struggled to completely shed even to this day—in order to bolster his arguments against the philosophy.

Part of the motivation was no doubt self-defense. The Epicurean school at this time was ascendant, and under the leadership of the prolific Apollodorus, who in addition to writing some four hundred books was nicknamed "the Garden Tyrant." We are told by Diogenes Laërtius that Apollodorus had taken to smearing Chrysippus, claiming that the Stoic had filled his books with quotes he had stolen from others. Such slander of the Stoa's great fighter would need to be addressed.

Diotimus chose to respond to slander with slander. He decided to commit a crime worse than what Apollodorus was falsely alleging against Chrysippus.

For a school that prized logic and truth as much as virtuous behavior, Diotimus's actions would have been inexcusable. Even if Epicureanism was now posing some kind of existential threat to Stoicism, it hardly justifies the commission of literary fraud. "If it is not right, do not do it," Marcus Aurelius would write in his encapsulation of Stoic doctrine, "if it is not true, do not say it." The Stoic is supposed to be beyond grudges, beyond revenge, beyond petty competition or the need to win arguments. Certainly, they're not supposed to do anything—let alone lie and mislead—out of spite. Somewhere, somehow, Diotimus went astray.

And to what end? To discredit a school that also earnestly sought to lead its students toward the good life?

It would be, then, Diotimus's sole contribution to the history of Stoicism, making himself a cautionary tale. He proved that the Stoics were hardly perfect, and that no matter how much training or reading we have done, a snap decision made in the moment can undo all of it.

What might Rutilius Rufus have thought, to know that at roughly the time he was being brought up on false charges by his political enemies, another Stoic was hard at work posthumously framing Epicurus? But such is life and history—complicated, contradictory, and often disappointing.

Athenaeus, citing Demetrius of Magnesia, says that Zeno of Sidon, who succeeded Apollodorus as head of the Epicurean school, tracked Diotimus down and filed suit against him. The court sided with Zeno of Sidon and sentenced Diotimus to death, which is a rather extreme form of justice—and certainly not one Rome would have countenanced.

While it's unlikely that the death penalty would have been given for something as common as slander, there can be no doubt that a strong fine and exile from Athens were imposed. And greater than that, a personal shame.

This is the mistake we make. We fight fire with fire and end up burning ourselves. Nobody remembers who started it and our scars stay forever, if we even manage to survive the conflagration. When we are angry, it's almost always better to wait and do nothing. And as far as our enemies go, if possible, we ought to let them destroy themselves.

Diotimus's infamy stained his fellow Stoics to enough of an extent, for example, that it prompted Posidonius to write what was certainly a more measured book against Diotimus's accuser, Zeno of Sidon, than he might have otherwise intended. It's not as if such an honorable man would have defended Diotimus's forgeries. Instead, it's likely that he needed to shift the focus away from the student and toward the school, clarifying what Stoicism's actual objections to the teachings of Epicurus were. Did Posidonius apologize for Diotimus? Did he disavow the man's despicable tactics? Did he correct Apollodorus's own slander against Chrysippus? One hopes, but does not know.

Still, it remains interesting that we have no record of any of the Stoics disavowing Diotimus's crime, at the time or in the generations after. Seneca, who writes expansively on all sorts of philosophers and their behaviors, and about the Epicureans more than eighty times across his surviving works, never once mentions this incident and the sad failing of his own school.

Perhaps the desperation of the intra-academic squabble hit too close to home.

It has never been easy to understand the bitterness of disputes between classical scholars, Samuel Johnson once observed. "Small things make mean men proud," he said, "and vanity catches small occasions; or that all contrariety of opinion, even in those that can defend it no longer, makes proud men angry; there is often found in commentaries a spontaneous strain of invective and contempt, more eager and venomous than is vented by the most furious controvertist in politics against those whom he is hired to defame."

He could not have captured the folly of Diotimus better. Nor could Shakespeare's funeral oration of Caesar be any more apt. For in that play, the once-Stoic Brutus's single deed—the assassination of Julius Caesar—would come to overwhelm and obscure everything else the man would do in his life. And so it went for Diotimus, a philosopher who may well have had many interesting and profound things to say about the pursuit of moral perfection and well-being, but instead is known to us only for his evil and vengeful decision to attempt to destroy the reputation of the founder of his rivals' school.

CICERO THE
FELLOW TRAVELER

(SIS-er-oh)

B. 106 BC

D. 43 BC

ORIGIN: ARPINUM

I t cannot be said that Cicero was a Stoic. Nor would he have claimed to be. It's undeniable, however, that he was a dedicated student of the Stoics. He spent time directly under Posidonius. The blind Stoic Diodotus lived with him for years and even died in Cicero's home, leaving his estate to the powerful young man he had long tutored. It was the Stoics who, Cicero deemed in his book *Tusculan Disputations*, "are the only true philosophers." In fact, it is through Cicero's writing that much of what we know about Stoicism in the ancient world survives.

But for all this, Cicero could never convince himself to actually *live* by the principles he would do so much to articulate and preserve. He was a fellow traveler, a man without a party, who for all his success and ambition would turn out to be deficient in the courage and character that his moment in history demanded—that Stoicism demanded he demonstrate.

He was, nonetheless, the great talent of the age.

The first century BC was a time in which the old way of doing things began to break down. There was political conflict and populist uprisings. Demagogues had amassed incredible power. The justice system devolved into a rigged game. The empire frayed at the edges and turned on itself.

This chaos could never slow down a striver like Cicero, but it would define his life.

Cicero was born into a wealthy equestrian family on January 3, 106 BC, in Arpinum, a provincial town about seventy miles southeast of Rome that had only recently received the rights of Roman citizenship. His family name derived from the Latin word for chickpea (*cicer*), which suggests they had, like Zeno's family, once been involved in trade.* Unlike the earlier Stoics who had been drawn to politics or public life out of a sense of duty, Cicero was looking for something else—upward social mobility.

How did this upstart country boy find his way into a book of Stoic lives? His inspiration was not the reluctant politics of Diogenes, the ethical bent of Antipater, the behind-the-scenes influence of Panaetius, or even his own Stoic teacher Posidonius. His first inspiration was instead the meteoric rise of Marius, the one whose last breaths had been observed by Posidonius, who had achieved—through raw ambition—immense power and fame even while lacking an illustrious bloodline. Marius too was an upstart from Arpinum. When friends suggested that Cicero change his name to hide his nouveau riche origins, he vowed instead to achieve fame so great that no one would ever say such a thing again. Indeed, he and Marius would both become *novi homines*, "new men," the first of their families to rise to senatorial power from outside the patrician ranks of Rome.

Cicero's life in Rome began in 90 BC, when at the age of sixteen he was sent there by his father to study public speaking and the law. He entered the capital with the benefit of his father's business connections, and immediately fell in love with what we might now call the life of the "elites." As biographer Anthony Everitt notes, "It was during these years that Cicero's ambition to become a famous advocate crystallized. . . . He

---

* Just as Zeno's incident with the lentils is loaded with class implications, so too is Cicero's association with the "lowly" chickpea.

was swept along by the almost unbearable excitement of the trials in the Forum and the glamour of the lawyer's job, very much like that of a leading actor."

While other young men in his position partied and enjoyed their wealth (and lack of parental supervision), Cicero studied like a man with something to prove. He was said to produce—as a deliberate homage to a philosophical hero, no doubt—as many as five hundred lines per night, just as Chrysippus was famed to do. Cicero wrote and read and observed. Did he love philosophy and literature? Of course. But he also saw it as a way to get ahead. It was the vehicle for realizing his potential, just as a natural athlete is drawn to sports and squeezes from the game every advantage they can. Cicero networked too, meeting other young men handpicked for great things, including a boy six years his junior, Gaius Julius Caesar.

Cicero's early years were almost like a training montage for the cinematic and pivotal events he would face in the prime of his life. And perhaps we see it like that because Cicero—himself the source of so much of what we know about him—was a conspicuous crafter of the narrative of his own rise.

The story goes like this: At eighteen, he attached himself to Philo of Larissa, head of the Platonic Academy who had fled Athens for Rome. He took on his first legal cases during the tumultuous reforms of Sulla, winning several impressive victories against the powers that be. He finished his first book on rhetoric—becoming a respected author at just twenty years old. Then he decamped to Athens for more studying under teachers of every school. Then he hit the road again to study Stoicism with Posidonius in Rhodes, where genius quickly recognized genius.

By the time Cicero returned to Rome at age twenty-nine, he was a man transformed by the crucible of many years of hard work and relentless drive. "And so I came home after two years," he wrote, "not only more experienced but almost another man; the excessive strain of voice had gone, my style had so to speak simmered down, my lungs were stronger and I was not so thin."

Notice he lists only attributes, not convictions.

That is the critical question of nearly everything Cicero did, as it is for so many talented, ambitious people: Were the motivations sincere? Or was it all part of some plan? Are they *training* or résumé building?

It was said that an oracle had warned Cicero early to let his conscience guide his life, not the opinions of the crowd, but for someone as driven as Cicero, such a warning was impossible to heed. Seneca would later write of the importance of choosing oneself "a Cato"—someone to use as a ruler to measure and guide oneself against. Cicero, who lived alongside a real Stoic like Cato, chose, for the most part, to look elsewhere for inspiration. Instead of Cato, Cicero had, in early life, chosen Marius, which is a little like choosing Richard Nixon or Vladimir Putin as one's lodestar.

It was a strange, revealing choice. As the Stoics were fond of saying, this character trait proved to be destiny.

Having checked all the boxes by the end of his twenties, it was time for Cicero to begin his political ascent, which he had planned for so long. At thirty, a Roman was eligible to stand for the office of quaestor— which translates to "the one who asks questions," but were simply those who drew up laws and answered to petitioners—and then become a member of the Senate. Cicero's family leveraged their wealth and contacts to make sure he won his first election handily. He wasn't just a natural, but a *worker*. Inspired by craftsmen who knew the names of each of their tools or instruments, Plutarch tells us, Cicero actively cultivated the habit of knowing not only the names of all of his eminent constituents, but the sizes of their estates, their businesses, and their needs.

Not *needs* in the Stoic sense, as in what was good for the *polis,* what was good for the state, but *needs* in the raw political sense. What did they want? What could he do for them? Where did their interests align, *quid pro quo.* There's no question that Cicero was an able politician. He was, in fact, the best in a generation. But he operated by a compass quite different from that of Diogenes or Antipater or Posidonius.

By 75 BC, Cicero was ensconced in office, and assigned as a tax collector and manager in Sicily. He took to administration quite easily and ably, but unlike the populists of his time, he remained a lover of high culture and philosophy. While in Sicily he tells the colorful story of tracking down the grave of Archimedes in Syracuse, which by this time was nearly a century and a half old and abandoned and overgrown. In his classic and rather egotistical style, Cicero would praise himself for his work in uncovering it: "So you see, one of the most famous cities of Greece, once indeed a great school of learning as well, would have been ignorant of the tomb of its one most ingenious citizen, had not a man of Arpinum pointed it out."

If the self-indulgence rings awkward now, imagine what it must have sounded like then.

Sicily had been only a way station for Cicero and served what later biographers would describe as his *philodoxia* and *philotimia*—loves of fame and honor, precisely what the oracles had warned him to be wary of. He took the job so he could become a senator, which in and of itself was a dizzyingly high honor for a man whose family just a few generations before was not even afforded the rights of citizenship. By no means sated by this accomplishment, Cicero quickly began planning to leap to higher and higher ones. In 71 BC, he took on as prosecutor the case of extortion brought by Sicilian citizens against Verres, hoping it would aid his next step in his *cursus honorum*—what the Romans referred to as the "ladder of offices" that the ambitious climbed—to the post of aedile, which regulated and enforced public order, in 70 BC. Cicero conducted a backbreaking fifty-day investigation and returned to Rome with a vast trove of documentary proof against the crimes of Verres.

It was a dramatic case. Verres had stolen forty million sesterces during his three years in Sicily, and Cicero had the proof. As he told the court in his opening statement, "It is this man's case that will determine whether, with a court composed of Senators, the condemnation of a very guilty and very rich man can possibly occur. And further, the prisoner is such that he is distinguished by nothing except his monstrous offences and immense wealth: If, therefore, he is acquitted, it will be impossible to imagine any explanation but the most shameful; it will not appear that there has been any liking for him, any family bond, any record of other and better actions, no, nor even any moderation in some one vice, that could palliate the number and enormity of his vicious deeds." Cicero knew the jury had been bribed, and yet he somehow secured a conviction. And now, holding the office of aedile, he was doubly victorious.

It was a great day for that Stoic virtue of justice—of fairness and truth—but was that why he struck it? Does it matter?

The constant theme in Cicero's life is movement—movement forward, movement *upward*. Nearly everything he did, including winning important corruption cases like the one against Verres, had a double motive. He often did the right thing, but he did it with more than half an eye on what it could do for him. It wasn't exactly Stoic . . . but it worked.

Since Cleanthes and Zeno, the Stoics had been, as a rule, indifferent to wealth and status. As much as Cicero respected them, he could not abide by this firmness. He would not abstain from luxury. He would chase it. An accomplished lawyer and politician, he first took Antipater's advice and married a wonderful and rich woman named Terentia and started a family. Then he used his wealth, both inherited and marital, to acquire property. Ultimately, he would own nine villas, along with other real estate investments—including a seaside resort in Formiae and, the most prized of all his villas, the one in Tusculum that had belonged to Sulla himself. In addition to his family's money and his wife's dowry, Cicero amassed a large fortune through what seems like unethical means. Cleanthes, at Zeno's direction, had rejected bequests offered to him. Marcus Aurelius would do the same for anyone who left him in their will. Cicero, on the other hand, seemed to be almost a professional son—a striver who wormed his way into people's estates so they might one day leave him money.

Near the end of his life, Cicero gave an astounding tally of this source of income: "Actually my account books show that I have received more than twenty million sesterces in bequests. . . . Nobody ever made me his heir unless he was a friend, so that any benefit there came along with a certain amount of grief." His Stoic teacher Diodotus could not have been too repulsed by this practice, for he too would leave every-thing to Cicero when he died in his home in 60 BC. But still, it's hard to not find the whole thing strange.

"If you have a garden and a library," Cicero would write in a letter to a friend as they discussed Chrysippus and Diodotus, "you have every-thing you need." Clearly there was a part of him that didn't fully believe that, that could not be content with the simple or the reflective life. Like many people, he seemed to believe that he needed wealth and fame too. Like many of us who crave those same things, he did not quite realize what they would cost him until he got them . . . and by then it was too late.

Still, to his credit, for all his ambitions and expensive tastes, Cicero drew a clear line at corruption. Unlike far too many Roman politicians, he would accept no bribes. An admirable and honest public servant, he refused to take legal fees for his services. Of course, this stand is easier to take when you inherit millions.

Having served as quaestor and then as aedile, the next office to be gained for Cicero was praetor, which he ran for and won at age thirty-nine in 67 BC—serving at the youngest age possible under law at age forty in 66 BC—due in no small part to his support of Pompey. This too was a launching pad for the final and most prized position, particularly as a "new man": consul. The Senate chairman and commander of the Roman army, the role of consul was almost exclusively reserved for Rome's most elite families. As the historian Gerard Lavery points out, in the final 150 years of the Roman Republic only ten *novi homines* were elected consul. Between 93 and 43 BC, Cicero would be the only one.

Cicero's path to the top would not be uncontested. He faced two rivals for the position, Catiline and Antonius. Playing to his strengths, Cicero began a blistering rhetorical campaign against "the murderous and corrupt" Catiline, warning the Senate and people of a brewing plot to usurp the Republic. It was enough to win Cicero the consulship. But the cost would be high—whether Catiline had been part of a plot before is up for debate, but after being on the wrong end of Cicero's slander, he was ready to burn the whole system down to exact his revenge.

Cicero took office in 63 BC in the midst of an economic crisis. Eastern trade routes had been closed off by Rome's enemies. Unemployment was high. Recession affected all walks of life in Rome. Tensions brewed, as they do in such times. Cicero promised *concordia ordinum*, the concord of the classes—but what he really meant was that he could keep everything from exploding. Actual fairness could not have ranked high on his list of concerns, even if he had been taught its benefits, its *virtue*, by Posidonius or Diodotus.

Cicero passed a law to increase the penalty for election bribery to ten years of exile—a good law, to be sure. But was it solely for the benefit of the people? Or was it a move against his political enemies? Catiline believed the law had been aimed at him and launched a plan to assassinate Cicero and his allies in the Senate. When a prominent Roman delivered letters purporting to show Catiline's scheme, Cicero convened the Senate and gave the speech of his life.

"When, O Catiline," he began, "do you mean to cease abusing our patience? How long is that madness of yours still to mock us? When is there to be an end of that unbridled audacity of yours, swaggering about as it does now?

"Shame on the age and on its principles!" Cicero called as he demanded the execution of his enemy. Catiline, who was in the audience for this harangue, meekly attempted to reply. He was no match for such a brilliant speaker. All he could do was fall back on the tropes of Rome's elitism. He pointed out that Cicero came from no great family. He questioned the credibility of a self-made man.

It didn't work.

So he fled—to the army he had in waiting, proving beyond a doubt that Cicero was right. Catiline was a traitor and a rebel. But how serious the threat actually was remains in doubt. Contemporaries and historians alike suspect that Cicero, always looking for power and the spotlight, may have significantly exaggerated the peril of the nation—for personal gain.

The Senate, trusting in Cicero, bestowed on him nearly dictatorial powers to put down the threat. The Republic and Cicero himself, like many empires believing they faced an existential threat to their institutions, warped under the pressure. Cato, the Stoic, urged Cicero to exact the full measure of the law from these criminals. It was only just, he said.

Cicero had absolute power in his hands. He hesitated, but not for moral reasons. He was, as always, thinking of his reputation. His wife, Terentia, proved an unexpected but decisive vote, interpreting a sacrifice that had frightened some others as a sign that her husband must wield the power that had been given to him.

The conspirators were put to death without trial by his order, and thousands more in their supporting armies died. In thanks, the Senate would bestow on him the title of "Father of His Country," but the extreme measures and the lives touched by so many deaths would hang over him for the rest of his life—and indeed, all of history.

What remained untouched through the ordeal was Cicero's sense of his own destiny and greatness. Plutarch tells us that within days, Cicero began a campaign to burnish his accomplishments. "One couldn't attend a Senate or public meeting," Plutarch wrote, "nor any session of the courts, without having to listen to the endless repetitions.... This unpleasing habit of his clung to him like fate." No amount of credit or praise was enough.

Cicero enshrined what he believed to be his own magnificence in writing as well. He tried to induce Posidonius to cover his consulship in his great fifty-two-volume history. When Posidonius declined, Cicero wrote a letter "the size of a book" to Pompey in 62 BC on the subject of his own achievements. Pompey acknowledged it with no more than a shrug. Cicero was undeterred—he was convinced he had saved the country. History, he thought, was in his debt.

The historian H. J. Haskell captures the contradictions in Cicero's character well. He was talented, he was brilliant, he was steeped in the wisest philosophy of every school, and yet "he was too sensitive, too vain, too dominated by personal feeling, too open to impression, to become a great leader of men. At times he saw both sides of public questions too vividly to enable him to make up his mind, close it to all doubts, and drive ahead. At other times, when his hatreds became engaged—and he was a fierce hater—he would plunge forward recklessly."

Cicero knew what the Stoics warned of the *passions*, but he did little work on reining in his own. And so, time and time again, they would come back to cause exactly the kind of suffering that the Stoics *since the days of Zeno* had been warning against.

Like the figures in Posidonius's writings, Cicero would get nearly everything he wanted . . . and come to regret it.

Cicero's consulship and brief moment of crisis leadership were the high-water mark of his life. It would be a staggered series of downhill declines from there. The country moved on, and as the oracle had predicted, the gratitude of the crowd was not enduring. Caesar, Pompey, and Crassus would form their Triumvirate in 60 BC, creating a front of enemies opposed to Cicero. The next consul, in 58 BC, turned openly against Cicero, passing a proscription against him for having condemned citizens to death without a trial. Cicero had to flee Rome in exile, while his property was destroyed.

It was Seneca who observed how quickly time and fate would afflict on Cicero "everything that a victorious Catiline would have done." In fact, his banishment was repealed a year later, but still, change—or dissolution—was in the air.

For the most part, Cicero steered clear of the city. He turned, as much as he could, back to writing and philosophy. He pored over the books at the library of Faustus Sulla near his villa in Cumae, which was once the home of the Stoic teacher Blossius. He worked on a book, *On Oratory* (56 BC), where he compared Cato's use of rhetoric to that of Rutilius Rufus, showing how Rufus's decision to maintain his Stoic brevity in the face of his accusers failed him at precisely the moment good rhetoric could have saved him. Worried about the future of Rome, he wrote two works, *Republic* and *Laws*, which drew on the Stoics Diogenes of Babylon and Panaetius.

But like many historians, and even readers today, he was missing what was staring him in the face: the *lives* these figures had lived. He was missing the common thread through those four Stoics. Character. Commitment. Purpose.

In 51 BC, Cicero was awarded the governorship of Cilicia—a

position well out of the fray of Roman politics, which helped to reburnish his reputation. Really, though, it was a brief respite from the chaos fate had in store for him and for Rome.

Cicero once wrote that the beginnings of things are small. He would also find in those few short years that the ends of things are surprising and fast. In early 49 BC, Caesar—Cicero's former friend and peer— would cross the Rubicon. Caesar's ambition had been slower burning than Cicero's, less self-aggrandizing, but far more aggressive and unbending—and it was backed by the wealth produced by an unmatched and deeply feared army in Gaul. Civil war ensued. By September 48 BC, Pompey—whom Cicero had praised in his first major political speech, and whom his teacher Posidonius had tried to instruct about virtue—would be dead.

Who could stop Caesar now? One would think that this would be the pivotal moment for such a student of philosophy, and a master orator like Cicero—when fate met the man whose time had come. But Cicero, the ambitious striver, was not prepared to meet it. We have, with the benefit of hindsight, the perspective to see that he had wasted himself on the wrong crisis. Thinking that the Catiline conspiracy was his moment to perform for history, he had moved too soon, too severely. He gained fame from it, but the victory was Pyrrhic.

Now the Republic really was hanging in the balance. Never before had Cicero's talents—his ability to persuade, to move the crowd, to tell a story that would drive people to the barricades—been more needed, but he could not summon an audience that would listen. He was impotent too, without much power. Spent, he could do nothing.

Or was he a coward? Offered a command of troops in the Republican cause, Cicero inexplicably turned it down.

Only Cato—the Stoic who wrote less but *lived* the ideas—was willing to fight. But it was not enough. By 46 BC, with Caesar ascendant,

Cato committed suicide in Utica, forever a martyr to the Republican cause. Cicero eulogized him, attempting to capture in words the power of this Stoic he both admired and judged, but whose commitment to principles he lacked. He, along with the rest of Rome, was ready to yield to Caesar and "accept the bridle," as Plutarch puts it.

Cicero's eulogy of Cato is a case in point—although only fifty words of the tribute survive, we know he censored himself for fear of angering Caesar and Caesar's supporters. Both Cato and Cicero cared about what was right—but Cicero cared about himself a little bit more. Cato believed in courage. Cicero believed in not getting killed.

The choice earned Cicero a few years of life, but the Stoics would ask—as we should ask of all self-preserving compromises—"At what cost?"

The one upside of Cicero's capitulation and his fair-weather commitment to philosophy is that by living he was able to continue writing, and to serve as a kind of bridge between Greek and Latin philosophical thought, especially in the area of ethics. And when it came to ethics, he knew of no better source in all of Greek and Latin literature than the Stoics. In the end it wasn't the accomplishments of public office that made his glory, or how Cicero lived his life, but what he set down in writing—wisdom from the Stoics that would endure to our own time.

In 46 BC, Cicero published the *Stoic Paradoxes*, dedicated to Marcus Brutus, who himself had strong Stoic leanings. In what was more a rhetorical exercise than a serious philosophical treatment, he explored six of the primary Stoic paradoxes:

1) that virtue is the only good;
2) that it is sufficient for happiness;
3) that all virtues and vices are equal;
4) that all fools are mad;

5) that only the sage is truly free;

6) that the wise person alone is rich.

These were not paradoxes in the logical sense, only in that they flew in the face of common sense. It was actually the counterintuitiveness of these ideas that the Stoics leaned on to catch people's attention: How can virtue be the only good if we need health and money to live? Is a lie really as bad as killing someone? Plenty of philosophers were visibly poor; how are they rich? The possibilities for discussion, for counterexamples, for *gotcha* moments, were endless—and Cicero loved noodling with the prompts laid down by Zeno and Cleanthes and Aristo and everyone else.

Ironically, what hurt Cicero in politics—the size of his ambition, his vacillation, his desire to please—suited him supremely well in the self-appointed task of being the first to give an eloquent and detailed account of Greek philosophy in the Latin language. While drawn to the rigor and precision of the Stoics, and to their well-developed ethical thinking, he danced with the Academic/Platonist school most regularly, with its skeptical method and insistence on arguing every side of any issue.

As an Academic, his opportunism made for great writing. So too his ability to talk and entertain ideas he didn't actually believe. He was a little like Carneades, arguing all sides of the discussion. This habit, infuriating to those around him, undoubtedly preserved all sorts of disparate sources for us that we can continue to enjoy today. It was beautiful writing, with ideas that would shape the world. Saint Jerome would later worry that he loved Cicero's works more than the Bible. Saint Augustine was converted to philosophy by reading Cicero's now lost work, the philosophical dialogue *Hortensius*. Seneca and other Stoics would read his works with great interest. But as a person, as a leader, his foot-in-both-camps mentality was a shameful vice.

Eventually the bill from the latter came due. The last years of Cicero's life were a mad dash to write and to escape the blows of fate. Indeed, with the exception of a book on rhetoric, *De Inventione,* composed at the early age of around twenty, his major books were all written in a twelve-year span between 56 BC and 44 BC, and in fact the bulk of them between 46 and 44 BC.

If Cicero had completely retreated into his books, we might admire him. Plutarch tells us that he made it a point to visit Rome and pay his respects to Caesar, and even awarded him honors. When Caesar rebuilt a torn-down statue of his own rival, Pompey, Cicero was there to flatter him, perhaps in the way that he himself had always wished to be flattered. *In setting up these statues of Pompey,* Cicero slobbered, *you have firmly established your own.*

Cato, whose martyred body lay fresh in the grave—as did Pompey's— would have been sick at the scene.

In 45 BC, Cicero's beloved daughter Tullia died. Here, Stoicism might have served him well, as he would later advise his friend Brutus over his own tragic loss in a few years. Instead, with nothing to fall back on, nothing to reassure himself, only the ideas in his books and his faltering ambitions, he was bereft and broken. His career seemed over. His life was falling apart.

So Cicero continued to write, but not live, philosophically. He continued to write about Stoicism, but declined to take any of it to heart. In a way, this would be a major contribution of his to the philosophy. By falling short of the doctrines he passed along from Zeno, from Chrysipus, and even from Stoic peers he wrote about like Rutilius Rufus and Cato, he was proving why the ideas matter. He was like Diotimus, showing us what *not* to do.

Cicero would dedicate his book *Tusculan Disputations* to his friend Brutus, and in 45 BC, Brutus in turn would write a book inspired by Stoicism, *On Virtue,* which he would dedicate to Cicero.

Unlike Cicero, Brutus wasn't just dabbling. Like Cato, like a real philosopher, he was prepared to risk everything to save the country he loved: He was going to assassinate Julius Caesar, now the dictator of the republic Cicero and Brutus had loved. When Brutus and Cassius and the other conspirators hatched their plot to kill Caesar, however, they left Cicero out of the loop. They believed he was too nervous, too untrustworthy, too likely to second-guess the plot or undermine it, unintentionally or not. In short, when the moment counted, Cicero couldn't be counted on. He wasn't Stoic enough.

Shakespeare renders it this way:

CASSIUS

But what of Cicero? Shall we sound him?
I think he will stand very strong with us. . . .

BRUTUS

O, name him not! Let us not break with him,
For he will never follow anything
That other men begin.

They feared their friend lacked courage and that his ego would hold them back. History would bear this out. Almost immediately after Caesar's death, Cicero began to take credit for the other men's deed, claiming that Brutus had shouted his name as he plunged the dagger in.

As Cicero would explain in a speech, "Now why me in particular? Because I knew? Quite possibly the reason [Brutus] called my name was just this: after an achievement similar to my own he called on me rather than another to witness that he was now my rival in glory."

What's past is prologue, Shakespeare would say, and so it was with his own life. His need for fame, his tendency to shift with the wind, would dog him to the end. In Caesar's wake rose young Octavian and Mark Antony. Cicero would again choose the wrong side and, conspicuously, decline to serve in the civil war he helped bring about.

Cicero's final work, surprisingly, would be on duty. He had never been a man whose career was about duty. Fame. Honor. Proving doubters wrong. That had been his drive. But with his twenty-one-year-old son, Marcus, just completing his first year of philosophical training in Athens, perhaps Cicero wished to instill in his boy a stronger sense of moral purpose than his own ambitious father had in himself. The work premises that Marcus, like Hercules at the crossroads, is being wooed by vice and at risk of forsaking the path of virtue. In response, Cicero took up the Stoic efforts of Diogenes, Antipater, Panaetius (above all), and Posidonius to not only lay down Stoic ethical theory, but give his wayward son the practical precepts he needed to keep him off the road to ruin.

In the work's dedication, he wrote to Marcus:

Although philosophy offers many problems, both important and useful, that have been fully and carefully discussed by philosophers, those teachings which have been handed down on the subject of moral duties seem to have the widest practical application. For no phase of life, whether public or private, whether in business or in the home, whether one is working on what concerns oneself alone or dealing with another, can be without its moral duty; on the discharge of such duties depends all that is morally right, and on their neglect all that is morally wrong in life.

They are words well written, as was nearly everything Cicero produced. What was missing, it seems, is any personal absorption of them.

In the end, it would be Cicero's love of rhetoric that would seal his personal fate. He had chided Rutilius Rufus for his brevity in the face of his accusers, saying that rhetoric might have saved him. But walking the plank in 44–43 BC, Cicero delivered fourteen orations against Mark Antony, one of the heirs to Caesar's power.

It would be one thing if Cicero had, as Cato would have, simply condemned excess and brutality where he saw it. Instead, his *Philippics*, as the speeches are now known, were a political ploy to play Mark Antony off Octavian, Caesar's nephew, both with equally authoritarian designs. Cicero was splitting the difference, not standing on principle. And considering his grandiose comparison of his own speeches to those made by Demosthenes more than two hundred years earlier, it's clear that once again he was motivated more by the limelight than by truth.

The remarks were his undoing. Caesar, though a tyrant, had always shown leniency and good humor—and love for the art of rhetoric. Mark Antony possessed no such gentleness. The Second Triumvirate debated Cicero's fate for several days, and then, deprived of a trial—as he had deprived his enemies so many years before—the sentence was in: death.

He tried to flee. Then wavered and returned. He contemplated a dramatic suicide like Cato and, shuddering at doing anything so final, struggled on.

Cicero had long talked a big game. He had written about duty; he had admired the great men of history. He had accomplished so much in his life. He had accumulated mansions and honors. He had been to all the right schools. He had held all the right jobs. He had made his name so famous that no one would ever care about his lowly origins again. He was not just a *new* man, he was, for a period, *the* man.

But he had compromised much to get there. He had ignored the sterner parts of Stoicism—the parts about self-discipline and moderation (as his chubby visage demonstrates), the duties and the obligations. He had ignored his conscience, in defiance of the oracle, to seek out the cheers of the crowd. If he had followed Posidonius and Zeno better, his life might not have turned out differently, but he would have been steadier. He would have been stronger.

Now, when it counted, there was nothing in him, nothing in his fair-weather personal philosophy that could have helped him stand up in this moment where cruel fate was bearing down on him. He could not rely on the inner citadel that countless Stoics had when they faced death, because he had not built it when he had the chance.

All Cicero could do was hope for mercy.

It did not come. Exhausted, like an animal that's been chased, he gave up the fight and waited for the killing blow. The assassins caught up with him on a road between Naples and Rome.

He was beheaded, his head, hands, and tongue soon impaled on display at the Forum and Mark Antony's house.

"Cicero is dead."

That's how Shakespeare rendered the sudden fall of this great man. It was abrupt, violent, and final.

One of Caesar's soldiers, Gaius Asinius Pollio, would write one of the most insightful epitaphs for Cicero:

> Would that he had been able to endure prosperity with more self-control, and adversity with more fortitude.... He invited enmity with greater spirit than he fought it.

Indeed.

CATO THE YOUNGER, ROME'S IRON MAN

(KAY-toe)

B. 95 BC

D. 46 BC

ORIGIN: ROME

E very few generations—or perhaps, every few centuries—a man is born with an iron constitution that consists of harder stuff than even his hardiest peers. These are the figures who come to us as myths and legends.

My God, we think, *how did they do it? Where did that strength come from? Will we ever see a person like that again?*

Marcus Porcius Cato was one of these men. Even in his own time it was a common expression: "We can't all be Catos."

This superiority was almost in his blood. He was born in 95 BC to a family that, despite its early plebeian origins, was, by his birth, firmly entrenched in Rome's aristocracy. His great-grandfather, Cato the Elder, began his career as a military tribune and rose through the ranks as quaestor, aedile, praetor, all the way to consul in 195 BC, all the while earning a fortune in agriculture and making his name fighting for the ancestral customs (*mos maiorum*) against the modernizing influences of an ascendant empire. Ironically, the one influence most important to Cato that his great-grandfather fought most stridently against with his conservative zeal was philosophy. It was he, after all, who had wanted to throw the Athenian philosophers from Diogenes's diplomatic mission out of Rome in 155 BC.

How perfect it was that his great-grandson, known as Cato the Younger, would become a famous philosopher, though we should note that Cato the Younger was no Carneades or Chrysippus. There would be no clever dialectics for him. He was cut from a different cloth than even a genius like Posidonius. Nearly every Stoic before and after was in part famous for what they said and wrote. Alone among them, Cato would achieve towering fame not for his words, but for what he did and for who he was. It was only on the pages of his life that he laid down his beliefs as a monument for all time, earning fame greater than any of his ancestors or his philosophical influences.

Not that you would have expected it at first.

As with Cleanthes before him and Winston Churchill nearly two thousand years after him, Cato's early school days were underwhelming. His tutor, Sarpedon, found him obedient and diligent, but thought he "was sluggish of comprehension and slow." There were flashes of brilliance—what Cato did understand stuck in his mind like it had been carved into stone. He was disruptive—not behaviorally (one struggles to imagine this disciplined boy ever acting out), but with his imperious and intense demeanor. He demanded an explanation for every task that was assigned to him, and luckily, his tutor chose to encourage this commitment to logic rather than beat it out of his young charge.

Physical force would have never worked on Cato anyway. There is a story about a powerful soldier visiting Cato's home to argue over some citizenship issue during his childhood. When the determined soldier asked Cato to take up his cause with his uncle, who was serving as his guardian as well as tribune of the plebs, Cato ignored him. The soldier, disliking Cato's lack of deference, attempted to frighten him. Cato, only four years old, stared back, unmoved. Next thing he knew, the soldier was holding him by the feet over a balcony. Cato remained not only un-afraid, but wordless and unblinking, and the soldier, realizing he had been beaten, set the boy down, saying that if Rome were filled with such men he'd never convince anyone. It was the first of a lifetime of battles of political will for Cato, and also a preview of the lengths his frustrated opponents would be forced to go to if they were ever to best him.

It was clear that beneath this determination, there was also an intense, almost radical commitment to justice and liberty. He did not stand for bullying, even in childhood games, and would step in to de-fend younger boys from older ones. Once after visiting the house of Sulla, Cato asked his tutor why so many people were there paying hom-age and offering favors—was Sulla really this popular? Sarpedon ex-plained that Sulla received these honors not because he was loved but because he was *feared*. "Why then didn't you give me a sword," he said, "so I could free my country from slavery?!"

It was likely this intensity—and a temper that Plutarch described as "inexorable"—that led Sarpedon to introduce Cato to Stoicism, hoping that it would help the young boy to channel his rage and his righteous-ness properly. Centuries later, inspired by and in fact cribbing from a play about Cato, George Washington would speak often of the work re-quired to view the intrigues of politics and the difficulties of life "in the calm light of mild philosophy." Washington, born with the same fiery temper, knew of the importance of subsuming his passions beneath a firm constitution.

Most strong-willed leaders have a temper. It's the truly great ones who manage to conquer it with the same courage and control with which they deal with all of life's obstacles.

Cato would study under Antipater of Tyre, who taught him the ba-sics of Stoicism. But unlike many Stoics of his time, the young Cato studied not only philosophy, but also oratory. Rutilius Rufus had been quiet in his own defense—that would never be Cato's way. Still, he did his great-grandfather proud with his circumspection and bluntness.

"I begin to speak," Cato once explained, "only when I'm certain what I'll say isn't better left unsaid."

When Cato did choose to break his silence, he was compelling. "Cato practiced the kind of public speech capable of moving the masses," Plutarch tells us. The rage and fury that had frightened Sarpedon was channeled through his training in Stoic philosophy and rhetoric into a fierce advocacy for justice that would stand out as a defining feature of his personal and political character. As Plutarch put it, "Above all, he pursued the form of goodness which consists in rigid justice that will not bend to clemency or favor." Armed with a resolute and fearless character, Stoic ethical principles, and a powerful proficiency in public speaking, Cato would become a formidable political figure—and a rare one, in that all knew his vote could never be bought.

But before he made his name as a politician, Cato was a soldier. In 72 BC, he volunteered for service in the Third Servile War, against Spartacus. It would have been unconscionable to let someone else serve in his place. To Cato, it was the *actions* one took, the sacrifices one was willing to make—especially at arms defending one's country—that made you a philosopher. And so in that war, as in the battles he fought in, he was fearless and committed, as he believed every citizen was obligated to be.

Fresh from this crucible, he was ready in 68 BC, at age twenty-seven, to stand for military tribune—the same position his father had served in before him. In fact, the Basilica Porcia, the public forum where the tribunes conducted their business, was named after its builder, his great-grandfather. Pregnant with respect for this legacy and always deeply committed to what he felt was *proper*, Cato would be the only candidate who actually adhered to the canvassing restrictions and campaign laws.

Corruption may have been endemic in Rome, but Cato was never one to buy the argument that "everyone else is doing it." It was a strategy that won him respect—at the very least, it made him stand out. As Plutarch recounts, "The harshness of his sentiments, and the mingling of his character with them, gave their austerity a smiling graciousness that won men's hearts."

That included the troops he led over the next three years as his military service took him across the empire, exposing him to the provinces. Some thought visits to these exotic locations might soften the man, or his iron grip on himself, but they were mistaken. And this in part is why he was so well liked—because he carried himself like a common soldier.

War, although it began as a grand adventure, would soon break Cato's heart. In 67 BC, a letter brought word that his beloved brother, Caepio, was ill. Cato and Caepio had always been different, Caepio favoring luxuries and perfumes that Cato would have never allowed himself. But sometimes when it's your brother you look the other way. Cato did more than that—he *idolized* Caepio and, hearing that he was near death, rushed to his side, braving wild and dangerous seas that nearly killed him, in a tiny boat with the only captain he could convince to take him.

Life is not fair and it cares little for our feelings or our plans. Cato had seen this wisdom written countless ways in the books of the philosophy he loved, but he landed in Thrace after a perilous journey to discover that he had missed, by hours, his brother's death. It was a crushing blow, and Cato mourned almost without restraint. "There are times," his biographers Jimmy Soni and Rob Goodman would write of Cato at his brother's deathbed, "when the mask will slip, when our resolve will fail, when our attachments will get the better of us." Yet much closer to Cato's time, Plutarch believed that those who found inconsistency in Cato's grief missed "how much tenderness and affection was mingled with the

man's inflexibility and firmness." Historians too seem to have over-
looked how the loss of his parents and then his cherished brother—
without an opportunity to say goodbye—might have hardened an
already hard man.

Certainly it didn't soften his incorruptibility and commitment to
his ideals. Even as Cato grieved, he politely declined expensive gifts that
friends sent for the funeral rites and repaid, out of his own pocket, what
others sent in the form of incense and ornaments. The inheritance went
to Caepio's daughter without a penny deducted for funeral costs. Cato
covered the expenses himself.

Emerging from his grief, Cato was ready at age thirty—firm and
without illusions—to stand for the office of quaestor. It was his first
entrance into the Senate and, more important, a larger platform for his
intractable dedication to eliminating corruption and returning Rome
to its core values. He used his term as quaestor to overhaul the treasury,
ousting corrupt clerks and scribes, and seeking to redress the ill-gotten
gains under Sullan proscriptions and to track down deadbeat debt-
ors. He was the first to show up for work each morning and the last to
leave, and seemed to relish saying no to the pet projects of politicians,
to needless diversions, and to state-funded luxuries. His commitment was so legendary that it became almost political cover for his less
stringent colleagues, Plutarch tells us. "It's impossible," shrugging politicians would tell constituents lobbying for handouts. "Cato will not
consent."

Did this strictness create enemies? Yes. It was inevitable. Like Cicero, he was at odds with Catiline and other powerful figures vying for
control in an increasingly kleptocratic state. Biographers tell us that
powerful people were hostile to Cato nearly all his life, because his very
essence seemed to shame them.

Even when Cicero aligned with Cato there was a distinction, for there was never a sense that Cato was benefiting from these reforms or that he was quietly accumulating his own wealth through them. In fact, despite his public positions and his wealthy family, Cato often looked like he had no money at all. He rejected the extravagant, brilliantly colored purple robes that were fashionable in the Senate and wore only a plain, ordinary dark robe. He never put on perfume. He walked Rome's streets barefoot and wore nothing underneath his toga. While his friends rode horses, he declined, and enjoyed walking alongside them. He never left Rome while the Senate was in session. He threw no lavish parties and declined to gorge himself at feasts—and was strict about reserving the choicest portions for others. He lent his friends money without interest. He declined armed guards or an entourage, and in the army he slept in the trenches with his troops.

He was a man, Cicero would say, who acted as if he lived in Plato's Republic, not "among the dregs of Romulus."

Cato's iron constitution may have been partly given to him at birth, but it's unquestionable that his choices forged additional armor plating and prepared him for the ordeals he was to face in the future. Plutarch says that Cato was "accustoming himself to be ashamed only of what was really shameful and to ignore men's low opinion of other things."

We naturally care what people think of us; we don't want to seem *too* different, so we acquire the same tastes as everyone else. We accept what the crowd does so the crowd will accept us. But in doing this, we weaken ourselves. We compromise, often without knowing it; we allow ourselves to be bought—without even the benefit of getting paid for it.

Of all the Stoics, it was Cato who most actively practiced Aristo's ideas about being *indifferent* to everything but virtue. Public opinion? Keeping up with appearances? His "brand"? Cato could have lived in great luxury, but he *chose* the Spartan life. And while there might have been a sliver of haughtiness to his demeanor, we are also told that his walks through the streets of Rome were filled with polite salutes to everyone he met and many unsolicited offers to help those in need. Reputation didn't matter. Doing right did.

This might be difficult, it might be exhausting, he said, but soon enough we forget about the hard labor. The results of doing well, though, "will not disappear as long as you live," he said. And conversely, even though taking a shortcut or doing something bad may bring a few seconds of relief, "the pleasure will quickly disappear, but the wicked thing will stay with you forever."

His job, Cato believed, in a tradition begun by Diogenes, was to serve the public good. Not himself. Not expediency. Not his family. But the nation. That's what *real* philosophy was about, whether his skeptical great-grandfather or fame-chasing friend Cicero understood it or not.

When Cato was sent on a mission to supervise the annexation of Cyprus—precisely the kind of opportunity Roman politicians liked to use to fill up their personal bank accounts—his conduct was irreproachable. His scrupulous sale of Cypriot treasures showed zero irregularities and raised some seven thousand talents for Roman coffers. The only thing he left unsold was a statue of Zeno, the founder of the philosophy to which he was so committed. There was one loss: his friendship with a man, Munatius Rufus, who resented that Cato refused to let Munatius enrich himself.

These were powerful gestures—countersignals—in an empire obsessed with status and demonstrations of power. In Cato's case, they were sincere. He was not playacting. He was *practicing*. His studies of Stoicism had taught him the importance of training, of actively resisting temptation and inoculating oneself from the need for comforts and externals. His forefathers had set down a firm example, and he intended to follow it—from the beginning to the end.

Not all Romans could be Catos, but Cato could represent them. In

63 BC, this austere man was named tribune of the plebs, now a powerful position he was eligible for because of his family's ancient plebeian origins—giving him the chance to balance the interests of the disenfranchised with those of the elites. Cicero was consul, and though they quickly joined forces in calling for the death penalty for the Catilinarian conspirators, they were not always in agreement. The trial of Murena—an officer in the Third Mithridatic War and later a consul—became a study in contrast between Cato and Cicero, the inflexible Stoic on one side, the more fluid and ambidextrous Academic on the other. Cicero on the defense, Cato for the prosecution. More bluntly, Cicero was defending an obviously guilty man, who had gained his offices through bribery.

Defending the guilty was inconceivable to Cato, even if earlier Stoics like Diogenes had supported it. Murena had done wrong, he had not played fair, and he must be driven from public life. It was the Stoic argument: What's right is right. Nothing else matters.

Cicero's argument, which comes to us through his published oratory *Pro Murena*, is more complex. As always with Cicero, there was both self-interest and ego involved. But mostly, he believed that Murena's defense was for the good of the state. With Catiline threatening violence against the state, could they really afford to tear themselves apart at the same time? If Murena was convicted and ousted from office, wouldn't the consulship fall into worse hands? Cicero respected Cato immensely, but it's impossible to read his arguments and not get the sense that he found the man's unflinching idealism to be naive. Stoicism was well and good, but not if it was so rigid and inflexible that it put the survival of the government at risk.

Indeed, this would be the continual knock on Cato and on Stoicism to this day: Where does commitment end and obstinance begin? Doesn't government—and life—require compromise? Aren't there times when we have to pick the lesser of two evils?

Cato seemed not to be so sure. Or rather, he was *sure*, and this black-and-whiteness presaged the battles and the destruction that were to come.

As a young boy, Cato had shut down the entreaties of that visiting soldier with quiet, unbreakable defiance. As a politician, he would deploy that same tenacity in a similar fashion. Believing himself to be an essential check on Rome's accelerating collapse and the abandonment of that *mos maiorum* beloved by his ancestors, he pioneered a political trick that remains in use: the filibuster. Using his voice and willpower as weapons, Cato effectively preserved the positions of his party by talking, talking, and talking. He was able to single-handedly prevent the delivery of tax collection contracts to corrupt parties and prevent laws that violated the spirit of Rome's old ways.

At the same time, his inherent conservatism also meant that he resisted necessary change. It is not extreme to say that Cato's one-man resistance fueled a sense in others that similarly unilateral moves would be necessary. When Caesar became consul, he would imprison Cato so as not to hear his marathon ramblings and so that the business of the state could resume.

If the contrast between Cato and Cicero was between personality types, between commitment and compromise, the contrast between Cato and Caesar was more ideological—between Republicanism and Caesarism. It was a battle of wills and a battle of philosophies.

The two were, each with his own excesses, incredible men. The historian Sallust, himself a Caesar supporter, highlighted both:

> But within my own memory there were two men of towering merit, though of opposite character, Marcus Cato and Gaius Caesar. . . . In ancestry, age and eloquence, they were almost equal; on a par was their greatness of soul, likewise their renown,

but each of a different sort. Caesar was considered great because of his benefactions and lavish generosity, Cato for the uprightness of his life. The former became famous for his gentleness and compassion; to the latter sternness had imparted prestige. Caesar gained renown by giving, by relieving difficulties, by forgiving; Cato by no conferral of lavish gifts. In the one was refuge for the unfortunate, in the other destruction for the wicked. The former's easygoing nature was praised, the latter's steadfastness. Finally, Caesar had made up his mind to work hard, to be alert; he devoted himself to the affairs of his friends at the neglect of his own; he refused nothing that was worthy of being given; he craved a major command, an army, a fresh war in which his merit might be able to shine forth. Cato, on the contrary, cultivated self-control, propriety, but above all sternness. He did not vie in riches with the rich, nor in intrigue with intriguers, but with the energetic in merit, with the self-restrained in moderation, with the blameless in integrity. He preferred to be, rather than merely to seem, virtuous; hence the less he sought renown the more it overtook him.

Caesar was motivated by power and control and change. Cato wanted things to go back to how they were in Rome's golden age, before the decadence, before the strongmen and the corruption. If he could not have that, he at least wanted them to stay as they were now—he would do his best to prevent them from getting worse. And so the unstoppable force met the immovable object, and the crash was, over a period of several years, explosive.

History can sometimes seem, especially from a distance, like a Manichean struggle between good and evil. In truth, there is always gray—and the good, even the Catos, are not always blameless. Cato's inflexibility did not always serve well the public good. For instance, after Pompey returned to Rome from his foreign conquests, he felt out potential alliances with Cato, a man whom he respected but often tangled with. It is said that Pompey proposed a marriage alliance with either Cato's niece or daughter. The women, we are told, were excited at the prospect of tying the two families together. Cato dismissed it, and did so rudely. "Go and tell Pompey," he instructed the go-between, that "Cato is not to be captured by way of the women's apartments."

Bravo.

But in so rejecting the alliance, Cato drove the powerful Pompey into an alliance with Caesar instead, who promptly married his daughter, Julia, to Pompey. United and unstoppable, the two men would soon overturn centuries of constitutional precedent. "None of these things perhaps would have happened," Plutarch reminds us, "had not Cato been so afraid of the slight transgressions of Pompey as to allow him to commit the greatest of all, and add his power to that of another."

But Cato was at least consistent in his obstinacy. As Caesar ruled Rome in the Triumvirate with Pompey and Crassus, Cato resisted them at every turn. While they campaigned for co-consul in 55 BC, he was the perpetual thorn in their side, championing the ancestral tradition of the Senate against the dangerous new forces that Caesar unleashed. He accused Caesar of war crimes in Gaul. He cleaned up electoral corruption and designed corruption courts. He insisted on his antibribery policy in elections, which encouraged the fraudsters to whip up votes against him. As Seneca beautifully described:

> In an age when the old credulity had long been thrown aside, and knowledge had by time attained its highest development, [Cato] came into conflict with ambition, a monster of many shapes, with the boundless greed for power which the division of the whole

world among three men could not satisfy. He stood alone against the vices of a degenerate state that was sinking to destruction beneath its very weight, and he stayed the fall of the republic to the utmost that one man's hand could do to draw it back.

It would be a mistake, however, to think that Cato was incapable of compromise or collaboration. Plutarch tells us that he was incapable of enmity. Yes, he was "stubborn and immovable . . . when it came to protecting the public welfare," but when it came to personal disagreements, he was always calm and friendly. Within him there was "an equal blend . . . of severity and kindness, of caution and bravery, of solicitude for others and fearlessness for themselves, of the careful avoidance of baseness and, in like degree, the eager pursuit of justice."

Cato was kind. Cato was tough. He was, in a way, the embodiment of an expression that a stoic in modern times, General James Mattis, would adapt as a motto of the 1st Marine Division: *No better friend, no worse enemy.* Where Rutilius had been a quiet paragon of political virtue, Cato was aggressive and would not be easy to beat. He would invite, only on a far greater scale, a martyr's fate as well. And unlike that of Rutilius, this fate would affect not just him, but the Republic itself.

After Cato lost his bid for consul in 52 BC—no doubt due to the machinations of his political enemies—he decided to push his hand. It was time, he felt, for the Senate to recall Caesar from Gaul. It was certainly the right thing to do, in the sense that Caesar had accumulated incredible power and his wealthy legions menaced the state with their undying loyalty to their master. But Cicero, more pragmatic, dreaded the implications. In 49 BC, Caesar did come up . . . and the 13th Legion followed him home, across the Rubicon, carrying civil war with them.

As with the failed potential alliance with Pompey, it's worth asking: Did it have to be this way? Could a less intransigent politician have navigated the crisis better? Or not forced it to the breaking point? Possibly. But it was not Cato's way to meditate on whether his insistence on *the right thing* had precipitated a much worse thing than the current status quo. Those questions were for the Ciceros of the world, of the theorists and sophists whom his great-grandfather had so despised.

For Cato, to compromise—to play politics with the bedrock laws of his nation at stake—would have been moral capitulation.

In protecting the Roman Republic, Cato may have hastened its destruction. Or perhaps he was drawing a line that should have been drawn by others long before. In any case, he was ready to go down fighting, as we all must be—if we are true philosophers—at some point in our lives.

After a long antagonism, and having spurned Pompey's entreaties years earlier, Cato and Pompey were suddenly on the same team, and both now bore arms in protection of their country. Cato had been a brave soldier early in life and he was again.

He was a selfless solider too. Pompey placed him in command of the military fleet—a massive armada of more than five hundred ships. But quickly, Pompey, thinking about the political situation after the war, reconsidered giving his former enemy so much power. Within days of Cato's appointment, Pompey revoked it. Yet Cato remained undaunted. Without a hint of bitterness, Plutarch tells us, he handed the command over. Indeed, on the eve of the next great battle, it was Cato—so recently demoted and betrayed—who stepped up to inspire Rome's troops in defense of their homeland. As Cato spoke of freedom and virtue and death and flame, Plutarch tells us, "there was such a shouting and so great a stir among the soldiers thus aroused that all the commanders were full of hope as they hastened to confront the peril."

A Stoic does the job that needs to be done. They don't care about credit.

Seneca observed that all ages produce men like Clodius and Caesar and Pompey, "but not all ages men like Cato." Few politicians would have risked their lives for something as abstract as principle, few would have kept going even when the cause spit in their face, few had the combined genius at arms, at leadership, at strategy to have brought his people so close to success.

But Cato did. Pompey hesitated and Caesar won the field in central Greece at Pharsalus in 48 BC. Cato would slip away to North Africa with the hope of fighting on, leading his army on a grueling thirty-day foot march across the hot desert to Utica where they prepared to make a last stand. It was desperate. It was violent.

Victory was not his to win.

Now, the Republic obviously lost, Cato stood and addressed the senators and officers who had so nobly resisted with him. It was time for them to make their way to Caesar and beg for clemency, he said. He asked only one last thing of them. *Do not pray for me,* he said, *do not ask for my grace.* Such pleas belonged to the conquered, and Cato had not lost. Where it mattered, he believed, in all that was honorable and just, he had beaten Caesar. He had defended his country. He had, for all his flaws, shown his true character.

So too, he believed, had Rome's enemies.

It is obvious in retrospect that Cato had already decided how the end would come. All that was left were the arrangements. He attempted to persuade his son to flee on a ship. He got many of his friends off to safety. And then he sat down to dinner with everyone who remained. It was, by all accounts, a wonderful meal. Wine was poured. Dice were rolled for the first cuts. Plates were passed. Philosophy was discussed, as it always was at Cato's table. Were only good men free? Were bad men, like Caesar, slaves?

It was one of those evenings where time passed quickly, where everyone present *was* present. With the specter of death looming, more than a few of them must have hoped the meal might go on forever. Cato, on the other hand, knew that it could not. So as the meal closed, he began to discuss the final travel arrangements and, quite out of character, expressed his worry for his friends embarking by sea. Then he hugged his son and friends and bade them good night.

In his chamber, Cato sat down with a dialogue of Socrates and read it leisurely. Then he called for his sword, which he noticed had been removed from his room, likely by a friend hoping to forestall what could not be forestalled.

It was time.

His son, knowing what his father wanted to do, sobbed, begging him to fight on, to live. Apollonides the Stoic was begged to convince Cato of the philosophical reasons against suicide, but words failed him, only tears came. Restored to his sword, Cato checked its razor edge with his finger. "Now I am my own master," he said, and then sat back down to read his book once more from cover to cover.

He awoke sometime in the early morning after dozing. Alone and ready, he thrust his sword into his breast. It was not quite a mortal blow, but Roman steel had pierced Rome's Iron Man. Still, he could not go quietly into that good night. Writhing, Cato fell, awakening his weeping and mourning friends as he raged against the dying of the light. A doctor rushed in and attempted to sew the wound shut while Cato drifted in and out of consciousness. In his final moments, Cato came to, and with the fierce and almost inhuman determination he had first exhibited as a young boy, he died at forty-nine years old, pulling his own wound open so that life could escape him more quickly.

He had lost his final battle—with Caesar, with the trends of his time, with mortality itself—but not before, as Plutarch would conclude, "he nevertheless gave Fortune a hard contest."

Why suicide? Montaigne would write admiringly that with Cato's unfailing constancy and commitment to principles, "he had to die rather than look on the face of a tyrant." Napoleon, who once displayed a bust of Cato in his "hall of heroes," and in the end faced defeat and lost all that he had striven for and considered suicide himself, would write of Cato's death much more disparagingly. He believed that Cato should have fought on, or waited, rather than seal his fate with his own hand.

"The conduct of Cato was applauded by his contemporaries," Napoleon said, "and has been admired by history; but who benefited from his death? Caesar. Who was pleased by it? Caesar. And to whom was it a tragedy? To Rome and to his party.... No, he killed himself out of spleen and despair. His death was the weakness of a great soul, the error of a stoic, a blot on his life."

But then again, in Napoleon's mind, Caesar was the great hero of the ancient world. He could not understand—not in the way that the true greats of the Enlightenment like Washington and Thomas Paine did—that there was more to this world than just power and accomplishment and winning. Who benefited from Cato's death? Generations that remain inspired by his conduct, which was true and consistent all the way to the end.

You will not find many statues of Cato in Rome or many books about him. For some reason, the honors go to the conquering generals and the tyrants instead. His great-grandfather had once said that it was better to have people ask why there *wasn't* a statue in your honor than why there was. In the case of Cato the Younger, it's even simpler: His character was the monument; his commitments to justice and liberty and courage and virtue are the pillars of the temple that stands to this day.

He was a living statue in his own time, Rome's Last Citizen and Rome's Iron Man, and, now as then, on these pages and in memory, his finger points directly at us.

PORCIA CATO
THE IRON WOMAN

(POUR-shya KAY-toe)

B. 70 BC

D. 43 OR 42 BC

ORIGIN: ROME

I t could be said that the conspicuous lack of credit given to women in the history of Stoicism is actually proof of their philosophical bona fides. Who better illustrates these virtues of endurance and courage, selflessness and duty, than the generations of anonymous wives and mothers and daughters of Greece and Rome who suffered, who resisted tyranny, who lived through wars, who raised families, and who were born and died without ever being recognized for their quiet heroism? Think of what they put up with, think of the indignities they tolerated, and think of the sacrifices they were willing to make.

But that's sort of the problem. We don't think about that. We think about Cato and his great-grandfather. We don't think about his mother or his wife.

The biographer Robert Caro, writing thousands of years after the fall of the Roman Empire about the rise of the American Empire, observed just what this unconscious bias misses. "You hear a lot about gunfights in Westerns," he said of the history of the frontier. "You don't hear so much about hauling up the water after a perineal tear."

While Rutilius Rufus deserves our respect for his brave stand against corruption, what about the forgotten woman who gave birth to him without anesthesia? What about his wife or his daughters, who too lost everything and went without complaint into exile with him? Surely, they deserved at least a mention from Plutarch or Diogenes.

Let us rectify this quickly by looking at the life of Porcia, the daughter of Cato, who seems to rival her father in steely determination and patriotism. Almost two centuries before Musonius Rufus would advocate that women be taught philosophy, Porcia was introduced to Stoicism as a child by her father and quickly dedicated herself to it. Her first marriage was to Marcus Calpurnius Bibulus, an ally of Cato. Bibulus would serve honorably and bravely with Cato in Rome's civil war, but would not survive it.

The only good news after the fall of the Republic that her family had so cherished, and the brutal suicide of the father she loved, was that Julius Caesar pardoned Porcia's brother, Marcus Cato. As the family attempted to pick up the pieces of their shattered lives, we are told she remained resolute. Somehow, her heart managed to find affection and she remarried to Brutus, the senator to whom Cicero had dedicated some of his writings. It appears she deeply loved her philosophical and principled husband, who must have reminded her of her father, and together they would have a son, though fate would once again visit tragedy on young Porcia.

As a knowing wife, she quickly intuited that Brutus was planning something in 44 BC, although what she wasn't sure. Instead of demanding that he explain himself, Porcia decided she would *prove* her trustworthiness to her husband and fortitude to herself—though one would think that her family tree was sufficient.

Plutarch tells us that Porcia took a small knife and stabbed herself in the thigh, and then waited to see how long she could stand the pain.

Bleeding profusely and shaking in near delirium from the wound, when Brutus finally came home, she grabbed him and said:

> Brutus, I am Cato's daughter, and I was brought into thy house, not, like a mere concubine, to share thy bed and board merely, but to be a partner in thy joys, and a partner in thy troubles. Thou, indeed, art faultless as a husband; but how can I show thee any grateful service if I am to share neither thy secret suffering nor the anxiety which craves a loyal confidant? I know that woman's nature is thought too weak to endure a secret; but good rearing and excellent companionship go far towards strengthening the character, and it is my happy lot to be both the daughter of Cato and the wife of Brutus. Before this I put less confidence in these advantages, but now I know that I am superior even to pain.

Shakespeare renders the same scene quite beautifully as well:

> Tell me your counsels, I will not disclose 'em:
> I have made strong proof of my constancy,
> Giving myself a voluntary wound
> Here in the thigh: can I bear that with patience,
> And not my husband's secrets?

As strange and nearly unbelievable as this story is to us today, Roman history is littered with examples of conspiracies revealed under torture and interrogation. It's not a stretch that Porcia might want to see how much suffering she could endure. Brutus was so moved by what he witnessed that he immediately informed his wife of the plot to kill Caesar and prayed that he would be able to prove himself worthy of her courage.

Of course, Plutarch was not content to show this impressive feat of female power without later counterbalancing it with "evidence" of the fragility of the female mind. We are told that on the Ides of March, Porcia nearly went out of her mind as she waited for word of events. Did her husband succeed? Had he been caught? Was no news good news? Did she need to flee?

"Porcia," Plutarch writes, "being distressed about what was impending and unable to bear the weight of her anxiety could with difficulty keep to herself at home, and at every noise or cry, like women in Bacchic frenzy, she would rush forth and ask every messenger who came in from the forum how Brutus was faring, and kept sending out others continually." He writes that she eventually fainted and rumor reached Brutus that she had died, but that with great strength, Brutus resisted rushing home and executed the violent deed to which they were both so committed.

Shakespeare, drawing on Plutarch and centuries of sexism, seems to think that Porcia is mentally strong but physically weak:

> I have a man's mind, but a woman's might.
> How hard it is for women to keep counsel!

It seems unlikely that the same woman who could hide a gushing leg wound, who had stoically endured so much loss and uncertainty in her life, would be unable to control her anxiety for a few hours. After all, Brutus was more trusting of his wife's ability to keep the secret than he and his conspirators were of Cicero, whom they kept in the dark because of his high-strung nature. But this is what the men who have written our history would have us believe.

In any case, the lessons stands: Deciding on a bold deed takes courage, but the execution matters too. Porcia and her husband would need to add patience and wisdom to the equation as well, for nothing racks the nerves quite like the moments, as Shakespeare would say, between decision and action.

The senators, led by Brutus, descended on Caesar with a savagery that surprised both their victim and themselves. Brutus's blows landed in Caesar's thigh and in his groin, another senator stabbed him in the face, another still in the ribs. Several senators wounded themselves in the frenzy, and Brutus himself was struck in the hand. Where was this violence when Cato needed it? When Caesar could have been stopped before he started?

And then, like a fit, the passion subsided and the deed was done. Brutus calmed his conspirators down quickly. No one else was to be killed, not even Caesar's most prominent supporter, Mark Antony. This seems noble, but it turned out to be a fatal error.

During the Catiline conspiracy, Cicero's wife urged him to execute his enemies, to destroy the cancer before it spread. We're told that Brutus, abhorring violence, was reluctant to shed any more blood. Porcia could have reminded him that deeds cannot be only half done—that sometimes mercy to the undeserving is a grave injustice to everyone else. Or perhaps she did and he refused to listen.

This restraint would prove to be the undoing of them and their cause.

As Caesar lay dead, civil war—led by Antony—returned to Rome. It must have been traumatic for Porcia to be experiencing this yet again, particularly since the last one had stolen from her both her husband and her father, as well as countless friends. Parting ways with Brutus, who had to flee to begin what would be the fight of his life, a friend quoted from the famous parting of Hector and his wife in the Trojan War. Brutus in turn quoted from the *Odyssey* in a way that reveals not just his love for his wife, but also his abiding belief that she was an equal to him in philosophical determination and courage. "But I, certainly, have no mind to address Porcia in the words of Hector," he said. "'Ply loom and distaff and give orders to thy maids,' for though her body is not strong enough to perform such heroic tasks as men do, still, in spirit she is valiant in defence of her country, just as we are."

Neither of their heroic efforts could stem the tide of history. Perhaps, had her father survived, his superior generalship could have been decisive. Or if Cicero had not vacillated again or danced with Octavian, his help might have saved the Republic for another generation of Catos. But it was not to be.

We have conflicting sources as to whether Porcia died before Brutus or Brutus before Porcia. Plutarch tells us that when Brutus's ashes were sent home to his mother, Servilia, Porcia resolved to depart from this earth, following the example of her father. Her attendants kept close watch over her, trying to prevent another Cato from suicide. But this was not a family easily stopped from doing what it believed was necessary. When her servants turned their backs, Porcia rushed to a fireplace, picked up glowing red coals, and quickly swallowed them, dying quite literally as the fire-eating lover of freedom her father had raised her to be. Other sources claim she died of illness before Brutus's death at the second battle of Philippi, while others still that it was illness and loneliness that drove her to suicide.

It would seem that Brutus was aware of his wife's loss, as there is a letter from Cicero in 43 BC consoling him about it. "You have suffered indeed a great loss (for you have lost that which had not left its fellow on earth)," he wrote, "and must be allowed to grieve under so cruel a blow, lest to want all sense of grief should be thought more wretched than grief itself: but do it with moderation, which is both useful to others and necessary to yourself."

Cicero's admonition to be stoic about Porcia's death is touching considering how wrecked he had been by the death of his daughter, Tullia, in 45 BC. It raises the eternal question of how one ought to respond to the loss of someone they love dearly. Can a philosopher shrug off this pain, like they might a wound in the thigh? Is indifference to grief actually possible? Is it perfectly understandable that such a loss might finally crack the hard exterior of the Stoic, the way it nearly had for Cato when he lost his brother, and when Marcus Aurelius would weep over the loss of his beloved tutor?

Shakespeare, always the astute observer of the human experience, explores this tension, having made his character Brutus a stand-in for all that he believed a Stoic philosopher was supposed to represent.

"I am sick of many griefs," Brutus tells a contentious ally, Cassius, who attempts to remind him of what the Stoics believed about accepting what was outside our control. "No man bears sorrow better," Brutus tells him with flat affect. "Portia is dead."

So is this Stoicism? A man who can spit out those painful words without flinching? *My wife is dead,* and then get on with a discussion about the upcoming battle? Perhaps.

But Brutus was no Porcia, who had always been all action and no talk. He had a flair for the theatric; he desired to be credited for those virtues that he made sure were conspicuous.

So when, a few minutes later, a messenger named Messala appears with news, Brutus sees an opportunity to perform for history. The word comes that Cicero is dead and a hundred senators have been executed. *Have you heard from your wife?* the messenger asks. Brutus replies that he hasn't. *Have you heard anything at all?* he asks. Again, Brutus pretends he does not know. "Tell me true," Brutus demands. So prompted, the messenger informs him that Porcia has died.

And then, whether for the sake of his reputation or to inspire others with his Stoic example, we get this:

BRUTUS

> Why, farewell, Portia. We must die, Messala.
> With meditating that she must die once,
> I have the patience to endure it now.

MESSALA

> Even so great men great losses should endure.

CASSIUS

> I have as much of this in art as you,
> But yet my nature could not bear it so.

BRUTUS

> Well, to our work alive. What do you think
> Of marching to Philippi presently?

Though Porcia departed from this earth as the Republic died its final death, she would live on as a powerful symbol of resistance for men and women forever. She had lived as her father and the Stoics had taught: We must do what needs to be done. We must not waver. We cannot be afraid.

More, she had proved that courage—and philosophy—don't know gender. They know only the people who are willing to put in what it takes and those who aren't.

ATHENODORUS CANANITES
THE KINGMAKER

(Ah-thee-na-DOOR-us
Kah-na-KNEE-tays)

B. 74 BC

D. 7 AD

ORIGIN: TARSUS

The Roman Republic bled out alongside Cato and Cicero. What emerged was the Roman Empire, a new political order that was all about power, increasingly concentrated in a single man. Not Caesar, but *a* Caesar—the title each successor bore for the next three hundred years. The first was Octavian, Caesar's nephew. He would begin the process of despotism slowly, refusing every title and power along the way, only to very cleverly usurp them all as his own over time.

One might think that Stoicism, having been born in the cradle of democratic Athens and then nursed for centuries against the backdrop of Alexander's warring generals, before finally coming of age in Rome's great Republic, would have trouble in this brave new world.

This is incorrect.

The Stoics were nothing if not resilient, and so it came to be that the new emperor's closest advisors were Stoics.

It makes sense. At the core of Stoicism is the acceptance of what we cannot change. Cato had given his life to defend the Republic and he had lost. Brutus had not only failed in his attempt to restore liberty to Rome, but had plunged the country into a second civil war. Now a new

state had been created and peace had returned, and the Stoics who survived believed it was their obligation to serve this state and ensure it
remained the same—and so they set out, as best they could, to mold
young Octavian into Augustus Caesar, the *emperor.*

The first Stoic to occupy that role in Octavian's life was Athenodorus
Cananites, another Tarsian Stoic, born in Canana, in what is today
southeastern Turkey, not far from the birthplace of Stoics like Chrysippus and Antipater. Athenodorus studied under Posidonius at his school
in Rhodes and then later lived in Athens, where he experimented with
oceanographic study like his teacher. He was later a correspondent of
Cicero's, and gave Cicero much of the research on Panaetius that would
go into his masterwork *On Duties.*

After completing his philosophical education under Posidonius,
Athenodorus traveled widely as a lecturer, reaching as far as Petra and
Egypt, along with other major cities in the Mediterranean, before assuming the role of young Octavian's teacher in Apollonia, on the coast
of modern Albania. It was here that this famous and widely respected
teacher, who was not quite thirty years old, became not only Octavian's tutor but his very close friend. When Caesar was murdered in 44
BC, Octavian returned to Rome as the nineteen-year-old named heir.
Athenodorus followed closely behind, charged with developing the kind
of mind required for supreme leadership.

Octavian was bright but by no means an easy student. He was
deeply superstitious, a trait that would have been repulsive to a rational
Stoic . . . and hardly a virtue in a king. We get a sense of Athenodorus's
teaching style—and his calm Stoic demeanor—by way of a ghost story
he would have almost certainly passed along to his Caesar. Renting a
large mansion in Athens that was purported to be haunted, Athenodorus,
undaunted by the stories, set about putting his house in order. Almost

immediately, he said, he was visited by a ghost clapped in irons and dragging heavy chains. Not to be disturbed from his writing session, Athenodorus motioned for the ghost to wait and returned to his work. When he finished, he got up and followed the apparition into the courtyard, where it suddenly vanished. Thinking fast, Athenodorus marked the spot where the ghost disappeared and then returned to tidy up his desk and go to bed. In the morning, he had workers return to the spot and ordered them to dig. Beneath the dirt they found ancient bones in chains, which Athenodorus had reburied with honors in a public funeral. The ghost was never seen again, by him or any other resident of the house.

Whether one believed in ghosts or the supernatural, as Octavian likely did, was beside the point. Stoics must *always* keep their head. Even the scariest situations can be resolved with reason and courage. And even if you believe in silly things like ghosts or superstitions, you can't let your life be ruled by them. *You* must be in charge—no excuses.

Temperance and wisdom, as well as diligence, were essential to Athenodorus, and they played an integral part in his teachings to his young emperor. "You will know you've been freed from all desires when you've reached the place where you will pray to God for nothing but things you'd ask for openly," he would say. "Live among men as if God were watching, and speak with God as if men were listening." In his book *On Taking Pains and Education*, he would speak of *spoudes*—the zealous effort—required to survive and thrive in life.

Seneca, who would advise emperors himself, studied Athenodorus's example and is the source for much of our knowledge of him. From him, we learn that Athenodorus balanced out his teachings on sobriety and hard work with a focus on the importance of tranquility, particularly for leaders. Yes, we must carefully follow public affairs, but it was also necessary to leave behind the grind of work and the stress of politics with retreats into the private sphere of friends. Athenodorus would note that Socrates would stop and play games with children in order to rest and have fun. The mind must be replenished with leisure, Athenodorus believed, or it was likely to break under pressure, or be susceptible to vices.

We know that Athenodorus offered similar advice to Octavian's sister, Octavia, after she lost her son, telling her to busy herself with practical matters rather than give in completely to grief and stress.

The difficulties and corruptions of a busy world made leisure an integral part of *euthymia*, the well-being of the soul, a core concern of Athenodorus and good advice from a Stoic who was advising a king.

Athenodorus's final lesson to Augustus was one Seneca would have appreciated. Asking to be relieved of his duties so that he might return to his home, Athenodorus offered one last piece of practical advice to the emperor—something he wanted him to follow always. "Whenever you feel yourself getting angry, Caesar," he instructed, "don't say or do anything until you've repeated the twenty-four letters of the alphabet to yourself."

Good advice for the ordinary. Essential for an emperor. And sadly ignored by leaders of all types—to the detriment of those who depend on and work with them.

Augustus knew this was true, which is why, upon hearing the advice, he begged his teacher to stay on for one more year. "I still need your presence here," he said. And Athenodorus, duty-bound by his philosophy to guide the state and work for his fellow citizens, gladly assented.

After giving Augustus one last year in Rome, Athenodorus returned to Tarsus around 15 BC, where he spent his final years cleaning up the political messes left by less enlightened rulers. Now, no longer the man behind the man, but leading himself, he applied the principles he had spent so long teaching and speaking about.

A lifetime of training prepares us for the moment of our final act. In Athenodorus's case, he was ready and he served his country well. Enough that the people of Tarsus loved him deeply, and, following his death at age eighty-two, honored him in a public festival every year after.

ARIUS DIDYMUS
THE KINGMAKER II

(AIR-ee-us DID-im-us)

B. 70 BC

D. 10 AD   ORIGIN: ALEXANDRIA

There was more than one great Stoic in Octavian's life. The other's name was Arius Didymus, and though we know a bit less about him, we know much more about what he believed and, through his writings, the central teachings of the Stoics.

We know that Arius had come into Octavian's life sometime around the year 44 BC and that he brought his young sons with him. His sons quickly became Octavian's "tent-companions," according to Suetonius, keeping the boy "well-versed in various forms of learning." Indeed, it was through this close relationship that Octavian would learn to read and appreciate the Greek language.

However Arius came into Octavian's circle, once in it, he was firmly lodged. He became, in his words, the emperor's "constant companion, and knew not only what all men were allowed to know, but all the most secret thoughts" of his heart.

When the thirty-three-year-old Octavian triumphantly entered Alexandria in 30 BC, he and Arius were walking literally hand in hand. The long civil war between Octavian and Antony had been violent and bloody, and the people of Alexandria—having been brought into the middle of it through Antony's obsessive affair with Cleopatra—feared for the worst. Octavian chose to publicly display his affection for Arius not only because it was sincere, but also because by aligning himself with this native Alexandrian, he could reassure the population that he meant no harm. We are told that Octavian delivered a speech in Greek, almost certainly written with Arius's help, announcing that he would spare the city, for a few reasons. The first, he said, was because Alexandria was great and beautiful. The second, because it had been founded and named after such a great man. "And thirdly," Octavian said with a smile, and motioning to Arius, "as a favor to my friend here."

Alexandrians saw immediately how much sway Arius had with their new conqueror. A philosopher named Philostratus who believed himself to be on Octavian's enemies list took to following Arius around the city, begging to be spared. "A wise man will save a wise man," he pleaded, "if wise he be." From Plutarch we hear that Octavian pardoned the man—mostly to save his teacher from the annoyance.

To be used as a symbol of peace is somewhat ironic given Arius's name (Arius Didymus translates literally as "Warlike Twin") and darker still given the Machiavellian—though pragmatic—advice that Arius would give his young charge. Whereas Athenodorus seemed to have mainly concerned himself with Octavian's education and his moral character, Arius instructed him directly on political matters too. The most urgent matter in Alexandria, in Arius's view, was mopping up the potential threats to the throne. Plutarch says Arius advised Octavian to kill Caesar's son with Cleopatra, the young Caesarion, telling him that "it's not good to have too many Caesars." Octavian would wait until Cleopatra had buried his former ally-cum-rival Antony and until she had poisoned herself to act on Arius's advice. Then he made the lethal move to eliminate Caesarion, not willing to risk the existence of any rival heirs, even if it meant killing the son of Caesar, whom he had claimed to love. Soon after, the Caesarium temple Cleopatra had built in Alexandria for Julius Caesar would be finished—except it would be dedicated to Augustus instead, his son's murderer and soon to be the first emperor of Rome.

It was dirty business, but Arius the Stoic advisor believed it needed to be done. With Cato and Cicero and Porcia in mind, he could not countenance another bloody civil war. Nor could Rome.

Since the early Stoic leaders, Stoicism had been moving toward politics and the centers of power, but through their proximity to Octavian, Arius and Athenodorus suddenly wielded more political power than any Stoics in history. Under the reign of Augustus, the empire added more territory than in any preceding period. Its population surged to some forty-five million inhabitants. Augustus now commanded all of it, facing only the most nominal checks and balances, and behind him, as his board of advisors, were two Stoic philosophers. At one point, Arius was offered the position of governor in Egypt but declined it, one suspects because he had far more influence in his informal role with Augustus than he would even governing one of the largest provinces in the empire. He preferred instead to remain within sight of the emperor and help Alexandria from afar, not unlike, Plutarch notes, the way Panaetius helped Rhodes through his friend Scipio.

Augustus had begged Athenodorus to stay another year when he had attempted to resign, but it's clear that he was deeply reliant on both teachers. We hear from the historian and statesman Themistius that Augustus claimed to value Arius as much as his powerful chief lieutenant, Marcus Agrippa. He valued Arius so much, he says, that he wouldn't insult or inconvenience the eminent philosopher by dragging him "into the stadium's dust" to watch the gladiatorial games.

Arius was close to Augustus's family too, famously writing a consolation—a letter to a grieving person—to Livia, the empress, when she lost her son Drusus, that was more moving, Livia said, than the thoughts and prayers of millions of Romans. "Do not, I implore you," he had written to her, "take a perverse pride in appearing the most unhappy of women: and reflect also that there is no great credit in behaving bravely in times of prosperity, when life glides easily with a favouring current: neither does a calm sea and fair wind display the art of the pilot: some foul weather is wanted to prove his courage. Like him, then, do not give way, but rather plant yourself firmly, and endure whatever burden may fall upon you from above; scared though you may have been at the first roar of the tempest. There is nothing that fastens such a reproach on Fortune as resignation." Instead, Arius said, join us in remembering fondly the memories of the young man they had lost and think of the children and grandchildren still living.

The Stoics would have never argued that life was fair or that losing someone didn't hurt. But they believed that to despair, to tear ourselves apart in bereavement, was not only an affront to the memory of the person we loved, but a betrayal of the living who still needed us.

That's not an easy message to deliver to a mother who has just buried her son, yet Arius managed to do it with sensitivity and grace and a compassion that she was forever grateful for.

Although we have just an example or two of Arius's realpolitik, we have much more evidence of his Stoic teachings. Several manuscripts of his writings survive—manuscripts that express not just his beliefs but summaries of centuries of Stoic doctrine. At the core of these writings are discussions of the four cardinal virtues: wisdom (*phronesis*), self-control (*sophrosune*), justice (*dikaiosune*), and bravery (*andreia*). Marcus Aurelius, very familiar with Arius's legacy—both politically and philosophically— would put those four virtues on the ultimate pedestal. If we ever find something better than "justice, honesty, self-control, courage . . . if you find anything better than that, embrace it without reservations," he wrote—they must be very special indeed.

To Arius, there was in fact nothing better than those four virtues. Everything that was evil lacked them and everything that was good contained them. Everything else was indifferent—or irrelevant.

In his writings, Arius sought to systematize all the commonly held virtues under this fourfold schema, as well as to account for their relation to other parts of Stoic doctrine. In doing it, he created a kind of road map for the aspiring Stoic, whether they were an emperor trying to control their passions or an ambitious young person setting out on a career in business.

His definitions were straightforward, essentially defining virtue as types of knowledge. As he simply defines it:

- Wisdom is the knowledge of what things must be done and what must not be done and what is neither, or appropriate acts (*kathekonta*). Within wisdom, we'll find virtuous qualities like soundness of judgment, circumspection, shrewdness, sensibleness, soundness of aim, and ingenuity.
- Self-control is the knowledge of what things are worth choosing and what are worth avoiding and what is neither. Contained within this virtue are things like orderliness, propriety, modesty, and self-mastery.
- Justice is the knowledge of apportioning each person and situation what is due. Under this banner Stoics placed piety (giving gods their due), kindness, good fellowship, and fair dealing.
- Bravery is the knowledge of what is terrible and what isn't and what is neither. This included perseverance, intrepidness, greatheartedness, stoutheartedness, and, one of Arius's most favored virtuous

qualities—one he illustrated well in his own life—*philoponia,* or industriousness.

In contrast to these four virtues, stupidity, lack of restraint, injustice, and cowardice are all the lack of this knowledge. It's an idea that matches up well with another set of categories Arius attempted to organize the world into, which he claimed came from Zeno. There are only two types of people in this world, he wrote, wise people and fools, or the worthwhile and the worthless. Worthless fools lack the knowledge that the wise use in the pursuit of virtue. It's black and white without much room for the gray of the world. One is tempted, for instance, to ask Arius which of the four virtues a person falls under—and whether it's the wise or the foolish—who murders young princes who might someday be rivals. Justice? Wisdom? Or is there perhaps another unlisted category entitled *political expediency?*

Certainly Zeno never said anything about that.

The point for Arius, though, was that while we have the natural ability to exhibit these virtues, it is in fact an active practice of cultivating and refining them that makes a person wise and good. At the core of it, he felt that living a virtuous life was about achieving a "disposition of the soul in harmony with itself concerning one's whole life."

Did he get there himself? We can't know. Did he and Athenodorus get Octavian—a man who took on absolute power and all the corruptive pressures that come along with it—a bit closer to virtue? Yes.

Augustus was nowhere near perfect, but he was not Nero. The sources show a man who got better over time, certainly not the rule among leaders or human beings, particularly those with absolute power. He seemed to earnestly strive to be great, to be in control of himself, and to live by those cardinal virtues. When, near the end of his life,

Augustus remarked that he had inherited a Rome of brick but left the world an empire of marble, he was not wrong. Buildings stand to this day that are a testament to that hard work, and by extension to the philosopher who exhorted him to follow that path.

Could he have done this without the lessons of his teachers and their philosophy? Can anyone? No. We need guidance and we need to love the process of getting better, the Stoics believed, or we will regress to the level of everyone else. Close to Arius's heart, Octavian was the epitome of *philoponia*—and seemed to genuinely love to toil on behalf of the good of everyone.

Few men and women who have had the royal life—or power and success—thrust upon them can have that said about them. Because few, then and now, put in the work.

"None of the worthless are industrious," Arius wrote. "For industriousness is a disposition able to accomplish unhesitatingly what is befitting through toil, and none of the worthless are unhesitating with regard to toil." Augustus worked hard—no one could accuse him of using the throne for rest. Nor is there any evidence that his teachers were, as Seneca would later be charged, corrupted by their proximity and access to power.

Would the *mos maiorum* and the *libertas* of Cato's Republic have been preferable to this new Augustan age? Almost certainly. Imperial power is good for no one, least of all the person wielding it. But by 27 BC, when Octavian became Augustus, a return to the old ways was no longer in the control of Arius or Athenodorus. All they could do was make the best of what they faced—and mold their charge into the best man they could.

As Arius would write, like Panaetius before him, we each have our own implanted gifts (*aphormai*), resources that can lead us to virtue.

Our personalities suit us differently to different paths of ethical development. We all have different launching points, but these inborn tools together with hard effort will get us to where we want to go.

We must focus on the task at hand, and waste not a moment on the tasks that are not ours. We must have courage. We must be fair. We must check our emotions. We must, above all, be wise.

This is what Arius and Athenodorus attempted to live and attempted to teach. It made them trusted advisors, at the highest level, and helped shape what would become Pax Romana. Their guidance—the proximity of Stoicism to the throne—not only shaped Augustus and then Seneca, but would inspire the philosopher king himself, Marcus Aurelius.

They would also, in the end, for all their power and influence, teach Marcus and us a lesson in humility and mortality. As Marcus wrote, summing up what was then an ancient era:

> Augustus' court: his wife, his daughter, his grandsons, his stepsons, his sister, Agrippa, the relatives, servants, friends, Arius, Maecena, the doctors, the sacrificial priests . . . the whole court, dead . . . someone has to be the last. There, too, the death of the whole house.

Athenodorus died. Arius died. Augustus died . . . and the wheels of time kept turning.

AGRIPPINUS THE DIFFERENT

(Agri-PEE-nus)

B. UNKNOWN

D. AFTER 67 AD   ORIGIN: UNKNOWN

W e don't know much about Paconius Agrippinus besides the fact that his father was executed by the emperor Tiberius, the successor of Augustus, on trumped-up charges of treason. We don't know what Agrippinus wrote, or where he was born—or even when he was born and when he died.

We know that he lived in the age of Tiberius's successors, two corrupt and violent emperors, Claudius and Nero, but where he went to school, or how he entered government service, remains a mystery to us.

Yet for all the unknowns about Agrippinus, he leaps out from the historical record as a kind of swashbuckling and distinctive figure, one who stood out even among the bravest and best-known Stoics of his time.

This was no accident. Because in a Roman Empire that had by the time of Claudius and Nero given itself over fully to avarice and corruption, anyone who truly lived by the Stoic principles—as Agrippinus did—would stand out.

According to Agrippinus, we are all threads in a garment—which means that most people are indistinguishable from each other, one thread among countless others. Most people were happy conforming, being anonymous, handling their own tiny, unsung role in the fabric. Who can blame them? Under a tyrant, the best strategy is usually to keep a low profile, to blend in so one does not catch the attention of the capricious and cruel ruler who holds the power of life and death.

But to Agrippinus, even having lost his father under such circumstances, this kind of compromise was inconceivable. "I want to be the red," he said, "that small and brilliant portion which causes the rest to appear comely and beautiful. . . . 'Be like the majority of people?' And if I do that, how shall I any longer be the red?"

Years later there would be a song by Alice in Chains, which would say in a nutshell what Agrippinus believed in his heart: "If I can't be my own, I'd feel better dead."

Individuality and autonomy, these are things many people pay lip service to—in fact, it's almost become a new form of conformity. We talk about being our unique selves, about letting our colors shine, but deep down we know this is just talk. Under pressure, when it really counts, we want the same things as everyone else. We do the same things as everyone else.

Not Agrippinus. He was willing to stand out—to be bright red— *even if it meant being beheaded or exiled.*

Nor was this desire driven by ego or a love of attention, as it unfortunately is even among those rare men and women who reject convention.

"It right to praise Agrippinus," Epictetus tells us, "because, although he was a man of the very highest worth, he never praised himself, but used to blush even if someone else praised him." It was standing on principle that brought fame to Agrippinus, and yet if he could have taken his stands in private, without attracting attention, he would have.

What he drew his fame from was his able service as the governor of Crete and Cyrene, surprising many with his dedication as an administrator, while others were using the same positions to line their pockets. Tacitus tells us that Agrippinus had inherited his "father's hatred towards emperors" after the injustice he had seen done to his "guiltless" father. It was an injustice indeed—for not only was his father likely innocent, his actual death sentence was finally executed after the highly sensitive emperor was teased by a palace dwarf for having waffled on the issue. It's remarkable this absurd mockery of the courts did nothing to diminish Agrippinus's commitment to the law and to applying it fairly and earnestly when the duty later fell to him.

"When Agrippinus was governor," Epictetus would recount admiringly, "he used to try to persuade the persons whom he sentenced that it was proper for them to be sentenced. 'For,' he would say, 'it is not as an enemy or as a brigand that I record my vote against them, but as a curator and guardian; just as also the physician encourages the man upon whom he is operating, and persuades him to submit to the operation.'"

This commitment was increasingly unusual in an empire where avarice was rewarded and principles were baggage. It does not seem to have occurred to Agrippinus, however, to be anything other than pure and committed and clear-eyed.

In a famous exchange, which is preserved to us by Epictetus, Agrippinus was approached by a philosopher who was wrestling with whether he should attend and perform at some banquet thrown by Nero, one that we can imagine Seneca had prepared a speech for. Agrippinus told the man he should go. But why, the man asked? *Because you were even thinking about it.* For me, Agrippinus said, it's not even a question.

To Agrippinus, there should be no hemming and hawing about the right thing. There should be no weighing of options. "He who once sets himself about such considerations," Epictetus said about Agrippinus, "and goes to calculating the worth of external things, approaches very near to those who forget their own character." Character is fate, is how

Heraclitus—one of the Stoics' favorite influences—put it. That was true for Agrippinus, as it had been for Aristo long ago and Cato too. He believed that only character decided difficult matters, and did so clearly and cleanly. No calculating, no consideration was necessary. The right thing was obvious.

When Agrippinus was eventually accused of conspiracy against Nero, he found himself brought up on charges just like his father. "I hope it may turn out well," he said to a friend as his trial began, and then, noting the hour, reminded him that it was time for their daily exercise. As the Senate decided his fate, as his life hung in the balance, Agrippinus worked out and then relaxed in a cold bath. Just as Cato had enjoyed one final dinner before his demise, so Agrippinus took a nice steam before news was brought to him: *You have been condemned.*

A normal person might have fallen on their knees or cursed the injustice. Agrippinus betrayed neither anxiety nor fear about his fate. He had only practical questions. Banishment or death? Exile, his friends said. Did they confiscate my property? No, thank god, they told him. "Very well," he said, "we shall take our lunch in Aricia."

Aricia was the first stop on the road out of Rome. Meaning: We might as well get this exile show under way. No use bemoaning or weeping about it. *Hey, is anyone else hungry?*

Certainly many people—including his fellow Stoics—have responded to better circumstances with worse. But that's who Agrippinus was—he was different. "I am not a hindrance to myself," Epictetus quotes him as saying. He did not add to his troubles by bemoaning them. He would not compromise his dignity or his composure for matters big or small, whether it was a meaningless party or a cruel miscarriage of justice. "His character was such," said Epictetus, "that when any hardship befell him he would compose a eulogy upon it; on fever, if he had a fever; on disrepute, if he suffered from disrepute; on exile, if he went into exile."

He saw life for what it was, exile for what it was, the cruelty of emperors for what it was, accepted it, and moved on.

And for what was Agrippinus sent packing? What crime had he committed and on what evidence was he convicted? Tacitus comes up empty, but provides a clue when he explains that at the same time, Nero had also driven from Rome a young, viceless, and venomless poet simply because he had been too talented. So it was the same for Agrippinus. He had dared to be different. He had been the bright red in an empire where Nero deemed himself the only one worthy of standing out.

Because that's the other expression that Agrippinus had either missed or decided he refused to be intimidated by: Yes, the beauty of the garment is made by the threads that stand out, but it's equally true that the nail that sticks up gets hammered down.

To a man like Agrippinus—and his father before him—this was a cost worth paying. Indeed, they did not even *consider* the alternative.

SENECA THE STRIVER

(SEH-ne-ka)

B. 4 BC

D. 65 AD   ORIGIN: CORDUBA, SPAIN

It would please Lucius Annaeus Seneca very much to know that we are still talking about him today. Unlike many of his fellow Stoics, who wrote of the worthlessness of posthumous fame, Seneca craved it, worked for it, performed for it, right down to the last moments of his life and the theatrical suicide that would rival Cato's.

Unlike Jesus, who was born the same year as Seneca in an equally far-flung province of the Roman Empire, there was little meekness or humility in Seneca. Instead, there was ambition and talent and a will to power that not only rivaled but surpassed Cicero's.

Contemporaries may have believed that Cicero was a better writer and speaker, but Seneca is the more widely read figure today, for good reason. No one has written more cogently and relatably about the struggles of a human being in the world—their desire for tranquility, meaning, happiness, and wisdom. The readership of the essays and letters Seneca wrote over his long life has not only eclipsed Cicero's, but in the long run likely all the other Stoics' combined as well.

Just as he aimed all along.

Born around 4 BC in Corduba, Spain (modern Córdoba), the son of a wealthy and learned writer known to history as Seneca the Elder, Seneca the Younger was destined for great things from birth. So were his brothers, Novatus, who became a governor, and Mela, whose son, Lucan, carried on the family's writing tradition.

Entering the world near the end of the reign of Augustus, Seneca was the first major Stoic with no direct experience of Rome as a republic. Seneca knew only of the empire; in fact, he would live through the reigns of the first five emperors. Never did he breathe in the freedom of Roman *libertas* that Cato and his predecessors had all enjoyed. Instead, he spent his entire life attempting to maneuver within the turbulent court regimes of increasingly autocratic and unpredictable power.

Yet for all these changes, his childhood remained more or less identical to those of the philosophers who had come before him. His father selected Attalus the Stoic to tutor his boy, primarily for the man's reputation for eloquence, wanting to imbue his son not just with a righteous mind but with one capable of communicating these ideas clearly and convincingly in Roman life. His son took to education with gusto—by Seneca's own telling, as a child he cheerfully "laid siege" to the classroom and was the first to arrive and last to leave it. We know that Attalus didn't tolerate "squatters," the kind of students who lounge around and listen, or at best take notes so as to memorize and repeat what they heard from the lectures. Instead, it was an active process, with debating and discussion, and involved both the teacher and the student. "The same purpose should possess both master and scholar," Attalus said of his methods, "an ambition in the one case to promote, and the other to progress."

By progress, Attalus had more in mind than just good marks and the appearance of being articulate. His instruction was as much moral as it was academic, as he spoke at length to his promising young student about "sin, errors, and the evils of life." He was an advocate for that core

Stoic virtue of temperance, instilling in Seneca lifelong habits of moderation in diet and drink, causing him to give up oysters and mushrooms,
two Roman delicacies. He poked fun at pomp and luxury as fleeting
pleasures that did not contribute to lasting happiness. "You must crave
nothing," Attalus told Seneca, "if you would vie with Jupiter; for Jupiter
craves nothing. . . . Learn to be content with little, and cry out with courage and with greatness of soul."

But the most powerful lesson that Seneca learned from Attalus was
on the desire to improve practically, in the real world. The purpose of
studying philosophy, he learned from his beloved instructor, was to
"take away with him some one good thing every day: he should return
home a sounder man, or on the way to becoming sounder."

Like countless young people since, Seneca experimented with different schools and ideas, finding value in Stoicism and the teachings of
a philosopher named Sextius. He read and debated the writings of Epicurus, from a supposedly rival school.* He explored the teachings of
Pythagoras and even became, for a time, a vegetarian based on Pythag-
orean teachings. It's a credit to Seneca's father, and a reminder to fathers
since, that he patiently indulged this period and encouraged a range of
study for his son. It can take a while for precocious young people to find
themselves, and forcing them to curtail their curiosity is expedient but
often costly.

What Seneca was doing was developing a range of interests and experiences that would later enable him to create his own unique practices. From Sextius, for example, he discovered the benefits of spending
a few minutes in the evening before bed with a journal, and combined

---

* It is interesting that the most cited writer in Seneca's works is Epicurus. Seneca said we
ought to read like a spy in the enemy's camp, always looking to learn from our intellectual
and philosophical opponents.

this with the kind of probing moral reflection that Attalus had taught him. "I avail myself of this privilege," he would later write of his journaling practice, "and every day I plead my cause before the bar of self. When the light has been removed from sight, and my wife, long aware of my habit, has become silent, I scan the whole of my day and retrace all my deeds and words. I conceal nothing from myself, I omit nothing. For why should I shrink from any of my mistakes, when I may commune thus with myself?"

This part of Seneca, his earnest commitment to self-improvement—firm but kind ("See that you don't do that again," he would say to himself, "but now I forgive you")—was beloved by his teachers and clearly encouraged. But they also knew why they had been hired, and that his father, no fan of philosophy, was paying them to train his son for an active and ambitious political career. So this moral training was balanced out by rigorous instruction in the law, in rhetoric, and in critical thinking. In Rome, a promising young lawyer could appear in court as early as age seventeen, and there is little doubt that Seneca was ready as soon as he was legally able.

Yet just a few years into this promising career, only in his early twenties, Seneca's health nearly cut it all short. He had always struggled with a lung condition, most likely tuberculosis, but some sort of flare-up in 20 AD forced him to take an extended trip to Egypt to recover.

Life takes our plans and dashes them to pieces. As Seneca would later write, we should never underestimate fortune's habit of behaving just as she pleases. Just because we have worked hard, just because we are showing promise and our path toward success is clear has no bearing on whether we will get what we want.

Seneca certainly wouldn't. He would spend something like ten years in Alexandria, in convalescence. While he didn't control that, he could decide how he would spend that time. So he spent the decade writing, reading, and building up his strength. His uncle Gaius Galerius served as prefect of Egypt, and we can imagine it was here that Seneca was given his first real education in how power operated. We can also imagine him pining for and plotting a return.

While he was away, he received news that would foreshadow the arc of his own life. Attalus had somehow run afoul of Tiberius, the emperor, who confiscated his property and banished him from Rome. Seneca's beloved tutor would spend the rest of his years making ends meet in exile, digging ditches. To be a philosopher in imperial Rome was to walk a razor's edge, Seneca was learning, and it was to accept that the fates were fickle and that fortune could be cruel.

Seneca's return to Rome at thirty-five in 31 AD would only reinforce this latter lesson. On the journey home, his uncle was killed in a shipwreck. He also arrived in time to see Sejanus, once among Tiberius's most trusted military commanders and advisors, condemned by the Senate and torn to pieces by the mob in the streets. It was a time of paranoia and violence and political turmoil. Into this maelstrom, Seneca took his first public office, serving as quaestor by virtue of his family connections.

Seneca kept his head down through Tiberius's reign, which lasted until 37 AD and through Caligula's, which was considerably shorter but just as violent. In his book *On the Tranquility of Mind*, Seneca would later tell the story of a Stoic philosopher he admired named Julius Canus who was ordered to be murdered when he fell afoul of Caligula. As Canus waited for the executioner, he played a game of chess with a friend. When the guard came to lead him away to his death, he joked, "You will testify that I was one piece ahead."

Seneca noted not only the quip's philosophical brilliance, but also the kind of fame it had won for its owner in this terrifying time.

He would have easily seen himself in Canus's shoes, for he too walked the razor's edge of life and death under such an unstable king.

According to Dio Cassius, Seneca was saved from execution—for what offense, we do not know—only by his ill health:

> Seneca, who was superior in wisdom to all the Romans of his day and to many others as well, came near being destroyed, though he had neither done any wrong nor had the appearance of doing so, but merely because he pleaded a case well in the senate while the emperor was present. Caligula ordered him to be put to death, but afterwards let him off because he believed the statement of one of his female associates, to the effect that Seneca had consumption in an advanced stage and would die before a great while.

It was out of the frying pan and into the fire. In a span of less than two years, Seneca would lose his father (in 39 AD at ninety-two years of age), get married (40 AD), then lose his firstborn son (40–41 AD). And then twenty days after burying his son, he would be banished from Rome by Claudius, the successor to Caligula.

What for? We are not sure. Was it blanket persecutions of philosophers? Did Seneca, in his grief, end up having an affair with Julia Livilla, sister of Agrippina? The record is murky, and, like scandals of our own time, beset with rumors and agendas and conflicting accounts. In any case, Seneca was brought up on adultery charges, and in 41 AD, at age forty-five, this grieving son and father was sent packing to the distant island of Corsica. Once again, his promising career was cut capriciously short.

Like his decade in Egypt, this would be a long time away from Rome—eight years—and although he started productively (writing *Consolation to Polybius*, *Consolation to Helvia*, and *On Anger* in a short span), the isolation would begin to wear on him. Soon, the man who had not long before been writing consolations to other people clearly needed some consoling himself.

He was angry, as any person would be, but rather than give in to that rage, he channeled the energy into a book on the topic, *De Ira* (or *On Anger*), which he dedicated to his brother. It's a beautiful, touching book clearly directed at himself as much as the reader. "Don't hang out with the ignorant," he writes. "Only speak the truth, but only to those who can handle it." "Walk away and laugh. . . . Expect to endure much." This kind of self-talk dates back in Stoicism to Cleanthes, but Seneca was applying it to one of the most stressful situations imaginable—being deprived of your friends and family, an unjust conviction, the theft of valuable years of one's life.

One of the most common themes in Seneca's letters and essays from this period is death. For a man whose tuberculosis loomed over him from an early age—at one point driving him to consider suicide—he could not help but constantly think and write about the final act of life. "Let us prepare our minds as if we'd come to the very end of life," he reminded himself. "Let us postpone nothing. Let us balance life's books each day. . . . The one who puts the finishing touches on their life each day is never short of time." While he sat in exile, he would comfort his father-in-law, a man who had just been deprived of his own job supervising Rome's grain supply, "Believe me, it's better to produce the balance-sheet of your own life than that of the grain market."

Most interestingly, he quibbled with the idea that death was something that lay ahead of us in the uncertain future. "This is our big mistake," Seneca wrote, "to think we look forward toward death. Most of death is already gone. Whatever time has passed is owned by death." That was what he realized, that we are *dying every day* and no day, once dead, can be revived.

It must have been a particularly painful insight for a man who was watching years of his life tick by—for the second time—due to events outside of his control. It might not have been Stoic to despair at this, but it was certainly quite human.

In a play Seneca wrote toward the end of his life, clearly from heartfelt experience, he captured just how capricious and random fate could be:

> If the breaking day sees someone proud,
> The ending day sees them brought low.
> No one should put too much trust in triumph,
> No one should give up hope of trials improving.
> Clotho mixes one with the other and stops
> Fortune from resting, spinning every fate around.
> No one has had so much divine favor
> That they could guarantee themselves tomorrow.
> God keeps our lives hurtling on,
> Spinning in a whirlwind.

Fate had caused him to be born to wealth and had given him great tutors. It had also weakened his health and sent him unfairly packing twice, just as his career was taking off. Fortune had behaved, all through his life, exactly as she pleased. For him, as for us, she brought success and failure, pain and pleasure . . . usually in exactly the form he was not expecting.

Little did Seneca know in 50 AD that this was going to happen again. His trials were about to improve and his life was about to be spun into a whirlwind that history has not quite yet fully wrapped its head around.

Agrippina, the great-granddaughter of Augustus, had grand ambitions for her twelve-year-old son, Nero. Having married Claudius, Caligula's successor, in 49 AD and convinced him to adopt Nero, one of her first moves as empress was to persuade Claudius to recall Seneca from Corsica to serve as their son's tutor. Plotting for him to be emperor someday, she wanted access to Seneca's political, rhetorical, and philosophical brain for Nero.

Suddenly, at fifty-three years of age, Seneca, long a subversive but marginalized figure, was elevated to the center of the Roman imperial court. A lifetime of striving and ambition finally produced the ultimate patron, and the entire Seneca family was ready to take advantage.

What did Seneca teach young Nero? Ironically, just as his father had hired Attalus to tutor Seneca in basically everything *but* philosophy, Agrippina wanted Seneca to teach Nero political strategy, not Stoicism. Seneca's lessons would have revolved around law and oratory—how to argue and how to strategize. Any Stoic principles would have been snuck into his lessons like vegetables baked into a child's muffin or sugar to cover the medicine.

Like Arius and Athenodorus with Octavian, Seneca was preparing the boy for one of the hardest jobs in the world: wearing imperial purple. In the days of the Republic, the Romans had been leery of absolute power, but now Seneca's job was to teach someone how to have it. Just a few generations earlier, the Stoics had been ardent defenders of the Republican ideals (Cato was one of Seneca's heroes), but by the death of Augustus most of these objections had become futile. As Emily Wilson, a translator and biographer of Seneca, writes, "Cicero hoped that he really could bring down Caesar and Mark Antony. Seneca, by contrast, had no hope that he could achieve anything by direct opposition to any of the emperors under whom he lived. His best hope was to moderate some of Nero's worst tendencies and to maximize his own sense of autonomy."

It makes sense, certainly, but the question remains: Could a more hopeful Seneca have had more of an impact? Or does accepting that one person is powerless to change the status quo become a self-fulfilling prophecy?

What Seneca did believe was that a Stoic was obligated to serve the country—in this case an empire that had already been through four emperors in his lifetime—as best one could, and surely he was willing to accept just about any role to get off the godforsaken island he had been stuck on.

Did he know what a Faustian bargain this would be? There were hints. Nero didn't seem to care about his education—not like Octavian, anyway—and he seemed to want to be a musician and an actor more than he wanted to be an emperor. He was entitled and cruel, spoiled and easily distracted. These were not traits that boded well. But the alternative to Nero was returning to exile in Corsica.

In 54 AD, roughly five years into Seneca's employment at court, Agrippina had her husband, Claudius, killed by way of poisoned mushrooms. Nero was made emperor at age sixteen, and Seneca was asked to write the speeches that Nero would give to convince Rome that it wasn't totally insane to give this dilettante child nearly godlike powers over millions of people.*

As if absolute power wasn't corruptive enough, Nero had clearly witnessed some nasty early lessons from his mother and adoptive father. As his teacher and mentor, Seneca attempted a course correction. One of the first things he gave the new emperor was a work he composed, entitled *De Clementia*, which laid out a path "for the good King" and that

---

* Seneca also took the time to write a vulgar satirical send-off to Claudius entitled *Apocolocyntosis*, or "the Pumpkinification," which was a final middle finger to the man who had taken so many years of his life in Corsica.

he hoped Nero would follow. And while clemency and mercy might seem like obvious concepts to us today, at the time this was quite revolutionary advice.

Robert A. Kaster, the classics scholar, writes that there was no Greek word for clemency. Philosophers had spoken of restraint and mildness, but Seneca was talking about something more profound and new: what one does with *power*. Particularly, how the powerful ought to treat someone without power, because this reveals who *they* are. As Seneca explained, "No one will be able to imagine anything more becoming to a ruler than clemency, whatever sort of ruler he is and on whatever terms he is put in charge of others."

It was a lesson aimed at Nero, as well as every leader who might read the essay after. The world would be a better place with more clemency in it—only a cursory look at history confirms this. The problem is getting leaders to understand it.

The dynamic between Seneca and Nero is an interesting one because it clearly evolved—or rather devolved—over time. But the essence of it is perhaps best captured in a statue of the two done by the Spanish sculptor Eduardo Barrón in 1904. Even though it depicts a scene some eighteen centuries after the fact, it manages to capture the timeless elements of the two men's characters. Seneca, much older, sits with his legs crossed, draped in a beautiful toga but otherwise unadorned. Spread across his lap and onto the simple bench is a document he's written. Maybe it's a speech. Maybe it's a law being debated by the Senate. Maybe it is in fact the text of *De Clementia*. His fingers point to a spot in the text. His body language is open. He is trying to instill in his young charge the seriousness of the tasks before him.

Nero, sitting across from Seneca, is nearly the opposite of his advisor in every way. He is hooded, sitting on a thronelike chair. A fine blanket rests behind him. He's wearing jewelry. His expression is sullen.

Both fists are clenched, and one rests on his temple as if he can't bring himself to pay attention. He is looking down at the ground. His feet are tucked behind him, crossed at the ankles. He knows he should be listening, but he isn't. He'd rather be anywhere else. Soon enough, he is thinking, *I won't have to endure these lectures. Then I'll be able to do whatever I want.*

Seneca can clearly see this body language, and yet he proceeds. He proceeded for many years, in fact. Why? Because he hoped some of it— *any of it*—would get through. Because he knew the stakes were high. Because he knew his job was to *try* to teach Nero to be good (he would literally die trying). And because he was never going to turn down a chance to be that close to power, to have that much impact.

In the end, Seneca made little progress with Nero, a man whom time would shortly reveal to be deranged and flawed. Was it always a hopeless mission? Was Seneca's steady hand a positive influence—one that Rome would have been worse off without? We cannot know. What we know is that Seneca tried. It's the old lesson: You can lead a horse to water, but you can't make it drink. You control what you do and say, not whether people listen.

All a Stoic can do is show up and do their work. Seneca believed he had to, and clearly, he wanted to also. As he would later write, the difference between the Stoics and the Epicureans was that the Stoics felt that politics was a duty. "The two sects, the Epicureans and the Stoics, are at variance, as in most things," Seneca wrote. "Epicurus says: 'The wise man will not engage in public affairs except in an emergency.' Zeno says: 'He will engage in public affairs unless something prevents him.'"

Nothing was preventing Seneca—least of all his own ambitions— so he kept trying.

Sources tell us that for the first several years, Seneca was the steady hand. While he was working with Burrus, the military leader also chosen by Agrippina, Rome was, for the first time in some time according to contemporaries, well run. In 55 AD, Seneca's brother Gallio was made consul. The following year, Seneca himself held that position.

Like the poem Seneca wrote about fate said, however, this was not to last. In fact, that seems to be the constant theme of Seneca's life—that peace and stability are fragile and punctured, quite capriciously, by events outside his control. Nero, driven by paranoia and the cruel streak he inherited from his mother, began to eliminate his rivals, starting with his brother Britannicus, who was dispatched with poison, just like Claudius. He forced out his mother and began to make designs to kill her too—failing several times to deliver a fatal dose of poison. One account has Nero attempting to have his mother killed in an elaborate boating accident. Finally, by 59 AD, the deed was done.

That early, restrained-but-waiting Nero captured in the Barrón statue was now released. In Tacitus's words, he deferred no more on long meditated crimes. With his power matured, and oxidized into his soul, he could do what he liked, no matter how depraved. It was a turning point noticed by Seneca, for sure. While Arius had advised Augustus to eliminate the other, "too many Caesars," Seneca had to remind Nero that it was impossible for even the strongest king, in the end, to kill every successor. Eventually *someone* would come next. But Nero didn't listen, and ultimately murdered every male in the Julio-Claudian line.

When Nero wasn't killing, it's not as if he was dutiful in attending to the business of the empire. He was racing chariots at a special track he liked outside Rome, with slaves dragooned into watching and clapping for him. He neglected the state so that he could perform onstage, singing and dancing like some cut-rate actor—a fact of which his attendants prevented him from knowing by, according to Suetonius, not allowing anyone "to leave the theatre even for the most urgent reasons."

Seneca was horrified, so why didn't he leave? How could he be a part of such an embarrassment?

One explanation is fear. His whole life he had watched emperors murder and banish with impunity. He had felt the hard hand of their injustice himself more than once. Imperial vindictiveness loomed over him. As Dio Cassius relates, "After the death of Britannicus, Seneca and Burrus no longer gave any careful attention to the public business, but were satisfied if they might manage it with moderation and still preserve their lives." Perhaps he thought, as people think today with flawed leaders, that he could do good *through* Nero. Seneca had always looked for the good in people, even someone as obviously bad as Nero. "Let's be kind to one another," he once wrote. "We're just wicked people living among wicked people. Only one thing can give us peace, and that's a pact of mutual leniency." Maybe he saw something in Nero up close, a goodness despite the flaws, that has been lost to the historical record.

Or maybe his very real fear and these blind spots were compounded by the tempting self-interest of Seneca's position. It's hard to get someone to see, the expression goes, what their salary depends on them *not* seeing.

Seneca had grown and continued to grow quite wealthy under Nero's regime. In just a few short years, he had amassed, largely through gifts from his boss, a fortune of some three hundred million sesterces. He was certainly the richest Stoic on earth, possibly the richest ever to live. One source notes that Seneca owned some *five hundred* identical citrus wood tables with ivory legs just for entertaining. It's an odd picture, thinking of a Stoic philosopher—descended from the frugal school of Cleanthes—throwing Gatsbyesque parties funded by the gifts of his murderous boss.

Although most art renders Seneca as lean and sinewy, in fact the real likeness of him survives only in the form of one statue, dating to the third century, which is actually a double bust of Seneca and Socrates. Seneca loved Socrates, marveling once that "there were thirty tyrants surrounding Socrates, and yet they could not break his spirit." Both men don the classic philosopher's toga. Curiously, Socrates's wraps both shoulders, while Seneca's right shoulder is bare—perhaps a nod to his line about how a man must realize how little he needs to be happy, it is "the superfluous things that wear our togas threadbare." But the portrait also reveals Seneca as the older man who had clearly enjoyed his share of sumptuous banquets, and had grown quite fat in Nero's service.

Much of our knowledge about Seneca's opulence and fortune comes to us via a man named P. Suillius, a Roman senator who was angry at Seneca, suspecting he was behind the revival of *Lex Cincia*, a law with a provision that lawyers plead cases without compensation. While Suillius's motives were quite suspect and he would later be convicted on serious criminal charges and banished from Rome, there was at least some truth to his written attacks on Seneca's hypocrisy. Even Seneca's response—in his essay *On the Happy Life*—seems to set up a standard to which he obviously falls short:

> Cease, therefore, forbidding to philosophers the possession of money; no one has condemned wisdom to poverty. The philosopher shall own ample wealth, but it will have been wrested from no man, nor will it be stained with another's blood—wealth acquired without harm to any man, without base dealing, and the outlay of it will be not less honourable than was its acquisition; it will make no man groan except the spiteful.

Cato was rich. So was Cicero. Neither of them grew rich in the service of someone as odious as Nero, however. Arius and Athenodorus were rewarded handsomely for their service to Augustus . . . but Augustus never murdered his own mother. Cato loaned much of his money to friends without interest, and did not seem interested in growing his fortune for its own sake. "What is the proper limit to wealth?" Seneca would later ask rhetorically. "It is, first, to have what is necessary, and second, to have what is enough."

Clearly he struggled with that idea of *enough*. Over several years, he lent out something like forty million sesterces at high rates to Rome's British colony. It was an aggressive financial play, and when the colony struggled under the debt, a brutal and violent rebellion broke out that eventually needed to be put down by Roman legions.

Seneca had said that a philosopher's wealth should not be stained in blood, but it's hard not to see the drops of red on his.

Why couldn't he stop himself? It's strange to say that his talent and brilliance were to blame, but it's true—as it is for so many ambitious people who end up with controversial fame and fortune. He had been groomed since birth for greatness, expected to become a leading man of his time. He had taken every opportunity that life had given him and tried to make the best of it, he had persevered through difficulties that would have sunk anyone who wasn't a Stoic, and he had enjoyed the good times too. He had not complained, he kept going, kept serving, kept trying to have impact and to do what he had been trained to do. What he had never done was stop and question any of it, never asked where this was leading him and whether it was worth it.

By 62 AD, it was harder to deny the compromises he was forced to make on a daily basis in Nero's world. Perhaps there was some lost event that broke him out of his stupor. Perhaps the moral conscience he had learned from Attalus finally won out in the battle with his desire to achieve.

Finally, finally, Seneca attempted to withdraw. We know he didn't confront Nero. That would have been too much. There is no evidence of a principled resignation, as the Stoic-inspired secretary of defense James Mattis would give to President Donald Trump in a disagreement over policy in Syria. Instead, Seneca met with the emperor and futilely attempted to convince Nero that he didn't need him anymore, that he was old and in bad health and ready to retire. "I cannot any longer bear the burden of my wealth," he told Nero. "I crave assistance." He asked Nero to take possession of all his estates and his wealth. He wanted to walk away clean into retirement.

It would not be so easy.

He'd gotten his hand bloody grabbing the money, and there would be blood getting rid of it.

A few days after their meeting, Nero murdered another enemy.

In 64 AD, the Great Fire struck Rome, and, boosted by strong winds, would destroy more than two-thirds of the city. One rumor spread that Nero had started the fire himself, or at least allowed it to burn for six days so that he could rebuild the capital as he liked. His reputation as a dilettante and a psychopath were fertile seeds for these conspiracy theories, and so, moving quickly, Nero found a scapegoat: the Christians. How many he ordered to be rounded up and killed we do not know, but one of them was a brilliant philosopher from Tarsus— the same intellectual ground that spawned Chrysippus, Antipater, and Athenodorus—who had earlier escaped death thanks to Seneca's brother during Claudius's reign. Saul of Tarsus, whom we know today as Saint Paul, was added to Nero's pile of bodies.*

As blood flowed and fires burned, could Seneca feel anything but guilt? *Tyrannodidaskalos*—tyrant teacher. That's what they called him.

---

* Seneca's brother Novatus, under his adoptive name, Gallio, makes an appearance in the New Testament (Acts 18:12–17).

It was true, wasn't it? Hadn't that been what he had done? Hadn't he shaped Nero into the man he had now clearly revealed himself to be? At the very least, it was hard to argue that Seneca hadn't lent credibility and protection to the Nero regime. Maybe it was despair that Seneca felt in those dark days—what he had tried to hold off for so long was now breaking loose.

"We've spent our lives serving the kind of state no decent man ought to serve," one of the Stoics says in *The Blood of the Martyrs*, Naomi Mitchison's haunting 1939 novel about the persecution of the Christians in Nero's court. "And now we're old enough to see what we've done."

Centuries before Seneca, in China, Confucius had been a teacher and an advisor to princes. He had danced the same dance as Seneca, trying to be a philosopher within the pragmatic world of power. His balancing principle was as follows: "When the state has the Way, accept a salary; when the state is without the Way, to accept a salary is shameful." It took Seneca much longer than Confucius to come to this conclusion. It's inexcusable—the shame was obvious the *first time* his boss tried to murder his mother . . . at least it should have been to someone trained in virtue.

But that was not how Seneca saw it, not for nearly fifteen years of service with Nero. In time, he would come to echo Confucius, writing that when "the state is so rotten as to be past helping, if evil has entire dominion over it, the wise man will not labor in vain or waste his strength in unprofitable efforts."

But he had done precisely that for far too long. Withdrawing as best he could, Seneca turned fully to his writing. In a remarkable essay titled *On Leisure*, published after he retired, he seems to be wrestling with his own complicated experiences. "The duty of a man is to be useful to his fellow-men," he wrote, "if possible, to be useful to many of them; failing this, to be useful to a few; failing this, to be useful to his neighbors, and, failing them, to himself: for when he helps others, he advances the general interests of mankind."

Only belatedly did it occur to a striver like Seneca that one can contribute to his fellow citizens in quiet ways too—for instance, by writing or simply by being a good man at home. "I am working for later generations," he explained, "writing down some ideas that may be of assistance to them. . . . I point other men to the right path, which I have found late in life. . . . I cry out to them: 'Avoid whatever pleases the throng: avoid the gifts of Chance!'" Seneca himself would note the irony that in communing with these future generations he was "doing more good than when I appear as counsel in court or stamp my seal upon a will or lend my assistance in the senate."

The primary form of this service came in the shape of philosophical letters, intended not just for his friend Lucilius, to whom they were addressed, but also for publication to a wide audience. If he couldn't impact the events of Rome directly, he figured, he could at least reach people through his pen—it could also help assure him the "immortal" fame he still craved. Succeeding on both counts, this collection, known as *Moral Letters*, sells many thousands of copies a year in countless languages.

Like Cicero, Seneca would spend three years (62–65 AD) completing all his letters and books, a fact for which the literary world is eternally grateful. We can imagine him liking the symmetry with such an illustrious peer, thinking even of how the theatrics of his retirement would play. It was also smart—turning to his writing was a convenient way to stay out of the fray of Nero's increasingly volatile ways. "My days have this one goal, as do my nights," he wrote, "this is my task and my study, to put an end to old evils. . . . Before I became old, I took care to live well; in old age I take care to die well." Sadly, far too much of Seneca's work before and after this period would be lost. Emily Wilson estimates that more than half of his writings did not survive, including all his political speeches and personal letters, as well as works on India and Egypt.

It was, for all the looming danger, a period of joy and creativity for him. He wrote of sitting in his rooms above a busy gymnasium, tuning out all the noise and just locking in on his philosophy. He wrote of the process of becoming, with time, a better friend to himself—an admission, perhaps, that his ambition may have been fueled by an early feeling of not being enough, of not being worth much. He said in one letter that only those who make time for philosophy are truly alive. Well, now he was actually doing that, and he was quite alive. Each day, as he wrote in his exile on Corsica, "I can argue with Socrates, doubt with Carneades, find peace with Epicurus, conquer human nature with the Stoics, and exceed it with the Cynics."

Seneca also spoke of philosophy as a way to look in the mirror, to scrape off one's faults. While we don't have any evidence that he directly questioned his work for Nero in his writings—serving was part of his political code, as it would be for General Mattis in our time—we can tell that he wrestled extensively with how his life had turned out. The closest Seneca would come to addressing a figure like Nero would be in a play he wrote called *Thyestes*, a dark, disturbing story about two brothers battling for the kingdom of Mycenae.* It's impossible to read this story today and not see it as a kind of dialogue between Seneca and Nero, a warning against the draws of power and the unspeakable things human beings do to each other in the pursuit of it.

---

*In the Middle Ages, it was thought that Seneca the tragedian was an entirely separate figure from Seneca the philosopher. James Romm marvels at Seneca's range: "It is as though Emerson had taken time off from writing his essays to compose the opera *Faust*." This is incomplete. It's as if Emerson founded Transcendentalism, wrote *Faust*, and served as Lincoln's vice president.

The most telling line in the play states a fact that Seneca had painfully come to understand: "Crimes often return to their teacher."

And so they had.

He writes in *Thyestes*, "It is a vast kingdom to be able to cope without a kingdom." This too he was painfully experiencing. For the third time in his life Seneca had lost next to everything. He believed, as he would now write to Lucilius, that "the greatest empire is to be emperor of oneself."

It was a realization a long time coming.

Seneca would again find that philosophy did not exist only in the ethereal world or only on the pages of his writings. Tacitus tells us that Nero's first attempt to kill Seneca—again by poison—was spoiled by Seneca's meager diet. It was hard to kill someone who had so turned away from their former life of opulence that he was eating mostly wild fruits and water from a burbling stream. But even this reprieve was short-lived.

In 65 AD, conspirators, including a Stoic senator named Thrasea (see "Thrasea the Fearless") and his brother's son, Lucan, began to plot against Nero's life. Seneca was not directly involved, not like Cato or Brutus had been involved, but he was at least more courageous than Cicero. One rumor had it that the conspirators planned to put Seneca back in charge after Nero's death. Is his involvement enough to redeem him? That he was finally willing to break decisively with the monster he had helped create? When the conspiracy failed, Seneca put his life on the line to try to cover for the more active participants.

This choice sealed his fate. Nero, a coward like Hitler in his last days, sent goons to demand Seneca's suicide. There would be no clemency, despite the essay Seneca had written for his student all those years ago.

Seneca's life had been a complex maze of contradictions, but now, staring at the end, he managed to summon a courage and a clarity that had long escaped him. He asked for something to write his will upon and was rejected. So he turned to his friends and said he could bequeath them the only thing that mattered: his life, his example. It was heartwrenching, and they broke down when he said these words.

It would seem absurd to say that Seneca had practiced for this moment, but in a way, he had. All his writing and philosophizing, as Cicero put it, had been leading up to death, and now it was here. He seized the opportunity to practice what he had so long preached. "Where," he gently chided his weeping friends as well as the audience of history, "are your maxims of philosophy or the reparation of so many years' study against evils to come? Who knew not Nero's cruelty? After a mother's and a brother's murder, nothing remains but to add the destruction of a guardian and a tutor."

Not long before, he had written to Lucilius that while it was true that a tyrant or a conqueror could suddenly send us off to our death, this was actually no great power. "Take my word for it," he had said, "since the day you were born you are being led thither." Seneca believed that if we wanted "to be calm as we await that last hour," we must never let the fact of our mortality slip from consciousness. We were sentenced to death at birth. For Seneca, all Nero was doing was moving up the timeline. Knowing this, he could now hug his wife, Paulina, and urge her calmly not to grieve for him too much and to live on without him.

Like so many other Stoic women, she was not content to be told what to do. Instead, she decided to go with him. Slitting the arteries in their arms, the couple began to bleed out. Nero's guards—apparently on Nero's orders—rushed in to save Paulina, who would live on for several more years.

For Seneca, death did not come as easily as he would have hoped. His meager diet seemed to have slowed his blood flow. So next, he willingly drank a poison he had kept for precisely this moment, but not before pouring a small libation to the gods. Could he have thought in that moment back to something Attalus had said so long ago? That "evil herself drinks the largest portion of her own poison"? It was proving true for Seneca, and it would prove true for Nero soon enough as well.

The man who had written so much on death was finding, with irony, that death did not come so willingly.* Did this frustrate him? Or did he have one eye on history, knowing fate was prolonging the scene he had long meditated on? When the poison did not work, Seneca was moved to a steam bath where the heat and dense air finally finished him off. There is an entire genre of paintings of the death of Seneca, including versions done by Peter Paul Rubens and Jacques-Louis David. Invariably they seem to show Seneca as perhaps he wished to be seen, no longer fat and rich but lean and dignified again. Everyone else in the room is hysterical, but Seneca is calm—finally the perfect Stoic he could not live up to in life—as he departs from the world.

Shortly after, his body was disposed of quietly without funeral rites, per a request he had made long before, which to Tacitus was proof that like a good Stoic, "even in the height of his wealth and power he was thinking of his life's close," as well as his eternal legacy.

But everything else he had gained in life was lost, except for the books we now have. And within a year, Nero would take his brother too, for crimes don't only return upon their teachers but also to the people and things they love.

---

* In 2018, James Romm would translate a selection of Seneca's writings entitled *How to Die*. It is 256 pages.

CORNUTUS
THE COMMON

(Cor-NEW-toos)

B. 20 AD
D. 68 AD   ORIGIN: LIBYA

T he line in Rome was that "we can't all be Catos." Meaning that few had his sheer, inhuman constancy and courage. But another way to look at that expression might be that we won't all achieve towering fame. Philosophers in modern times speak of the concept of "moral luck"—how the time we were born and the situations we find ourselves in determine how heroic we'll turn out to be.

Lucius Annaeus Cornutus turns out to be such a Stoic—not a Cato or an Agrippinus, but an ordinary man in extraordinary times who did the best he could. Born around 20 AD in Libya, Cornutus was a Phoenician like the Stoic founder Zeno, but his life's impact was much closer to that of the second Zeno than the first. He ultimately came to Rome through the auspices of Seneca's family—hence the name Annaeus—very likely through his brother Mela, as Cornutus taught his son Lucan.

With a wide grasp of diverse topics, including orthography, theology, grammar, rhetoric, linguistics, logic, physics, and ethics, Cornutus was an imposing figure. His reputation was such that Emperor Claudius took his advice and introduced a new letter to the Roman alphabet (the digamma, which looked like an *f* and made a *w* sound) in

48 AD. We can't all be Catos, all our accomplishments are ephemeral, but introducing a new letter to the alphabet is pretty cool.

It must have been strange for Seneca's family to see a Stoic like Cornutus thrive in Rome under the same emperor who had driven their beloved son and brother so far away from them. In any case, Cornutus seemed mostly to keep his head down, and down inside his books. His friend the poet Persius wrote fondly of "spending long days . . . and plucking the early evenings" with Cornutus, working and relaxing together in "seriousness at a restrained table." They were, he said, "in harmony with a fixed bond and are guided by one star." It's a beautiful image and one worth remembering anytime you hear that the Stoics were without joy or friendship or fun.

In 62 AD, Persius died tragically young and Cornutus inherited from him an enormous library, including the full seven hundred volumes of Chrysippus's books, as well as a great deal of money. Cornutus returned the money to his friend's sisters, saying that the books were more than enough.

But it was impossible, by the time Nero came along, for even the most innocent and bookish philosophers to avoid offending the sensitive emperor. Caesar had had a sense of humor. Augustus loved the arts. Rome was a long way from living under such an emperor. When editing some of the late Persius's poems, Cornutus took pains to change a line that compared Nero's ears to those of a donkey. It was a compromise that Agrippinus would never have considered. Cornutus believed he had no choice.

The trouble with appeasement is that it never works. Nero soon found something else to be offended by. Dio Cassius tells us that Nero, like his stepfather, had sought out Cornutus's advice, specifically about an epic history he planned to write about Rome. As Nero grandiosely explained, he planned to tell Rome's narrative across four hundred volumes. Cornutus advised that this was far too many. One of Nero's henchmen demanded an explanation—hadn't Chrysippus written more than that? Didn't Cornutus own them himself? How could he say such a thing? It's not a fair comparison, Cornutus replied, for the Stoics wrote to "help the conduct of men's lives."

Perhaps Cornutus knew how this remark would land, or perhaps he said it with an academic's ignorance of the subtleties of the art of courtiership, but the result was the same regardless. We are told Nero had to restrain himself from having this impudent philosopher executed on the spot.

He decided on banishment instead.

Where and when Cornutus was sent—to an island unnamed by Dio Cassius, somewhere between 66 and 68 AD—and ultimately what happened to Cornutus is lost to the historical record. His resistance to tyranny was hardly as heroic as that of Cato or the conspirators who plotted against Nero, and his ability to navigate the fraught politics of his time was certainly less impressive than Seneca's, but his fate helped make a small contribution to the rising Stoic opposition.

The egregiousness of Nero's overreaction to such a minor slight helped galvanize the plans of Thrasea and Lucan, Cornutus's former student. We can't place the events perfectly, but if Seneca was still around when Cornutus and Nero clashed, it must have weighed heavily on him. Here his own student was banishing his nephew's teacher, just as Attalus had been driven off in his own childhood. It was one thing for Nero to eliminate his own family members, but now he was attacking a member of Seneca's extended relations.

To anyone watching, it was clear that Nero's sanity was getting harder and harder not to doubt.

Meanwhile, Cornutus drifted off into obscurity, not unlike Rutilius Rufus, far from home but at the same time blissfully removed from the carnage of a country tearing itself to pieces.

GAIUS RUBELLIUS PLAUTUS THE MAN WHO WOULD NOT BE KING

(GUY-us Ru-BELL-ee-us PLOW-tuss)

B. 33 AD

D. 62 AD

ORIGIN: TIVOLI

For generations, Stoics had been in close proximity to power. In Athens, they had been diplomats and the teachers of the best and the brightest. In the Republic, they had been generals and consuls. Since Arius and Athenodorus, they had been the advisors to the young princes of the empire.

But none had actually *been* a sovereign. Gaius Rubellius Plautus, born in 33 AD, was the first Stoic with royal blood. The great-grandson of Tiberius through his mother, Julia, and because of Tiberius's adoption, a great-great-grandson of Augustus, he was in line for the throne from the rival Julio-Claudian line.

Yet for all his wealth and prestigious lineage, we're told that Plautus lived an austere and quiet life. His study of philosophy had made him an old soul, a living embodiment of the old *mos maiorum*, one who commanded respect from all who met him. He did not lust for power; he did not abuse his wealth. He was, then, quite a contrast not just to his great-grandfather Tiberius, but to nearly all the emperors to come after them both.

Would he be the first Stoic emperor? The philosopher king that Plato had spoken of so long before?

It was possible, but it would not be an easy road. In the way that Cato seemed to create enemies unintentionally—his virtue an inherent rebuke to the corrupt and the tyrannical—Plautus was, by his very nature, fated to clash with Nero. Two men of high birth, they were otherwise opposites. One, through his mother, had grand ambitions. The other wished to maintain his studies and live by his internal code. One was willing to do anything—no matter how depraved—to achieve those aims. The other would do nothing to betray his.

It should not surprise us then that Nero began to make designs against his third cousin, or that his paranoia would make this man a rival. It must have been obvious to everyone, including Plautus. First, Nero murdered his stepbrother, Britannicus, after his mother, Agrippina, had threatened that she would side with Britannicus if Nero did not straighten out. Then a rumor spread that Agrippina might marry Plautus to replace Nero on the throne. Whether it was true or not, this was the pretext he used to drive his mother from Rome and what eventually fixed it in his mind that he must kill the woman who had birthed him.

Although the Stoics had written of the dangers of superstitions and believing in silly, supernatural signs, clearly Seneca failed to instill that lesson in Nero. Between August and December of 60 AD, an unbelievably bright comet stretched across the sky above Rome, one like none seen before. It was an omen, people believed, that a change in monarchy was coming. Nero would be replaced. Around this same time, Tacitus tells us that a tremendous bolt of lightning struck the dinner table at Nero's enormous lakeside villa at Sublaquaeum. Due to the proximity to Plautus's birthplace, Nero and the guests took this as a dangerous portent: Plautus was to replace Nero.

The Stoic would be king.

Or would he?

In response, Nero attempted something out of character: He simply wrote to Plautus that Rome would be more peaceful if he took his leave to his grandfather Drusus's estates in Asia. Perhaps this unusual bit of restraint—at least in a matter more grave than petty—was the result of Seneca's intervention, one of the last bits of moral influence he was able to exert. Plautus decided it was an offer he could not refuse.

So he, accompanied by his wife, Antistia, and their children, along with "a few of his intimate friends," went into exile in Syria. Tacitus suggests that the great Stoic teacher Musonius Rufus, who counseled Plautus in Syria "to have courage and await death," accompanied him into exile, where Plautus attempted to busy himself with philosophy. Cicero popularized the story of the "Sword of Damocles"—the threat of death and uprising—that intimidated all kings. So it was for Plautus . . . without the benefit of actually being one.

But this is what Stoicism trains us for: to be able to focus in even the most distracting of situations, to be able to tune out anything and everything—even creeping death—so that we lock in on what matters.

With Seneca on the outs, Nero was unmoored and, as in today's time, ambitious and shortsighted politicians sought to wield this volatile man to their own ends. One such figure, Tigellinus, stoked Nero's paranoia to eliminate enemies and to keep Rome in chaos. Tacitus recounts him whispering to Nero, "Plautus, with his great fortune, did not even affect a desire for peace, but, not content to parade his mimicries of the ancient Romans, had taken upon himself the Stoic arrogance and the mantle of a sect which inculcated sedition and an appetite for politics."

It was all Nero needed to hear: The order to kill Plautus was set.

Part of what had motivated Nero must have been the knowledge that many people would have supported Plautus had he actually acted on the ambitions that Nero projected onto him. That is our deepest fear anyway: that the people we loathe are actually better than us, and that we loathe them not because they are inferior but because they have something we lack.

There was an irony in Nero's attack on Plautus that he would not have appreciated but Seneca had long predicted. As he wrote in *Oedipus*, "He who indulges empty fears earns himself real fears." Plautus had not had designs on the throne, but now Antistius Vetus, Plautus's father-in-law, wrote to him to gather forces and take up arms. Others advised the same. It took some time for the assassins to reach Asia, long enough for rumors to spread that Plautus did in fact rise up and defend himself. Revolution, it seemed, was in the air.

But that was not Plautus's style. Although he had the money to fund an entire army, he decided not to. Perhaps he would have rather been the victim of a tyrant than to be responsible for another bloody war in which countless others died. Perhaps it was Musonius's advice that convinced him: "Choose to die well while it is possible, lest shortly it may become necessary for you to die, but it will no longer be possible to die well."

Unmoved by the calls for civil war, Plautus prepared himself for the end. The Stoic would not be king. He would not even live to see thirty.

Like Agrippinus before him, Plautus refused to let the threat of death deter him from his daily routine. It was on a quiet afternoon in 62 AD, as he stripped to exercise, that Nero's killers arrived. They would not even offer him the dignity of suicide. A centurion cut down this young philosopher while a court eunuch watched to confirm that the deed had been done. Together they brought back the severed head as proof.

Nero's depravity had reached sadistic levels. Holding Plautus's head before an audience, he referred to himself in the third person. "Nero, why did you fear a man with such a nose?" Not finished with his humiliation, he wrote to the Senate to inform them that Plautus had been an unstable figure who had threatened Rome (remember the tactic from Rutilius Rufus's time: Accuse the good man of exactly what you, the evil man, are yourself guilty of). Nero lacked the courage to own his dirty work, but he demanded credit for protecting the peace.

Perhaps we cannot fault Seneca—then trying to retire from public life—too much for his enabling of Nero, because it was clearly endemic to the times. The Senate rubber-stamped Nero's smear and did him one better, choosing to expel Plautus from their ranks posthumously, simply to please their petulant king. Within weeks, Nero divorced his wife, tossing her Plautus's confiscated estate in the settlement, and prepared to remarry.

Although Seneca—inexplicably—still seems not to have had enough, and would remain loosely in Nero's service for a few more years, Thrasea, one of the few remaining Stoics in Rome, pulled an Agrippinus and declined to attend the wedding.

Nero had invented an enemy in Plautus and given himself a real one in Thrasea. Now he would have something, someone to fear.

THRASEA
THE FEARLESS

(THRA-see-ah PAY-toos)

B. 14 AD

D. 66 AD

ORIGIN: PADUA

Thrasea Paetus was a man born out of step with his time. Born in Padua around the time of the death of Augustus, he belonged to a wealthy and noble family. As was common in the stories of many of the Roman Stoics, he was given the best and most respected tutors who instilled in him a talent for rhetoric, for the law, and, most of all, for principled living.

Where other Stoics had figured out a way to adjust to the changing times or smartly withdrew, Thrasea was a senator of old. It had been decades since Cato's courage and commitment had cast a shadow in Rome, but so deep was Thrasea's love of history and philosophy that the figures of the Republic's distant past were almost alive and real to him. As Zeno had been told by the oracle that he could commune with the dead—through philosophy—so too could Thrasea.

Seneca would later write about how philosophers needed to "choose [themselves] a Cato"—a person who could serve as a kind of ruler to measure and straighten themselves against. Plutarch tells us that from an early age, Thrasea chose Cato as his Cato and later even wrote a book about him.

Thrasea was likely also inspired by the Scipionic Circle—which he would have seen depicted in Cicero's writings—as we're told that Thrasea's house became a meeting place of like-minded poets, philosophers, and politicians. His dinner table was the setting, as Cato's had been and Scipio's too, for long discussions about virtue and duty and, sadly, the worrying state of affairs of their beloved country. On any given evening, many of the Stoics in the later pages of this book might have been seen at Thrasea's home—from Seneca to Helvidius Priscus— and just as present would have been the ghosts of the Stoics who had lived before them.

Even his wife's family brought their own heady legacy to the table: His wife, like Porcia, came from serious Stoic stock. In 42 AD, his mother-in-law committed suicide at the order of Emperor Claudius. Her last words were "See, it doesn't hurt" to her husband, who was forced to follow suit.

With all this swirling about Thrasea—his early influences, his philosopher friends, his deep commitment to the public good—it was unlikely that he was ever going to go along to get along, no matter who was emperor. But Nero? Everything about Thrasea's life made it impossible for him to tolerate such as his master. Nothing about him could simply accept what Rome had become—and he would be utterly fearless in this rejection of the status quo.

As Thrasea's senatorial career grew, like Rutilius Rufus and Cato, he used his power to take up cases of extortion. In 57 AD he vigorously supported a case brought by Cilician envoys who had come to Rome to accuse their ex-governor, Cossutianus Capito, of extortion. As Tacitus put it, this "was a man stained with much wickedness," and in fact, one who openly embraced his corruption. At trial, he didn't bother to defend himself and was convicted and stripped of his senatorial rank.

In a sane political environment, this would have been the end of

Capito's career, but Rome under Nero was not sane. Within just a few years, Capito's rank was restored and somehow saw him pursuing civil cases *against* other people, including one against a poet who had criticized Nero. The Senate sentenced the poet to death, only to be stopped by the intervention of Thrasea, who, like Seneca in his famous work *On Clemency*, argued for mercy and restraint. Nero acceded, but one gets the sense he could not have been happy letting even petty criticism go unpunished.

And yet as pesky as Thrasea was to Nero, Nero could not help but begrudgingly respect the tenacity of his opponent. When someone once criticized Thrasea for judging a case unfairly to Nero—likely expecting appreciation from their king—they were admonished for their sycophancy. "I wish," Nero said, "Thrasea were as excellent a friend to me as he is a judge."

It had been inevitable that Cato and Caesar, with their enormous gravitational pulls, would eventually clash. So it went for Thrasea and Nero, one a senator, the other Caesar; one restrained and principled, the other unmoored and consumed by ego. One demanding accommodation, the other refusing to even consider such a thing.

In 59 AD, when Nero murdered his mother, Thrasea was appalled. While Seneca seemed to be willing to overlook it, Thrasea's fellow senators did him one better—not only accepting Nero's preposterous explanation, sent in a letter to the Senate, that he needed to kill her because she was a traitor who had planned to kill him, but actually deciding to award him honors for committing matricide. Thrasea was so disgusted that he walked out and refused to vote.

In our times, senators sometimes abstain from voting as a form of political cover—if they don't vote, they won't be on the record either way. Thrasea's abstention was something different. It was not cowardice but courage. He was refusing to dignify brazen corruption and evil.

Cato had fought against Caesar and Pompey with filibusters, but that was when Rome was still nominally a republic. All Thrasea could do now was try to exert some moral authority, to tell people, "This is not normal." So he did, refusing consent, refusing to rubber-stamp, whatever little that was worth.

Nor was he afraid of who might take offense at that . . . or any stand he took.

He refused to vote for divine honors that Nero attempted to give to his new wife, Poppea—the one some contemporaries claimed he had murdered his mother for not approving of. At the trial of Claudius Timarchus—a robber baron "whom immense wealth has emboldened to the oppression of the weak," as Tacitus put it—Thrasea called aggressively for exile. His speech was "hailed with great unanimity," we are told, only to be set aside by the emperor, who seemed constitutionally incapable of doing anything that served the common good. For three long years he stood openly opposed to Nero, who in turn began to more openly oppose him. In 63 AD, Nero refused to accept Thrasea's entrance into his home when he accompanied his fellow senators to Nero's palace to congratulate him on the birth of his daughter.

A Stoic must learn when to walk away when the cause is hopeless. Seneca realized this too late, well after he was complicit in enabling Nero. Thrasea had no such blood on his hands. When the Senate allowed Nero to reject Thrasea—one of their colleagues—he came to see that the state was long past helping. He would spend the next three years in semi-retirement, working on his writings about Cato and studying his philosophy, with little regard for the death sentence he figured would soon find him.

Tacitus tells us that Nero was simply looking for the right pretext. Capito, the man Thrasea had driven from the Senate years before, helped give it to him. Thrasea had allegedly refused to show support at the funeral of Poppea in 65 AD, and to this Nero and Capito took great offense (ironic, given the likelihood that Nero was involved in her death). In any case, with "a heart eager for the worst wickedness," Tacitus says Capito's charges were aimed at carrying out Nero's yearning "to put Virtue itself to death" by killing off one of the few men in Rome not cowed by Nero's tyranny. "The country in its eagerness for discord is now talking of you, Nero, and of Thrasea, as it talked once of Gaius Caesar and Marcus Cato," Capito whispered with insidious intent.

It was a malicious, evil thing to say, and yet also the highest praise that Thrasea could have ever imagined. Such is life: Sometimes our enemies, by nature of their fears and their designs, pay us the ultimate compliment.

Thrasea refused to give Nero the pleasure of undermining him in secret. He wrote him directly: Name your charges and let me defend myself. Nero opened the letter expecting fealty, assuming that Thrasea would cower and beg for mercy. Instead, he found "the defiant independence of the guiltless man." For Thrasea there was no other way to be.

For the Stoic, for us, there is nothing else worth being.

Now, as with Caesar and Cato, a fatal conflict was set in motion. Nero crossed his Rubicon by calling for Thrasea's head, and the Senate, now decayed by five emperors over the last century, was more than willing to go along with the side of tyranny. Only Arulenus Rusticus, a fellow Stoic philosopher, dissented and offered to block the Senate's decree and save Thrasea's life. Thrasea asked him not to intervene. "You're only at the beginning of your career in office," he told this young man. "Consider well what path you will walk, in times like these, through politics."*

---

*Arulenus Rusticus lived to see six more emperors, until Domitian put him to death in 93 AD for a book praising Thrasea's courage and example. His grandson, Junius Rusticus, would attend the lectures of Epictetus and become the philosophy teacher of Marcus Aurelius.

Thrasea did not need anyone's protection. He had decided, like Cato, to bear whatever fate would bring to his door.

A defense went deliberately unoffered, as it had for Rutilius Rufus's show trial so many years before.

The Senate voted to kill him, and to send his son-in-law, Helvidius Priscus, into exile.

When the first rumors of the news came, Thrasea was sitting with his friends in his gardens, as they had for so many years—poets, philosophers, and magistrates. Epictetus tells us that Thrasea, deep in a conversation on the immortality of the soul with Demetrius the Cynic, met the news with sardonic resignation: "I would rather be killed today than banished tomorrow."

Nero offered Thrasea the same courtesy he had offered Seneca: He could choose the manner of his own death. For Thrasea, it was another moment for a conversation with the great dead men who were so real to him. Socrates. Cicero. Cato. Even the recently departed Seneca. "Nero can kill me," Thrasea said, echoing Socrates's last words, "but he cannot harm me."

As he prepared to die, the first thing Thrasea did was urge his loved ones to leave, saying his goodbyes and asking them to take care of themselves. Then he pleaded with his wife, who wanted to follow in her mother's footsteps and die alongside her husband. Thrasea, proving to be more empathetic than Seneca once again, begged his wife to persevere for the sake of their daughter, since she would be losing her own husband with Helvidius's exile.

When the officials arrived with the death decree, Thrasea retired to his bedroom with Demetrius the Cynic and Helvidius Priscus. Perhaps they talked philosophy for a few minutes, or maybe Thrasea advised Helvidius to carry on the fight from a distance. Eventually, they got down to business. Thrasea asked his companions to open the veins on both his arms.

As he lay bleeding out, he—in a nod to Seneca's famous suicide only a year before—offered a prayer of libation to Jupiter the Deliverer and said to the young man who had delivered his death sentence, "You have been born into times in which it is well to fortify the spirit with examples of courage." Then he turned to Demetrius and uttered his last words, which, like Thrasea and the rest of us, were writ on water and disappeared into the abyss of history.

Nero had eliminated another enemy, and a potential check against his excesses. But as Seneca had warned him, crimes return upon those who commit them, and no one can murder or kill enough to make themselves invincible.

As with all despots and gangsters, Nero's support eroded slowly, and then all at once. The plot against him that Seneca had been caught up in showed that the people had begun to turn on their deranged king. Conspirators, facing certain death, began delivering the truth that Nero had long sought to avoid: "No one in the army was more loyal to you than I," Sabrius Flavus told him, "when you deserved our love. But I began to hate you, after you became the murderer of your mother and wife, a chariot driver, an actor and an arsonist." Another soldier, when asked why he would try to kill the emperor, explained, "It was the only way I could help you."

Even the willingness of Rusticus to stand with Thrasea was a sign of dissension inside a Senate that had been hitherto unanimous in its support of Nero's excesses. But still, these were only flickers. The final years of Nero's life were marked by more murders and more indulgent performances. Rigging singing contests so he could win, he toured the empire lapping up praise from increasingly exhausted citizens.

Eventually, it was the army that first turned on him. Suddenly, Nero had lost the beam on top of which his intimidation rested. Now he could not even flee Rome with protection from previously loyal henchmen.

It was an anonymous Praetorian guard who would give the final hint to Nero: "Is it as awful as that, to die?" he asked. Nero awoke one morning to find that most of his bodyguards had abandoned their posts. James Romm describes what would have awaited him were he captured: "Nero would be held immobile with his neck in the fork of a tree, then beaten to death with stout rocks. His ravaged corpse would be flung from the Tarpeian Rock, in imitation of the death deserved for Rome's worst criminals."

Nero, who had so long ignored Seneca's lessons on dying, and who had driven Thrasea to suicide and executed Plautus among countless others, now tested two daggers against his flesh. He hesitated and resheathed them, hoping to wait just a little longer. He took the time to ask his remaining companions to make sure that he not be decapitated after his death—a shameful hypocrisy from the man who had hoisted Plautus's head up by the hair and mocked the dead man's nose.

Then, steeling himself, Nero grabbed one of the knives and stabbed himself in the throat.

One of the conspirators against Nero in 65 AD had joked, when staring at the hastily dug grave Nero's goons had prepared, "Not even this is up to code." Nero's malevolent incompetence extended to his own suicide: He had picked the most painful way to possibly do it . . . and failed anyway. Finally, Epaphroditus, a former slave and Nero's aide, stepped forward and jiggled the dagger, which nicked the artery enough to begin the end of Nero's reign. His second-to-last words, as blood filled his throat, were typical Nero nonsense. "*This*," he burbled, "is loyalty."

Just then, the soldiers returned, hoping to deliver the kind of public death sentence to which Nero had sentenced to so many others. As a centurion attempted to stop the bleeding, Nero laughed and said, "Too late."

He was dead.

Many Stoic philosophers had gruesomely preceded him—Rubellius Plautus, Barea Soranus, Seneca, and of course Thrasea—to almost no point but Nero's ephemeral satisfaction. Yet no one who heard of Nero's death or saw him alive would have thought he got the better end of the deal.

Thrasea said that Nero had the power to kill but not harm, which was true, with one exception. Nero had harmed himself over and over again, and filled his thirty years with a kind of living death that stands to this day as an example of the worst kind of leadership.

Cato. Thrasea. Those two names are watchwords for courage, for wisdom, for moderation, and for justice.

Nero? A pejorative for excess, incompetence, delusion, and evil. Proof of William Blake's line that the most potent poison ever known rests in a Caesar's laurel crown.

HELVIDIUS PRISCUS
THE SENATOR

(Hel-VID-ee-us PRISS-cuss)

B. 25 AD

D. 75 AD

ORIGIN: CLUVIAE

The story of the child who works their way from humble origins to the great body of government of their country is not a new one. The politician who comes from nothing, achieves great power, and uses it to reach back down and help the people they came from is the story of Abraham Lincoln and Henry Clay. It's the story of Margaret Thatcher and Angela Merkel. It's the story of Helvidius Priscus too.

Helvidius was born the son of a soldier stationed in the southern Italian lands of the Caraceni tribe of the Samnium region, in the town of Cluviae. Helvidius Priscus would rise from these humble plebeian origins to be a major figure in Roman life, with a career that spanned the reigns of five emperors.

Given the dates of his first political office, we can be confident he was born in 25 AD or earlier, and must have, from a young age, been a dedicated and earnest student. Tacitus tells us that from his early days he "devoted his extraordinary talents to higher studies, not as most youths do to cloak a useless leisure with a pretentious name, but that he might enter public life better fortified against the chances of fortune." From Tacitus we also learn that his early teachers were Stoics, who counted "only those things 'good' which are morally right and only those things 'evil' which are base, and who reckon power, high birth, and everything else that is beyond the control of the will as neither good nor bad."

Like Seneca's brother Gallio, and like Scipio several generations before, Helvidius was adopted into a wealthy and powerful family, likely that of Helvidius Priscus, who served as a legate under the Syrian governor Quadratus. How young Helvidius—who took his new family's name—met these allies we are not sure. Perhaps his adoptive father served in the army with his family, perhaps the bright up-and-comer dazzled the heirless couple with his educational promise.

In any case, he was no longer the plebeian son of a nobody, but someone on the rise. Fortune does that, Seneca had written, brings us low, as well as proud. Breaks our hearts as well as gives us lucky breaks.

What matters is what we do with either one, and Helvidius, trained as a Stoic, would not waste the material life gave him.

After achieving the first rung of magistracy by winning the post of quaestor in Achaea, the young Helvidius distinguished himself enough in character and success that he married Thrasea's daughter Fannia. It would have been like marrying into the Cato family, as Brutus had, except the old man was still there to teach and to inspire. As Tacitus tells us, from Thrasea, Priscus learned everything about "the spirit of freedom" and how to, "as citizen, senator, husband, son-in-law, and friend," prove "equal to all of life's duties, despising riches, determined in the right, unmoved by fear." Priscus and his new wife moved to a beautiful home in Rome, a startling transition from his early life in the camps on the Roman frontier.

By 56 AD, Helvidius won the office of tribune of the plebs, where he distinguished himself by defending the poor against a punitive young treasurer, Olbutronius Sabinus, who abused his authority to liquidate their assets. Priscus made a convincing enough case against Sabinus that

Nero stepped in to declare that future treasury officers would be held to a higher standard.

It was a begrudging reform that Nero could not have enjoyed having to make.

The specifics of Helvidius's political career, as for several other Stoics, are a mystery to us until it careened off course and into open conflict with the ruling regime. In 66 AD, Thrasea was brought up on charges for plotting against Nero. Helvidius's alleged sympathies for Brutus and Cassius of Julius Caesar's time—perhaps heard in an offhand remark, or in something he had written—were used as evidence against his beloved father-in-law.

Shortly thereafter, Helvidius was asked to help Thrasea commit suicide. No sooner had Thrasea's blood poured from his body than Helvidius and his grieving wife were sent with their two children to distant Macedonia in exile.

After two years and Nero's death, Helvidius was recalled to Rome by the emperor Galba. Unlike Rutilius Rufus, who had chosen to stay where he was, free of Rome's insanity, Helvidius was hopeful enough to return. Perhaps Nero had been only a bad dream—a passing tyranny—and the new emperor would be better.

Certainly Helvidius's first actions reveal a naive faith in the stability of Rome at that time. Almost immediately, he brought impeachment charges against Eprius Marcellus, the man who had persecuted Thrasea and himself. This faith in the institutions of his country were quickly shaken—how many other senators shared guilt with Marcellus, how fair-weather was the new emperor's support of the son of an executed traitor—and Helvidius ended up dropping his charges. Within months, Galba was dead, and thus began the so-called "Year of the Four Emperors," in which the throne resembled a game of musical chairs.

Otho, the next emperor, would serve for barely three months—just enough time for Helvidius to receive permission to bury Galba. After the death of Otho, Helvidius gained the office of praetor, where he quickly found himself at odds with the new emperor, Vitellius, who himself lasted only eight months. In what must have seemed like an endless series of unresolved but exhausting battles of wills, Helvidius found himself cornered in 70 AD, in opposition to the new emperor, Vespasian, over whether the Senate or the emperor controlled the empire's spending.

While these conflicts for legislative supremacy were real, certainly Helvidius's Stoic disdain—which some might call impudence—for sovereigns undoubtedly heightened the tension. We are told that Helvidius, who had learned from Thrasea that nothing unearned is worth respect, took to calling the new emperor by his private and not his imperial name. Indeed, at the height of Vespasian's fame, following his triumphal return from Syria, Helvidius was the only senator who chose to address the man as if he was a commoner. In all his edicts as praetor, Helvidius refused to recognize Vespasian by his royal titles.

Was it recklessness or a sincere refusal to bow before someone he believed was not his superior? Or was it simply exhaustion with the endless parade of two-bit leaders that the Senate had been forced to put up with?

We know that in time this disrespect became more pronounced. Suetonius tells us that Helvidius began to speak out directly against Vespasian. Epictetus provides us an exchange that portrays the man as utterly fearless:

When Vespasian sent for Helvidius Priscus and commanded him not to go into the senate, he replied, "It is in your power not to allow me to be a member of the senate, but so long as I am, I

must go in." "Well, go in then," says the emperor, "but say nothing." "Do not ask my opinion, and I will be silent." "But I must ask
your opinion." "And I must say what I think right." "But if you do,
I shall put you to death." "When then did I tell you that I am immortal? You will do your part, and I will do mine: it is your part
to kill; it is mine to die, but not in fear: yours to banish me; mine
to depart without sorrow."

You do your job, I'll do mine, the Stoic says. You be evil, I'll be good.
Let everything else come what may.

Helvidius must have known that this approach was not long for this
world, or at least for Rome. He hung on long enough to oversee the con-
struction of the new Capitol building and the dedication of the new
temple of Jupiter Capitolinus. In Tacitus, we see Helvidius Priscus standing as a kind of lonely but hopeful figure, trying to reach backward or
forward to more peaceful times, where the common good was served by
the state and a functioning republic would eclipse imperial excesses and
the bloody succession of the Flavians.

It was not to be.

Vespasian, tired of being toyed with and undermined, decided to
banish Helvidius once again. It likely says something about the power
Helvidius still held that Vespasian kept the exile close so that he could
keep an eye on him. In truth, it was more like a death row holding cell.

Not long after, Vespasian ordered Helvidius's execution.

Helvidius's wife would later commission a celebration of her husband's life, but as with the best of the Stoics, it was not words that defined
his legacy but his actions. Epictetus was inspired by him. Marcus Aurelius held him up as an example. And then, 1,927 years later, another man
who had also grown up poor and had been adopted, but came to fall

in love with the legislative body of his country—the senator Robert Byrd*—would take to the floor of the Senate at eighty-five years old to protest the overreaches in the name of "security" of his own president:

> Helvidius Priscus spoke his mind; the emperor Vespasian killed him. In this effeminate age it is instructive to read of courage. There are members of the U.S. Senate and House who are terrified apparently if the president of the United States tells them, urges them, to vote a certain way that may be against their belief. So in this day of few men with great courage—relatively few—let us take a leaf out of Roman history and remember Helvidius Priscus.

When asked why he gave this speech, Byrd managed to unintentionally provide the perfect lesson from Helvidius Priscus's life and those of the brave Stoics who had died opposing the reigns of Nero and his successors:

> To me, that question misses the point, with all due respect to you for asking it. To me, the matter is there for a thousand years in the record. I stood for the Constitution. I stood for the institution. If it isn't heard today, there'll be some future member who will come through and will comb these tomes.

---

*It should be said that Byrd could have used a lesson in the Stoic virtue of justice and fairness earlier in life, for in the early 1940s he joined the Ku Klux Klan. Though maybe he did later get the message, repeatedly apologizing for this sin and actively supporting the efforts of the NAACP.

MUSONIUS RUFUS
THE UNBREAKABLE

(Mu-SOWN-ee-us ROOF-us)

B. 20–30 AD

D. C. 101 AD   ORIGIN: VOLSINII, ETRURIA

C ato may have been Rome's Iron Man, but in the end he was challenged by only one emperor. Thrasea was utterly fearless, but his friend Gaius Musonius Rufus was also unafraid, and, as it happens, endured a life so challenging as to make Thrasea's ordeal under Nero seem fun.

Born a member of the equestrian class, in Volsinii, Etruria, during the reign of Tiberius, Musonius Rufus quickly made his reputation as a philosopher and as a teacher. Even in a time and after a long history of brilliant Stoics, Musonius was considered above the rest. Among his contemporaries, he was the "Roman Socrates," a man of wisdom, courage, self-control, and a marrow-deep commitment to what was right. It was fame that transcended his times, and we find Musonius mentioned admiringly by everyone from Christians like Justin Martyr and Clement of Alexandria to Marcus Aurelius.

But unlike Seneca and Cicero, who relished their places at the top of the heap of Roman society, Musonius was a far more humble figure. He was not born to the senatorial rank or to great wealth. He did not marry into a well-connected family. He did not seek out fame or power. Nor, it seems, did he think these things were particularly important.

He believed that praise and applause were wastes of time—for both the audience and the philosopher. "When a philosopher," he said, "is exhorting, persuading, rebuking, or discussing some aspect of philosophy, if the audience pour forth trite and commonplace words of praise in their enthusiasm and unrestraint, if they even shout, if they gesticulate, if they are moved and aroused, and swayed by the charm of his words, by the rhythm of his phrases, and by certain rhetorical repetitions, then you may know that both the speaker and his audience are wasting their time, and that they are not hearing a philosopher speaking but a flute player performing."

To Musonius, the sign of a successful philosopher was not the loud cheering of supporters. It was silence. Because it meant the audience was actually thinking—it meant they were wrestling with the difficult ideas that the speaker was getting across.

And so we can imagine this Roman Socrates drawing large crowds— not because of his showmanship, but through the reputation of his teachings—who sat in respectful silence, even as he challenged their most deeply held assumptions.

His most provocative belief in first-century Rome? That women deserved an education as much as men. Two of Musonius's twenty-one surviving lectures (*That Women Too Should Study Philosophy* and *Should Daughters Receive the Same Education as Sons?*) come down strongly in favor of treating women well and of their capabilities as philosophers.

This was not a conventional view, but then again, the right thing rarely is.

It should not surprise us that Musonius held it or that he had the courage to argue it at a time when most believed that women were no more than property. A core precept of Stoic training is independent thinking, and here Musonius was illustrating an ability to see what was just, outside the context of his times. "It is not men alone who possess eagerness and a natural inclination towards virtue," he wrote, "but women also. Women are pleased no less than men by noble and just deeds, and reject the opposite of such actions. Since that is so, why is it appropriate for men to seek out and examine how they might live well, that is, to practice philosophy, but not women."*

Even his view of marriage was modern, calling for the "perfect companionship and mutual love of husband and wife, both in health and in sickness and under all conditions." A good marriage, he believed, was one where a couple strove to outdo each other in devotion. He spoke of the kind of "beautiful union" that Brutus and Porcia had, where two souls stick with each other through the adversity of life and inspire each other to greater virtue. What was Musonius's marriage like? We don't know—but it would be incredible to think that a man who wrote so movingly about the benefits of this kind of marriage would not be speaking from experience, and more impossible still that Musonius could have endured the adversity he was soon to face without a life partner of courage and virtue.

At the core of Musonius's teachings was a belief in the importance of hard work and endurance. He was a man cut from the same cloth as Cleanthes, who centuries before had supported his philosophical studies with manual labor. In a lecture entitled *What Means of Livelihood Is Appropriate for the Philosopher*, Musonius would speak highly of that kind of hard work, believing very little was beneath our dignity, if done well and with the right work ethic.

Hardship, he believed, was simply a part of life. "In order to support

---

* The Stoics were very early on equality between the sexes. Three centuries earlier, Cleanthes had written a book titled *On the Thesis That Virtue Is the Same in a Man and a Woman*.

more easily and more cheerfully those hardships which we may expect to suffer in behalf of virtue and goodness," he said, "it is useful to recall what hardships people will endure for unworthy ends. Thus for example consider what intemperate lovers undergo for the sake of evil desires, and how much exertion others expend for the sake of making profit, and how much suffering those who are pursuing fame endure, and bear in mind that all of these people submit to all kinds of toil and hardship voluntarily."

So if we're going to suffer, ought we not suffer in a way that gets us somewhere worth going?

Suffer and endure *toward* virtue—that's the core of Musonius's teachings. As he said, "And yet would not anyone admit how much better it is, instead of exerting oneself to win someone else's wife, to exert oneself to discipline one's desires; instead of enduring hardships for the sake of money, to train oneself to want little; instead of giving oneself trouble about getting notoriety, to give oneself trouble how not to thirst for notoriety; instead of trying to find a way to injure an envied person, to inquire how not to envy anyone; and instead of slaving, as sycophants do, to win false friends, to undergo suffering in order to possess true friends?"

It is fitting that he would write and speak so much on this topic, because he—like many of the Stoics—would find that life had challenges and hardships in store.

Musonius's first brush with trouble came from his association with the Stoic Opposition, including Gaius Rubellius Plautus, for whom Nero's paranoid delusions made him a marked man. It was Musonius who would accompany Plautus into exile to Syria in 60 AD. It was Musonius's first brush with the capriciousness of fate, and by no means his last.

Musonius would advise his dear friend "to have courage and await death," and was likely there when Plautus fell to Nero's angry sword.

Musonius was allowed to return to Rome, briefly, but in 65 AD when the fallout from the Pisonian conspiracy claimed Seneca, Musonius was banished by Nero to the desolate island of Gyara.

It was there that Musonius sat, some seven hundred miles from home, wondering if he would need to follow his own advice and courageously wait for death.

Why didn't he kill himself? As he had suggested to Thrasea? He had reminded Thrasea that there is no reason to choose a heavier misfortune if we can make do with the one in front of us. We can train ourselves to be satisfied with the difficulties fortune has chosen to give us. Besides, Musonius believed he still had living to do. "One who by living is of use to many," he said, "has not the right to choose to die unless by dying he may be of use to more."

So he lived and studied—as we must—as long as it was in his control to keep doing so well and for the greater good.

Gyara is a very dry, harsh island that today is unpopulated, but Musonius seized every opportunity he could to live by his teachings and to be of use to people around him.* According to one source, he discovered an underground spring on the island, earning him the eternal gratitude of his fellow residents, most of whom were also political exiles. It's clear that he believed that exile was not an evil or a hardship, but merely a kind of test—a chance to move closer to virtue if one so chose. So he did, rededicating himself to teaching and writing, playing advisor to the philosophers and dignitaries who visited him from across the Mediterranean.

A testament to Musonius's growing fame and the inspirational example he cast in those dark times is seen in the fictional letters of a man

---

*Modern Greece actually kept leftist political agitators in Gyara from 1948 to 1974. For all the passage of time, people don't change that much.

named Apollonius of Tyana. In one exchange, Apollonius says he dreams of boldly rescuing Musonius from Gyara. Musonius writes back to say that he won't need it, because a true man undertakes to prove his own innocence and therefore has control of his own liberation. Apollonius replies that he worries that Musonius will die like Socrates. Musonius has no intention of going so quietly. "Socrates died because he was not prepared to defend himself," he supposedly says, "but I will."

Another exchange captures Musonius's fighting spirit. We are told that Demetrius the Cynic—who had been with Thrasea during his last moments—encountered Musonius, bound in chains and digging with a pickaxe on a chain gang for one of Nero's canals. "Does it pain you, Demetrius," Musonius was said to reply, "if I dig the Isthmus for the sake of Greece? What would you have felt if you had seen me playing the lyre like Nero?" The dates on this encounter make it hard to trust, as the canal was being constructed during the time of his confinement to Gyara, but these stories nonetheless give us an insight into the reputation of Musonius's character.

Whether he was providing for thirsty islanders or digging a canal for the benefit of Greece, the hardship of exile was not enough to break the will of a true philosopher. But what of all the comforts he was deprived of? Musonius chose to think about what he still had access to— the sun, water, air. When he missed the amenities of Rome, friends, or the freedom to travel, he reminded himself and his fellow exiles that "when we were home, we did not enjoy the whole earth, nor did we have contact with all men." And then he got back to spending his time in Gyara doing what he did best—finding opportunities to do good.

Because for a Stoic, this chance is always there. Even in the worst of circumstances. As bad as exile—or any adversity—is, it can make you better, if you so choose.

"Exile transformed Diogenes from an ordinary person into a philosopher," he said later, speaking not of the Stoic but of the famous Cynic from before Zeno's time. "Instead of sitting around in Sinope, he spent his time in Greece, and in his practice of virtue he surpassed the other philosophers. Exile strengthened others who were unhealthy because of soft living and luxury: it forced them to follow a more manly lifestyle. We know that some were cured of chronic illnesses in exile. . . . They say that others who indulged in soft living were cured of gout, even though they previously had been laid low by it. Exile, by accustoming them to live more austerely, restored their health. Thus, by improving people, exile helps them more than it hurts them with respect to both body and soul."

Musonius would have never been so conceited as to claim he was improved by his own exile, but the fact of the matter is that he was.

Where did this incredible strength and skill come from? Musonius Rufus believed that we were like doctors, treating ourselves with reason. The power to think clearly, to get to the truth of a matter, that was what nursed that rock-hard, unbreakable citadel of a soul that he had. He was not interested in shortcuts, he said, or smelling salts that "revive . . . but do not cure the disease."

And he was a serious proponent of the "manly" life that exile necessitated. When he was in Rome, even at the height of his powers, Musonius sought out cold, heat, thirst, hunger, and hard beds. He familiarized himself with the uncomfortable feelings these conditions brought about and taught himself to be patient, even happy, while experiencing them. By this training, he said, "the body is strengthened and becomes capable of enduring hardship, sturdy and ready for any task." Exile did come, and he was ready body and soul. Good times returned as well, and for this he was ready too.

When Galba succeeded Nero in 68 AD, Musonius was allowed to return to Rome and resume his teaching. His stature would grow over the next decade, and eventually Epictetus, a long-suffering former slave of one of Nero's secretaries, would be added to the ranks of his students. Could a teacher who had experienced less adversity, who was less determined and self-sufficient, have reached a student like that—who had had such a difficult life?

When the student is ready, the teacher appears . . . and sometimes the perfect student is exactly what's needed to bring out the best in a teacher.

Musonius had a habit of turning away students to test their resolve. We can imagine him trying this tactic on Epictetus, who, after three decades of being told what he could and could not do, would have risen to the challenge. "A stone, because of its makeup, will return to earth if you throw it up in the air," Epictetus recounts Musonius telling him. "Likewise, the more one pushes the intelligent person away from the life he was born for, the more he inclines towards it."

Like Epictetus, he had cultivated a distinct distaste for the rich and the corruptions of their money. So he liked to taunt them. We're told by one witness that Musonius once awarded a thousand sesterces to a charlatan posing as a philosopher. When someone stepped in to say that this man was a liar and unworthy of such a gift, Musonius was amused. "Money," he replied, "is exactly what he deserves."

One might think that after two painful exiles, Musonius would spend some time lying low. That's certainly how Seneca or Cicero would have played it. Rome was in a state of flux and fear—three more emperors would follow Galba within months—but Musonius made no effort to hide what he thought was the proper way to live and act.

In fact, his entire approach was to be indifferent to who was in power.

In the waning days of Vitellius's reign, with the looming threat of Vespasian's armies marching on Rome, Musonius agreed to serve as an emissary to forestall the conflict. His partner in the mission, Arulenus Rusticus—whom Thrasea had advised with some of his last words to consider what kind of politician he would be—was badly wounded in a scuffle. Tacitus tells us that Musonius threw his own body into the fray and was nearly trampled to death by the troops he was attempting to warn against engaging in civil strife.

Musonius's calls went unheeded—in fact he was heckled—and soon blood flowed in the streets. Vitellius was torn limb from limb by an angry mob not far from where his predecessor, Galba, had died. Now Vespasian was the emperor and Rome was yet again under the command of a strongman.

Would Vespasian hold Musonius's service to Vitellius against him? Would he be exiled once more? Or finally killed for his association with the Stoic threat? None of these considerations had stopped Musonius from trying. None of it would break his commitment to what was right.

This commitment to justice, as it had for Cato, played no favorites. Not long after escaping with his life from the civil conflict between Vitellius and Vespasian, Musonius engaged in civil conflict of his own, in this case against a fellow Stoic. Sometime around 70 AD, he undertook the prosecution of Publius Egnatius Celer, who had been an informant for Nero about other Stoics and contributed to the execution of one named Barea Soranus. It was an epic case that pitted Musonius not only against a Stoic traitor, but also against Demetrius the Cynic, who chose to represent Celer.

It was a hard-won victory for justice, in a time where such a thing had become rare. A remaining fragment from Musonius captures why he would have pursued such a case. "If one accomplishes some good though with toil, the toil passes, but the good remains," he said. "If one does something dishonorable with pleasure, the pleasure passes, but the dishonor remains."

We must do the right thing, no matter how difficult, Musonius was saying. A Stoic must avoid doing the wrong thing, even if the reward for it is great.

Musonius must have known that justice against Celer would come at a cost. No matter the verdict, to attack an informant of an emperor—even one as reviled as Nero—was a risky move. Perhaps wishing to be rid of the Stoics entirely, a year or so later Vespasian would issue a blanket banishment to all philosophers. Although Musonius was originally exempted, he would not long after be exiled personally by Vespasian for a term of three years.

The good Musonius had done remained while he himself was sent away.

For what? We do not know, but it is fitting, because Musonius would have shrugged off the reasons anyway. Was he angry? He certainly deserved to be. Now, for the third time, he was being driven away from his home, returning to life as a refugee, and why? Because a despot decreed he must?

Even this, Musonius found a way to be philosophical about. Another surviving fragment gives us a sense of his view: "What indictment can we make against tyrants when we ourselves are much worse than they? For we have the same impulses as theirs but not the same opportunity to indulge them."

Or perhaps he recalled how his exile had gone before and the good that had come from it. "Do not be irked by difficult circumstances," he once said, "but reflect on how many things have already happened to you in life in ways that you did not wish, and yet they have turned out for the best."

Once again in Syria, far away from home, Musonius held court and taught. Once again, he did what a Stoic seeks to always do: make the best of a bad situation.

He might not have been able to reach or help the deranged sovereigns who controlled Rome, but he did find willing royal students abroad. In a lecture, *That Kings Also Should Study Philosophy,* Musonius refers offhandedly to a Syrian king whom he advised.* Just as comfortable lecturing freed slaves as he was the grandson of Herod the Great, Musonius kept his teachings the same no matter how powerful or powerless his students. As he had learned from his own struggles, there is no position so high or so low that it is not improved by the four virtues: justice, temperance, wisdom, and courage.

"The ruin of the ruler and the citizen alike," Musonius told him, "is wantonness." And so he spoke to this king at length about the power of self-control, the danger of excess, and the need for justice. These were things that he had experienced firsthand. In fact, it was these exact deficiencies in the parade of incompetent emperors that had brought him to Syria in the first place, so his lessons must have been convincing and deeply personal. No doubt the king listened with the rapt silence that Musonius had long ago defined as the sign of a student whose mind was being blown. "Is it possible for anyone to be a good king unless he is a good man?" Musonius asked. "No, it is not possible. But given a good man, would he not be entitled to be called a philosopher? Most certainly, since philosophy is the pursuit of ideal good."

When Musonius wrapped up his lectures, the young king was spellbound, and unlike those Roman emperors who had been so cruel to Musonius, he was grateful. As a thanks, he offered him anything—wealth, power, pleasure—that it was in his power to offer. "The only favor

---

* Given the dates of his exile, this is mostly likely Aristobulus of Chalcis, husband of Salome.

I ask of you," Musonius replied, "is to remain faithful to this teaching, since you find it commendable, for in this way and no other will you best please me and benefit yourself."

Eventually, Musonius was recalled from exile by Vespasian's son Titus in 78 AD. Within a year, Titus was emperor, and within three, he was dead. His successor, Domitian, was another king who could have listened to the lessons Musonius had given the Syrian king. Instead Domitian chose to be violent, ruthless, and paranoid. Musonius persevered—now taking Epictetus on as a student and training him to become an equally formidable Stoic teacher.

Yet once again, an emperor had the Stoics in his sights. Eventually, in 93 AD, Domitian ordered a death sentence for Arulenus Rusticus for his support of Thrasea many years earlier. He murdered the son of Helvidius Priscus. He then killed Epaphroditus, the former slave who had owned Epictetus and helped Nero kill himself twenty-five years earlier. Domitian even banished every philosopher from Rome, including Epictetus.

If Musonius was still alive by this point, it would have marked his *fourth* exile. Whether he survived until this final trial of fate or had died shortly beforehand, we don't know. Considering the murderous tyrants he had lived under, it is incredible that he survived this long—into his seventies or eighties. Countless people and situations had conspired to break him, but each had failed. He was repeatedly deprived of his country, he said, but no one would take away his "ability to endure exile."

No one can take away our ability to remain undaunted. Which is why Musonius was committed to what he believed up until he drew his last breath, wherever he drew it—in Rome or on whatever rock he was sent to.

"Philosophy is nothing else than to search out by reason what is right and proper and by deeds put it into practice." Rufus had said this, but more important he had lived it. As an exile. As a teacher. As a husband and father, and finally as a dying man. However old he lived to be, simple longevity had never been Musonius's goal. "Since the Fates have spun out the lot of death for all alike," one of his fragments explains, "he is blessed who dies not late but well."

Undoubtedly, whenever the end did come for Musonius, he was ready, and ready to die well. The man who had witnessed the end of so many other Stoics, who had advised them in some cases to go when it was their time and others to hold on because they still had work to do, would have known that eventually his number would come up. He had tried to live that way, saying, "It is not possible to live well today unless one thinks of it as his last."

Now his number was up and Musonius passed—an inspiration to all of us—from this earth with the same dignity and poise with which he had faced all the adversity in his life.

EPICTETUS
THE FREE MAN

(Epic-TEE-tuss)

B. 55 AD

D. 135 AD

ORIGIN: HIERAPOLIS

There are the Stoics who talked about what it means to be free, and then there is Epictetus.

For nearly half a millennium, from Zeno to Thrasea, these philosophers had written about freedom. They had resisted tyrannical governments and they had faced the prospect of exile. Yet one cannot help but feel the privilege dripping from most of their writings.

Most of these men were rich. They were famous. They were powerful.

Cato was. Zeno had been. Posidonius and Panaetius never had to work a day in their lives.

So when each spoke about freedom, they meant it abstractly. They were not literally in chains. While Seneca would speak, with surprising relatability, about slave owners who became owned themselves by the responsibility and management of their slaves, or other Stoics would congratulate themselves for their humane treatment of their human chattel, Epictetus actually was one.

Freedom was not a metaphor for this Stoic philosopher. It was his daily battle.

Born in 55 AD in Hierapolis, Epictetus knew slavery from birth. His name, in Greek, is quite literally "acquired one." Somehow, despite this, his tenacity, his perspective, and his sheer self-sufficiency would make Epictetus—not just in his life, not just to the emperors he influenced, but in history and for all time—the ultimate symbol of the ability of human beings to find true freedom in the darkest of circumstances.

And they were dark circumstances. Epictetus was born the son of a slave woman in what is now modern Turkey, in a region that as part of the Roman Empire was subject to its brutal laws. One of those laws, *Lex Aelia Sentia*, made it impossible for slaves to be freed before their thirtieth birthday. It's a disturbing irony that Augustus, then, who passed the law and was advised by not one but *two* Stoic philosophers, stole three decades from Epictetus's life. As a young boy, Epictetus was purchased by a man named Epaphroditus—a former slave himself—who went on to become Nero's secretary and served alongside Seneca. Two emperors, with three Stoic philosophers advising them, and apparently not so much as a question about whether it was right to own a human being.*

Hardly a shining moment of courage, justice, temperance, or wisdom...

Epictetus had little time to ponder the fairness of his fate. He was too busy *being* a slave. What he could do and couldn't do was overtly controlled. The fruits of his labor were stolen, and his body abused— Rome was not known for treating its slaves gently. He was a vessel to be used up and then discarded, like a horse that was ridden into the ground and then put down.

That he even survived into adulthood is a surprise.

Even by Roman standards, Epictetus had a cruel master. Later

---

* The dye Zeno's family traded in was made by slaves in backbreaking conditions. Seneca owned slaves, and so did Marcus Aurelius. Though to be fair, Epictetus himself, at least from his writings, was fine to openly discuss slavery and never questioned its fairness or morality.

Christian writers portray Epictetus's master as violent and depraved, at one point twisting Epictetus's leg with all his might. As a punishment? As a sick pleasure? Trying to get a disobedient young kid to follow instructions? We don't know. All we hear is that Epictetus calmly warned him about taking it too far. When the leg snapped, Epictetus made no sound and cried no tears. He only smiled, looked at his master, and said, "Didn't I warn you?"

Why does this make us shudder? Empathy or pain? A horror at the senselessness? Or is it at the sheer self-mastery?

With Epictetus it is all this and more.

All his life, Epictetus walked with a limp. We can't be certain whether it came from this painful incident or another, but undoubtedly he was hobbled by slavery, yet somehow unbroken all the same. "Lameness is an impediment to the leg," he would later say, "but not to the will."

The Stoics believed we decided how we would react to what happened to us. Epictetus, as we each hold the power to do, *chose* to see his disability as only a physical impairment, and in fact it was that idea of *choice*, we shall see, that defined the core of his philosophical beliefs.

To Epictetus, no human was the full author of what happened in life. Instead, he said, it was as if we were in a play, and if it was the playwright's "pleasure you should act a poor man, a cripple, a governor, or a private person, see that you act it naturally. For this is your business, to act well the character assigned you; to choose it is another's."

And so he did.

In Nero's court in the 60s AD, Epictetus would have seen all of the opulence, insanity, and contradictions of Rome at that time. He would later tell a story of witnessing a man come to Epaphroditus begging for help because he was down to his last million and a half sesterces (at least $3 million in today's dollars). Was it with sarcasm or genuine bafflement that Epictetus's rich owner replied, "Dear man, how did you keep silent, how could you possibly endure it?"

It must have also been revealing for Epictetus to watch Epaphroditus—this man who had incredible power over him—contorting himself to remain on Nero's good side, down to flattering even the man's cobbler in hope of winning favor. He saw aspiring candidates for the office of consul working themselves to the bone to earn the position. He saw the gifts that were expected, the spectacles that had to be put on, the chain of offices that needed to be held for years in order to get ahead. *That's freedom?* he must have thought. "For the sake of these mighty and dignified offices and honors you kiss the hands of another man's slaves," he wrote, "and are thus the slaves of men who are not free themselves."

The rich in Rome were no different than the rich today: Despite all their wealth, ambition turns even a powerful person into a supplicant in the hope of gaining more.

"Freedom is the prize we are working for: not being a slave to anything—not to compulsion, not to chance events," Seneca had written. What would Epictetus have thought watching Seneca in the flesh—whose works would have been featured in the home of a well-read man like Epaphroditus—working for such a deranged boss? As a writer, Seneca may well have been the person who introduced Epictetus to Stoicism, but by his example he clearly influenced Epictetus even more: Freedom is more than a legal status. It's a state of mind, a way of living.

Seneca, unable to walk away from Nero's service, ultimately forced to submit to suicide, was not trapped in the same slavery as Epictetus, but he was not free all the same.

What we know is that Epictetus was horrified by what he saw in the palaces and imperial offices of Rome, and resolved to live differently. "It is better to starve to death in a calm and confident state of mind," he would say, "than to live anxiously amidst abundance." Seeing someone like Agrippinus—whom Epictetus likely also met—would have been a powerful counterexample, reminding him that those who marched to their own beat could be free despite the tyranny that surrounded them. "For no man is a slave who is free in his will," Epictetus would later say, sounding much more like Agrippinus in practice than Seneca on the page.

At some point, Epictetus came formally to philosophy, though we are not sure when. By 78 AD, though, when Musonius Rufus returned from his third exile, Epictetus was there to study under him. Did he sneak off to his lectures? Did Epictetus's master let him attend out of guilt?

We don't know, but clearly Epictetus found a way. He would not be stopped, not even by Musonius, who was a difficult teacher. Musonius said that silence was a sign of attentive students, but Epictetus, who would have been in his twenties by the time he met Rufus, would later recount that Rufus also believed that if a student praised him, it meant they had utterly missed the challenge his lectures had aimed at them.

This was not a general challenge either. Like the best teachers, Musonius made each of his students feel like he truly understood them at their core. Musonius had said a good teacher should "seek to penetrate to the very intellect of his hearer," and that's what clearly happened with Epictetus.

Epictetus would describe a teaching style that was so pointed and so personal that it felt as if another student had whispered all of your weaknesses in the teacher's ear. Once, after making an error, Epictetus tried to make an excuse. "It is not as bad as if I had set fire to the Capitol," he said. Musonius shook his head and called him a fool. "In this case," he said, "the thing you missed *is* the Capitol." This was a teacher who demanded the absolute best from his students. To make a mistake, to use weak logic, to fail to spot your own inconsistency was to fail philosophy entirely. And to then try to minimize it? To Musonius, that was as bad as burning Rome and dancing on the ashes.

It was from this kind of teacher that Epictetus came to understand philosophy not as some fun diversion but as something deadly serious. "The philosopher's lecture-hall is a hospital," he would later say to his own students. "You shouldn't walk out of it feeling pleasure, but pain, for you aren't well when you enter it."

Although Musonius Rufus was not a slave, he and Epictetus had long conversations about the human condition. Both, clearly, had experienced the worst of what men could do to each other—Musonius with his repeated exiles, and Epictetus living through bondage. Yet instead of taking bitterness from this, instead of losing their sense of agency over their lives, they were both pushed by these painful events toward realizing that the only power they actually had was over their mind and their character. "If a person gave away your body to some passerby, you'd be furious," Epictetus said, yet we so easily hand our mind over to other people, letting them inside our heads or making us feel a certain way.

Which of these forms of slavery is more shameful? Which of these can we stop right now?

At some point, in his thirties, Epictetus was made free by fact and law as well as spirit. Now life presented him with new choices, the same choices each of us gets when we enter the world as adults: What would he do for a living? How would he spend his freedom? What would he do with his life?

Epictetus chose to dedicate himself fully to philosophy. Unlike the other Stoics, who had been senators and generals, advisors and wealthy heirs—professions that were influenced by their philosophy—

Epictetus was one of the first to choose what today we might call the academic route.

It would be a life closer to Cleanthes's or Zeno's than Athenodorus's or Cato's.

Almost immediately, Epictetus gained a large following. His school and his standing were enough that by 93 AD, when Domitian banned philosophers from Rome, Epictetus was one who was driven to exile. In a way, it was fitting that he chose Greece—a city called Nicopolis—because this idea of returning to *teaching* philosophy was a return to the Greek Stoicism that Zeno and Cleanthes had helped pioneer. Epictetus's life was no soft affair and he could expect no tenure, but in choosing to teach, he was explicitly turning away from the Stoicism of the imperial court.

He would not be complicit in some deranged emperor's plans. He would not suffer vainly to rein in their worst impulses. He would not be a cog in the enormous imperial hegemon. He would instead pursue truth where it could be found.

This hardly meant he was fleeing the responsibilities or the reality of the world—he just had no interest in political machinations or acquiring wealth. It was wisdom he was after: how to get it, how to apply it, how to pass it on to others. "If we philosophers," he said, "apply ourselves to our own work as zealously as the old men at Rome have applied themselves to the matters on which they have set their hearts, perhaps we too could accomplish something."

Epictetus's most powerful insight as a teacher derives directly from his experiences as a slave. Although all humans are introduced at some point to the laws of the universe, almost from the moment he was born, Epictetus was reminded daily how little control he had, even of his own person. As he came to study and understand Stoicism, he adopted this lesson into what he described as our "chief task in life." It was, he said, simply "to identify and separate matters so that I can say clearly to my-self which are externals not under my control, and which have to do with the choices I actually control." Or, in his language, what *is* up to us and what is *not* up to us (*ta eph'hemin, ta ouk eph'hemin*).

Once we have organized our understanding of the world into this stark categorization, what remains—what was so central to Epictetus's survival as a slave—is to focus on what *is up to us.* Our attitudes. Our emotions. Our wants. Our desires. Our opinions about what has happened to us. Epictetus believed that as powerless as humans were over their external conditions, they always retained the ability to *choose* how they responded. "You can bind up my leg," he would say—indeed, his leg really had been bound and broken—"but not even Zeus has the power to break my freedom of choice."

"Every situation has two handles," Epictetus taught. One of these handles was weak and one of them was strong. No matter our condition, no matter how undesirable the situation, we retain the ability to choose which one we will grab. Are we going to choose to see that our brother is a selfish jerk? Or are we going to remember that we share the same mother, that he's not this way on purpose, that we love him, that we have our own bad impulses too?*

This decision—which handle we grab, day in and day out, with anyone and everyone we deal with—determines what kind of life we have. And what kind of person we will be.

While it should not surprise us that in times as tough and cruel as Rome in the first century AD, students would flock to hear the insights of a man who had triumphed over so much adversity, it is interesting how affluent and powerful Epictetus's audiences became, even as he taught

---

* Thomas Jefferson would later incorporate Epictetus's rule into the "Canon of Conduct" he wrote for his son, saying, "Take things always by their smooth handle."

more than five hundred miles from Rome. From all over the empire, parents sent their children to be schooled about life by a man who in the hustle and bustle of the court they would have dismissed as a mere slave.

Even the powerful themselves came to sit at his feet. At some point a young Hadrian, the future emperor, passed through Nicopolis and met Epictetus. How many lectures he sat in on, what kind of questions he asked, we do not know, but the historical record shows us that he admired this Stoic, and when he became all-powerful, he tacitly endorsed him (the *Historia Augusta* tells us that Hadrian was known for dismissing unfit philosophers from the profession entirely). Soon enough, Epictetus's lectures would make their way to a young Marcus Aurelius, Hadrian's adopted grandson and future king.

Epictetus's focus on powerlessness was not only an insight about the power structures of his time. He was looking at what makes us fundamentally human. So much is out of our hands. And yet so much remains within our grasp, provided that we decline to relinquish it.

If a person wants to be happy, wants to feel fairly treated, wants to be rich, according to Epictetus, they don't need life to be easy, people to be nice, and money to flow freely. They need to look at the world right. "It's not things that upset us," he would say, "it's our judgment about things." *Our opinions determine the reality we experience.* Epictetus didn't believe it was possible to be offended or frustrated, not without anyone's consent. "Remember, it is not enough to be hit or insulted to be harmed, you must believe that you are being harmed," he said. "If someone succeeds in provoking you, realize that your mind is complicit in the provocation. Which is why it is essential that we not respond impulsively to impressions; take a moment before reacting, and you will find it easier to maintain control."

It's a message that everyone ought to learn as a kid . . . or before they become king.

And what of the situations that are outside our control? How is one supposed to deal with that?

Exactly as Epictetus did while he was a slave—with endurance and equanimity. It is from Aulus Gellius that one of Epictetus's most famous sayings is preserved:

> [Epictetus] used to say that there were two faults which were by far the worst and most disgusting of all, lack of endurance and lack of self-restraint, when we cannot put up with or bear the wrongs which we ought to endure, or cannot restrain ourselves from actions or pleasures from which we ought to refrain. "Therefore," he said, "if anyone would take these two words to heart and use them for his own guidance and regulation, he will be almost without sin and will lead a very peaceful life. These two words," he said, "are ἀνέχου (persist) and ἀπέχου (resist)."

Persist and resist.

The ingredients of freedom, whatever one's condition.

For every rich student Epictetus taught, he would have seen others who had been as impoverished and disadvantaged as he was. He would have seen men—and if he listened to Musonius, as we expect he did, he taught women too—who had been kicked around by fate. His message to them was the same as it was for emperors and future senators: Figure out how to make the most of the hand you have been dealt, play the role assigned to you with the brilliance of a character actor.

The ability to accept life on life's terms, the need to not need things to be different, this was power to Epictetus. "Remember," he said, "that it's not only the desire for wealth and position that debases and subjugates us, but also the desire for peace, leisure, travel, and learning. It doesn't matter what the external thing is, the value we place on it subjugates us to another. . . . Where our heart is set, there our impediment lies."

For Epictetus, then, ambition should not be focused on externals but on internals. A Stoic's greatest, most impressive triumph, he said, is not over other people or enemy armies but over oneself—over our limitations, our tempers, our egos, our petty desires. We all have these impulses; what sets us apart is if we rise above them. What makes us impressive is what we are able to make of this crooked material we were born with.

How rare but glorious the man or woman who manages to do so. How much better are the lives of those who try to rise above than those of the masses, who complain and whine, who sink to the level of their basest instincts. "From now on, then," Epictetus said, "resolve to live as a grown-up who is making progress, and make whatever you think best a law that you never set aside. And whenever you encounter anything that is difficult or pleasurable, or highly or lowly regarded, remember that the contest is now: you are at the Olympic Games, you cannot wait any longer, and that your progress is wrecked or preserved by a single day and a single event."

It was the experience of having been deprived of so much that formed Epictetus's detachment from worldly possessions. It was as if he said to himself, "No one will ever take anything from me again."

We know that one evening a thief entered Epictetus's home and stole an iron lamp that he kept burning in a shrine in his front hallway. While he felt a flash of disappointment and anger, he knew that a Stoic was not to trust these strong emotions. Pausing, checking with himself, he found a different way through the experience of being robbed. "Tomorrow, my friend," he said to himself, "you will find an earthenware lamp; for a man can only lose what he has."

You can only lose what you have. You don't control your possessions, so don't ascribe more value to them than they deserve. And whenever we forget this, life finds a way to painfully call it back to our attention.

It says something about the fame of this frugal teacher that after his death, an admirer—who clearly didn't mind having something that could be taken from him—would purchase Epictetus's earthen lamp for three thousand *drachmas.*

Yet even with this rejection of materialism, Epictetus was cautious not to let his self-discipline become a vice, to become some sort of contest with other people. "When you have accustomed your body to a frugal regime," he said, "don't put on airs about it, and if you only drink water, don't broadcast the fact all the time. And if you ever want to go in for endurance training, do it for yourself and not for the world to see." Progress is wonderful. Self-improvement is a worthy endeavor. But it should be done for its *own sake*—not for congratulations or recognition.

Epictetus never had children, but we know he adopted a young orphan and raised him to adulthood. It is haunting then, to imagine him practicing steeling himself against the loss even of the joy being a father brought him. As we learn from Marcus Aurelius, who himself would lose seven children in his lifetime:

> As you kiss your son good night, says Epictetus, whisper to yourself, "He may be dead in the morning." Don't tempt fate, you say. By talking about a natural event? Is fate tempted when we speak of grain being reaped?

It cannot have been easy for Epictetus to think these thoughts about a boy he loved, but he knew from experience that life was cruel. He wished to remind himself that his precious son was not his *possession,* nor were his friends or his students or his health. The fate of these things remained, for the most part, outside his control. Which for a Stoic means only one thing: Cherish them while we have them, but accept that they belong to us only in trust, that they can depart at any moment. Because they can. And so can we.

This was what Epictetus practiced philosophy for. A man who had seen life in real and hard terms had no room or time for dialectics or for sophistry. He wanted strategies for getting better, for dealing with what was likely to happen to a person in the course of a day or in an empire ruled, far too often, by tyrants.

If this practical bent put him at odds with other Stoics, so be it. "What is the work of virtue?" he asked. "A well-flowing life. Who, then, is making progress? The person who has read the many works of Chrysippus? What, is virtue nothing more than that? To have attained a great knowledge of Chrysippus?"

Action was what mattered. Not reading. Not memorization. Not even publishing impressive writing of your own. Only working *toward* being a better person, a better thinker, a better citizen. "I can't call a person a hard worker just because I hear they read and write," Epictetus said, "even if working at it all night. Until I know what a person is working for, I can't deem them industrious. . . . I can, if the end they work for is their own ruling principle, having it be and remain in constant harmony with Nature."

As a thinker and a teacher, Epictetus preached humility. "It's impossible to begin to learn that which one thinks they already know," he said. In Zen, there is a parable of a master and a student who sit down to tea. The master fills up the cup until it overfills. This cup is like your mind, he says. If it is full, it cannot accept anything more. "It's this whole conceit of knowing something useful that we ought to cast aside before we come to philosophy," Epictetus would say, ". . . otherwise we will never come near to making any progress, even if we plow through all the primers and treatises of Chrysippus with those of Antipater and Archedemus thrown in."

So each morning Epictetus had a dialogue with himself, checking his progress, evaluating whether he had properly steeled himself for what may come. It was then that he journaled or recited philosophy to himself. "Every day and night keep thoughts like these at hand," he advised, "write them, read them aloud, talk to yourself and others about them."

While other Romans were getting up early to pay obeisance to some patron or to further their careers, Epictetus wanted to look in the mirror, to hold himself accountable, to focus on where he was falling short. "What do I lack in order to achieve tranquility? What to achieve calm?" he would ask. "'Where did I go wrong?' in matters conducive to serenity? 'What did I do' that was unfriendly, or unsocial, or unfeeling? 'What to be done was left undone' in regard to these matters?"

Epictetus would die around 135 AD. Although he had been born into anonymity and slavery and would die of causes and in circumstances not known to us, it was never in doubt that his legacy would survive.

In the vein of Socrates and Cato, Epictetus neglected to publish a single word in his lifetime. Yet his teachings traveled widely even in his own time. Marcus Aurelius would be loaned a copy of Epictetus's lectures by his tutor Junius Rusticus. Hadrian had studied Epictetus and now his chosen protégé would drink deeply from that same source of wisdom.

If Epictetus declined to write, how did so many of his teachings survive? Because one student, Arrian—a biographer who would achieve a consulship under Hadrian—would publish eight volumes of notes from Epictetus's lectures. But it's Arrian's choice of title of an abridged form of these volumes that best captures what Stoicism and Epictetus's teachings were designed for. He called it *Encheiridion*, literally meaning "to have at hand."

A. A. Long, a later translator of Epictetus, explains this word choice:

> In its earliest usage *encheiridion* refers to a hand-knife or dagger. Arrian may have wished to suggest that connotation of the work's defensive or protective function. It fits his admonition at the beginning and end of the text to keep Epictetus's message "to hand" (*procheiron*). In obvious imitation, Erasmus in 1501 published a work in Latin with the title *Enchiridion militis Christiani* (A Christian soldier's manual).

Shakespeare has Casca say in *Julius Caesar* that every slave holds the source of their freedom in their hand, and it is with that weapon that Brutus would free himself of Caesar's reign in 44 BC. Epictetus, some four generations later, would be an actual slave and under much more serious tyranny. He would not need to resort to murder. He would not need a literal weapon.

Instead, he would create another kind of freedom, a deeper freedom—that Arrian graciously replicated—that could also be possessed in one's hand.

And so it was that Toussaint Louverture would be in part inspired by Epictetus's ferocious commitment to freedom—literal and otherwise—when he rose up and led his fellow Haitian slaves to freedom against Napoleon's France. Just as it was that in 1965, as Colonel James Stockdale was shot down over Vietnam, knowing he would almost certainly be taken prisoner, he would arm himself with Epictetus's teachings, which he had studied as a student at Stanford, and say to himself while he parachuted down, "I am leaving the world of technology and entering the world of Epictetus."

So two thousand years apart the same teachings were helping a man find freedom inside captivity and making him unbreakable despite the worst circumstances.

Which is the only way future generations can possibly thank or pay the proper homage to someone like Epictetus.

Forget everything but action. Don't talk about it, be about it.

"Don't explain your philosophy," Epictetus said, "embody it."

JUNIUS RUSTICUS
THE DUTIFUL

(JUNE-ee-us ROOS-ti-cuss)

B. 100 AD
D. 170 AD

ORIGIN: ROME

In 66 AD, as Thrasea faced an almost certain death sentence, Arulenus Rusticus had offered to dissent and save him. No, Thrasea had said, it is too late for me. But there was still time, he had said to that courageous young man trying to save him, to think about what kind of politician he would be.

Rusticus would go on to raise a son who in turn would have a son who by and large proved that faith to be well founded. He would also prove, it seems, how often history hinges on small events.

Junius Rusticus, the grandson of Arulenus, was born around 100 AD, less than a decade after the murder of his grandfather. He would become the tutor who introduced Marcus Aurelius to Stoicism and helped form, in so doing, the world's first philosopher king—the kind of leader who was the opposite of the men Arulenus had bravely stood against.

It would have made sense for Junius to want to turn away from this violent world, to hide in his books and in theories. We are told by one ancient writer that there was a part of Junius that would have been content to be a "mere pen-and-ink philosopher," that he would have liked to stay at home and compose his theories in peace. But the sense of duty—instilled by the example of his grandfather, as it had been for Cato—called him to higher things.

It's an example that should challenge every talented and brilliant person: You owe it to yourself and to the world to actively engage with the brief moment you have on this planet. You cannot retreat exclusively into ideas. You must *contribute*.

Junius, for his part, became a soldier and a general. In his early thirties, he was a consul under Hadrian. At some point he met Arrian, who had studied under Epictetus. It's perfectly possible, modern scholars like Donald Robertson speculate, that Junius himself attended Epictetus's lectures and wrote his own notes of what the great sage taught to students.

In any case, it would be a personal copy of Epictetus's sayings that made its way from Junius's library directly into the hands of a young Marcus Aurelius and changed the course of a man's life.

A book given. A book read. Such a simple exchange, but done between the right two people at the right time—as it was here—can be enough to change the world.

At some point in the boy's early twenties, Junius became Marcus Aurelius's official tutor. It was, from the looks of it, a transformative period of study. As Marcus would later reflect, he learned from Junius matters big and small, from how to carry himself with dignity to how to write clearly and effectively.

"From Rusticus," he reflected later in life,

> I learned to become aware of the fact that I needed amendment and training for my character; and not to be led aside into an argumentative sophistry; nor compose treatises on speculative subjects, or deliver little homilies, or pose ostentatiously as the moral athlete or unselfish man; and to eschew rhetoric, poetry, and fine language; and not to go about the house in my robes,

nor commit any such breach of good taste; and to write letters without affectation, like his own letter written to my mother from Sinuessa; to show oneself ready to be reconciled to those who have lost their temper and trespassed against one, and ready to meet them halfway as soon as ever they seem to be willing to retrace their steps; to read with minute care and not to be content with a superficial bird's-eye view; nor to be too quick in agreeing with every voluble talker; and to make the acquaintance of the remembrances of Epictetus, which he supplied me with out of his own library.

From Junius, Marcus Aurelius learned all that Seneca was supposed to but failed to impart to Nero. Indeed, it's a remarkable parallel. Nero had been attached to Seneca as a teenager, after the death of his father. Marcus began to study with Junius at age twenty-five, after the death of his mother. And when Nero became emperor, Seneca was drawn into more serious governmental affairs. In 161 AD, when Marcus became emperor, Junius was drawn into the role of magistrate and advisor. He, like Seneca, would go on to serve as consul.

Unlike Seneca, Junius seemed to be willing to deliver hard truths to his pupil. Marcus relates that he was "often upset with Rusticus," but the teacher and student always reconciled. It's a credit to both of them that Marcus was able to say he never became so angry with Junius's criticism or methods that he did something he later regretted.

Nero had been a truculent student, a boy who was biding his time so he could do whatever he wanted when he got his power. The respect he had had for Seneca when he was young transmogrified with time into a kind of resentment and disgust. Seneca seemed to be willing to go along with this, to say his piece and hope it landed, and was otherwise unalarmed enough to allow Nero to get that power he so craved.

Marcus, on the other hand, was eager to learn and remained so for the rest of his days, even when the power dynamic between him and his tutor shifted. In the *Historia Augusta*, we're told he greeted Junius with a kiss, always, and honored him before anyone else on his staff. He sought counsel in private and in public, and genuinely revered his teacher, to whom he considered himself a "disciple." Rusticus had managed to do the thing that so few teachers manage, even with lowly pupils: He *reached* Marcus Aurelius.

Plutarch would talk later talk about how many politicians sought to govern as an exemption from being governed by others. Perhaps what made Marcus so special was that he seemed to place an advisor and a philosopher like Rusticus above himself, despite the fact that his power as emperor was nearly absolute. Why did Marcus remain good while so many other rulers have broken bad? His relationship and deference to a wise, older man like Rusticus explains a lot of it.

Almost immediately after Marcus became emperor, Junius was given major roles serving the state. In 162 AD, he served his second term as consul (almost thirty years after his first). For five years, he was urban prefect, essentially the mayor of Rome, supervising its police, legal enforcement, public works, and the city's food supply. Given the vast corruption that had been endemic in Rome, this was a position of immense responsibility and trust. By all accounts, he acquitted himself honorably.

It would also put Junius on a collision course with an event that would, unfortunately, define his legacy for most of history. In 165 AD, a seemingly minor court case came to Junius's desk. A Christian philosopher named Justin Martyr and a Cynic philosopher named Crescens had become involved in some sort of nasty dispute that had spilled out into the streets. Denounced by Crescens, who accused these Christians of being atheists, Justin and six of his students were charged and brought in to face questioning.

Justin had in fact studied under a Stoic teacher in Samaria but left the school in favor of the burgeoning Christian faith. Many of Justin's writings would evoke similarities between the Stoics and the Christians and he may well have been familiar with Junius's own philosophical work. He quite reasonably expected a favorable ruling from his Stoic judge. As a devout Christian, he knew that a century before, Seneca's brother had fairly judged and and freed Saint Paul in Corinth.

But this was Rome in a very different time, and Rusticus was not simply a pen-and-ink philosopher. His job was to protect the peace. These Christians refused to acknowledge the Roman gods, the supremacy of the Roman state. That was crazy, disruptive, dangerous. Wasn't Rusticus's job to enforce the laws? To prevent these kinds of things from happening? And, perhaps, with Marcus away at the front and no one to check him, Rusticus was a little lost in the sway of his own power.

In her 1939 novel about Christianity in ancient Rome, written as fascism was crushing religious minorities in Europe, Naomi Mitchison has a Stoic philosopher, Nausiphanes, attempt to explain this collision course between the Stoics and the Christians. "[The Christians] were being persecuted," he says, "because they were against the Roman state; no Roman ever really bothered about a difference of gods; in religious matters they were profoundly tolerant because their own gods were not of the individual heart but only social inventions—or had become so. Yet politically they did and must persecute: and equally must be attacked by all who had the courage."

We think we are doing the right thing. We think we are protecting the status quo. We do terrible things in the process.

The proceedings of the trial, and its all too modern undertones, are recorded in *The Acts of Justin*. Rusticus gets right down to business, demanding an account of how Justin is living. Is he a Christian?

Yes. *Yes*, I am, he says, admitting that he knows his beliefs are seen as a threat by the powers that be. That power is not Rusticus, but the empire he represents. Even so, Rusticus seems to take personally Justin's claim that that it is the Romans who "hold fast in error." "Are the [Christian] doctrines approved by you, wretch that you are?" Rusticus demands, and their encounter spirals out of control from there.

As pride goeth before the fall, contempt goeth before injustices and moral failings.

Seneca had written his famous essay *On Clemency* to Nero in 55–56 AD. It's likely, given how Nero turned out, that Rusticus was not a big admirer of Seneca's philosophy. Yet in this case, the thrust of that essay—about how the decisions that the powerful make in regard to the powerless define who they are—was desperately relevant. Here, Rusticus controlled the full weight of the Roman legal system. Justin was just a small man, one man dissenting against a widely held belief. His example mattered very little. He could have been allowed to go free.

He deserved mercy. Most everyone does.

Rusticus was too frustrated to give it. He was baffled by Justin's faith, by his firm belief in something that the Roman system did not countenance. That's why Justin was sitting in court before Rusticus in the first place.

"Listen," Rusticus says, "if you were scourged and beheaded, are you convinced that you would go up to heaven?" Justin replies, "I hope that I shall enter God's house if I suffer that way. For I know that God's favor is stored up until the end of the whole world for all who have lived good lives."

Marcus said that from Rusticus he had learned "to show oneself ready to be reconciled to those who have lost their temper and trespassed against one, and ready to meet them halfway as soon as ever they seem to be willing to retrace their steps." Where was that readiness with

Justin? How much better would Rusticus have come off if he had managed to muster it?

He gave Justin a chance to repent, to submit to the law and go on his way. Justin didn't have to mean it. He just had to do as every other Roman was expected to do. "Now let us come to the point at issue," Rusticus said, "which is necessary and urgent. Gather round then and with one accord offer sacrifice to the gods." The punishment for not doing so would be the same as for any Roman who dared impiety, who spurned the gods whose favor the empire believed it needed.

He was presenting Justin with the same choice offered to Agrippinus, to Cato, to Thrasea, to Helvidius. Go along to get along. Thrasea had faced it, had a chance at reprieve, but refused even help from Arulenus, Rusticus's grandfather. Now, years later, the roles were reversed. It was not a tyrant demanding obeisance from a Stoic. It was a Stoic demanding it of a Christian.

This time, the Christian would be the brave one. "No one who is right thinking stoops from true worship to false worship," Justin replied. And in so doing, chose to die for what he believed in rather than compromise and live.

Holding the immense power of the state in his hands, Rusticus chose to use it. "Let those who have refused to sacrifice to the gods and to obey the command of the emperor," he ordered, "be scourged and led away to suffer capital punishment according to the ruling of the laws."

In the name of Marcus Aurelius, at the order of Rusticus, this poor man was sent off to be cruelly beaten, whipped until the skin was torn from his body, and then beheaded.*

---

* Almost unbelievably, Justin's bones would be discovered in a church safe in Baltimore in the 1960s, and finally buried in the 1980s.

It would be a stain on two otherwise flawless reputations.

Even if Justin had been totally and indisputably wrong on this matter of religion, might the Stoics instead have considered that idea of *sympatheia*, which dated back to Zeno and Chrysippus? How could they have forgotten that we are all part of one large body, each with our own role, our own part to play? Marcus Aurelius would write beautifully that even the misinformed, even the selfish, even the shameless and stupid fit in that equation, and that we shouldn't be surprised when we meet them. It would have been an idea he and Rusticus had discussed countless times.

Was a world of one hundred percent agreement on anything possible? Wasn't it inevitable that some people would dissent, particularly on matters of religion? What was so shocking about the existence of the occasional heretic? What if—gasp—the heretic knew something you didn't? What if most people, even the disruptive ones, were genuinely sincere in whatever they were doing?

Okay, Rusticus might have told himself as he presided over Justin's trial, *this man is one of those people who must exist in the world. Let me slap him on the wrist and let him go.* But he didn't. He was too lost in the black-and-whiteness of the legal case in front of him: Justin was refusing to comply with sacrificial ordinances, a daily practice in Roman life. This was civil disobedience and the law was clear. So he ordered one of the most famous executions in Christian history in 165 AD.

But only in retrospect.

This "martyrdom" was barely notable at the time. Rome was in the middle of the Parthian War and a conflict with Germanic tribes on the border was bubbling up. A plague was ravaging the empire. Millions would die. A death sentence for one lawbreaker would not seem like the kind of thing that history would remember.

History is like that. Just as the unremarkable decision to hand Marcus Aurelius a book would have outsize consequences, so too would this tiny case, which probably seemed at the time to be utterly indistinguishable from hundreds of others.

Just as it did not occur to the Stoics to question the institution of slavery, true religious freedom was an utterly inconceivable concept. But to martyr oneself for one cause, to refuse to compromise even under the threat of death? This should have been at least begrudgingly respected by someone as well versed in Stoicism as Rusticus.

Sadly, he could not do so. All he saw was a threat to the public order, a threat to his power. It was, ironically, the same thing that had motivated a paranoid emperor to kill Rusticus's grandfather.

Duty-bound, Rusticus had done what he believed he had needed to do. Justin Martyr, the same. For the former's failure to see a bigger picture, he would be a villain to millions of Christians for the rest of history. The latter, the victim, inspires the persecuted to this day.

In 168 AD, Junius left his position as urban prefect. Within two years he would be dead. Even as Marcus waged a brutal war hundreds of miles from Rome, he took the time to order the Senate to confer honors over his longtime teacher and friend, with whom he'd closely spent nearly half of his life. The *Historia Augusta* says that statues to Rusticus were placed around Rome—honoring a man not given to arguments, spectacles, or sermons, but only to the training of his character and public duty.

But the real monument to Rusticus—outshining even his own infamous court case—would be found in the life of the student he trained, the Stoic who would, finally, be king.

MARCUS AURELIUS
THE PHILOSOPHER KING

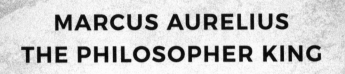

(Marcus Au-REE-lee-us)

B. 121 AD

D. 180 AD

ORIGIN: ROME

Since Plato, it had been the dream of wise men that one day there might be such a thing as a philosopher king. Although the Stoics had been close to power for centuries, none of them had come close to wielding supreme command themselves. Time and time again they had hoped the new emperor would be better, that this one would listen, that this one would put the people before his own needs. Each one would prove, sadly, that absolute power corrupts absolutely.

Caesar. Octavian. Tiberius. Claudius. Nero. Trajan. Vespasian. Domitian.

The list of flawed and broken kings was long, stretching back not just past Rome but to the kings of Zeno and Cleanthes's time. Just as the Christians had prayed for a savior, so too had the Stoics hoped that one day a leader cut from their own cloth would be born, one who could redeem the empire from decay and corruption.

This star, born April 26, 121, was named Marcus Catilius Severus Annius Verus, and for all impossible expectations and responsibilities, he would manage, to paraphrase his great admirer Matthew Arnold, to prove himself worthy of all of it.

The early days of the boy who would become Marcus Aurelius were defined by both loss and promise. His father, Verus, died when he was three. He was raised by both his grandfathers, who doted on him, and who clearly showed him off at court. Even at an early age, he developed a reputation for honesty. The emperor Hadrian, who would have known young Marcus through his early academic accomplishments, sensing his potential, began to keep an eye on him. His nickname for Marcus, whom he liked to go hunting with, was "Verissimus"—a play on his name Verus—*the truest one.*

What could it have been that Hadrian first noticed? What could have given him the sense that the boy might be destined for great things? Marcus was clearly smart, from a good family, handsome, hardworking. But there would have been plenty of that in Rome, and there have been plenty of "true" teenagers. That doesn't mean they'll be good heads of state.

By the time Marcus was ten or eleven, he had already taken to philosophy, dressing the part in humble, rough clothing and living with sober and restrained habits, even sleeping on the ground to toughen himself up. Marcus would write later about the character traits he tried to define himself by, which he called "epithets for yourself." They were "*Upright. Modest. Straightforward. Sane. Cooperative. Disinterested.*" Hadrian, who never had a son and had begun to think about choosing a successor (just as he had been selected himself by the heirless emperor Trajan), must have sensed the commitment to those ideas in Marcus from boyhood on. He must have seen, as they hunted wild boar together, some combination of courage and calmness, compassion and firmness. He must have seen something in his soul that Marcus likely could not even see himself, because by Marcus's seventeenth birthday, Hadrian had begun planning something extraordinary.

He was going to make Marcus Aurelius the emperor of Rome.

We don't know much about Hadrian's stated reasons, but we know about the plan he settled on. On February 25, 138, Hadrian adopted an able and trustworthy fifty-year-old administrator named Antoninus Pius on the condition that he in turn adopt Marcus Aurelius. Tutors were selected. A course of successive offices laid out. Even after Marcus became a member of the imperial family, we're told, he still went to the residences of his philosophy teachers for instruction, though he could have just as easily demanded they come to him. He continued to live as if his means and his status had not irrevocably improved.

By the time Hadrian died a few months later, destiny was set. Marcus Aurelius was to be groomed for a position that only fifteen people had ever held in Rome—he was to wear the purple, he was to be made Caesar.

It was not an altogether dissimilar path to the one that Nero's mother had charted for her boy. Would the results be different?

Unlike most princes, Marcus did not yearn for power. We're told that when he learned he had officially been adopted by Hadrian, he was greatly saddened rather than overjoyed. Perhaps that's because he would have rather been a writer or a philosopher. There was an earnestness to his reticence. One ancient historian notes that Marcus was dismayed at having to leave his mother's house for the royal palace. When asked by someone why he was downcast about such an incredible bounty of fortune, he listed all the evil things that kings had done.

Reservations are not the same thing as cowardice. The most confident leaders—the best ones—often are worried that they won't do a good enough job. They go into the job knowing it will not be an easy one. But they do proceed. And Marcus, around this time, would dream a dream that he had shoulders made of ivory. To him it was a sign: *He could do this.*

At age nineteen, Marcus Aurelius was consul, the highest office in the land. At age twenty-four, he held it again. In 161, at age forty, he was made emperor. The same position held by Nero and Domitian and Vespasian and so many other monsters.

Being chosen to be king—having enormous power thrust upon him at so early an age—somehow seems to have made Marcus Aurelius a better person. This utterly anomalous event in human history—how one man did not go the way of all kings—can only be explained by one thing: Stoicism.*

But it would be an injustice to Marcus Aurelius not to give him the full credit due for the *work* he had to put in. And we know it was conscious, deliberate work. He recognized, quite openly, the "malice, cunning and hypocrisy that power produces," as well as the "peculiar ruthlessness often shown by people from 'good families,'" and decided he would be an exception to that rule. "Take care not be Caesarified, or dyed in purple," he was still writing to himself as an old man, "it happens. So keep yourself simple, good, pure, serious, unpretentious, a friend of justice, god-fearing, kind, full of affection, strong for your proper work. Strive hard to remain the same man that philosophy wished to make you."

It wasn't just the headwind of power that Marcus faced in life. From his letters, we know he had recurring, painful health problems. He became a father at age twenty-six—a transformative and trying experience for any man. In Marcus's case, though, fate was almost unbelievably cruel. He and his wife, Faustina, would have thirteen children. Only five would survive into adulthood.

His reign, from 161 to 180, was marked by the Antonine Plague—a

---

* Gregory Hays, one of Marcus Aurelius's best translators, writes, "If he had to be identified with a particular school, [Stoicism] is surely the one he would have chosen. Yet I suspect that if asked what it was that he studied, his answer would not have been 'Stoicism' but simply 'philosophy.'"

global pandemic that originated in the Far East, spread mercilessly across borders, and claimed the lives of at least five million people over fifteen years—and some nineteen years of wars at the borders. As the historian Dio Cassius would write, Marcus Aurelius "did not meet with the good fortune that he deserved, for he was not strong in body and was involved in a multitude of troubles throughout practically his entire reign."

But these external things don't deter a Stoic. Marcus believed that plagues and war could only threaten our life. What we need to protect is our character—how we act *within* these wars and plagues and life's other setbacks. And to abandon character? That's real evil.

Perhaps the copy of Epictetus that Junius Rusticus had given him had so landed with Marcus Aurelius because they both were dealt hard blows by fate. It is a striking contrast, an emperor and a slave sharing and loving the same philosophy, the latter figure greatly influencing the former, but it is not a contradiction—nor would it have seemed odd to the ancients. It's only in our modern reactionary, divisive focus on "privilege" that we have forgotten how much we all have in common as human beings, how we all stand equally naked and defenseless against fate whether we possess worldly power or not.

Both Marcus Aurelius and Epictetus were, to borrow Epictetus's metaphor, assigned difficult roles by the author of the universe. What defined them was how they managed to play these roles, which neither of them, Marcus especially, would ever have chosen.

Consider the first action that Marcus Aurelius took in 161 AD when his adoptive father, Antoninus Pius, died. When Octavian had become emperor, Arius Didymus, his Stoic advisor, had suggested that he get rid of young Caesarion, the son of Julius Caesar and Cleopatra. "It's not good to have too many Caesars," the Stoic had told his boss, joking as he suggested murder. Nero had eliminated so many rivals that Seneca had to remind him that no king had it in his power to get rid of *every* successor. Marcus Aurelius found himself in an even more complex situation. He had an adoptive brother, Lucius Verus, who had even closer ties to Hadrian's legacy.* What ought he do? What would *you* do?

Marcus Aurelius cut this Gordian knot with effortlessness and grace: He named his adoptive brother co-emperor.

The first thing Marcus Aurelius did with absolute power was voluntarily share half of it. This alone would make him worthy of the kind of awe that King George III felt upon hearing that George Washington would return to private life—"If he does that, sir, he will be the greatest man in the world"—but it was just one of several such gestures that defined Marcus Aurelius's reign.

When the Antonine Plague hit Rome, and the streets were littered with bodies and danger hung in the air, no one would have faulted him for fleeing the city. In fact, it might have been the more prudent course of action. Instead, Marcus stayed, braving it like the British royal family during the Blitz, never showing fear, reassuring the people by his very presence that he did not value his safety more than the responsibilities of his office.

Later, when due to the ravages of the plague and those endless wars, Rome's treasury was exhausted, and Marcus Aurelius was once again faced with a choice of doing things the easy way or the hard way. He could have levied high taxes, he could have looted the provinces, he could have kicked the can down the road, running up bills his successors would have to deal with. Instead, Dio Cassius tells us, Marcus "took all the imperial ornaments to the Forum and sold them for gold. When the barbarian uprising had been put down, he returned the purchase price to those who voluntarily brought back the imperial possessions, but

---

*Lucius was the son of an earlier chosen heir of Hadrian who had died before he could succeed the emperor.

used no compulsion in the case of those who were unwilling to do so." Even though as emperor he technically had unfettered control over Rome's budget, he never acted as such. "As for us," he once said to the Senate about his family, "we are so far from possessing anything of our own that even the house in which we live is yours."

Finally, toward the end of his life, when Avidius Cassius, his most trusted general, turned on him, attempting a coup, Marcus Aurelius was faced with another test of all the things he believed when it came to honor, honesty, compassion, generosity, and dignity. He had every right to be angry.

Incredibly, Marcus decided the attempted coup was an *opportunity*. They could, he said to his soldiers, go out and "settle this affair well and show to all mankind there is a right way to deal even with civil wars." It was a chance "to forgive a man who has wronged one, to remain a friend to one who has transgressed friendship, to continue faithful to one who has broken faith." An assassin would soon enough take down Avidius, hoping almost certainly to impress himself to Marcus, and in the process revealing just how different a plane Marcus Aurelius was operating on. As Dio Cassius writes, Marcus "was so greatly grieved at the death of Cassius that he could not bring himself even to look at the severed head of his enemy, but before the murderers drew near gave orders that it should be buried." He proceeded to treat each of Avidius's collaborators with leniency, including several senators who had actively endorsed this attempted coup. "I implore you, the senate, to keep my reign unstained by the blood of any senator," Marcus later appealed to those who wanted vengeance on his behalf. "May it never happen."

His dictum in life and in leadership was simple and straightforward: "Do the right thing. The rest doesn't matter." No better expression or embodiment of Stoicism is found in his line (and his living of that line) than: "Waste no more time talking about what a good man is like. Be one."

Yet there is, in studying Marcus's life, an impression that he was somehow different, made of special stock that made his many difficult decisions easier. The common perception of Stoicism only compounds this—that somehow the Stoics were beyond pain, beyond material desire, beyond bodily desires.

But Marcus would not have accepted this explanation, for it sells short the training and the struggle he experienced as he worked to get better. "Alone of the emperors," the historian Herodian would write of Marcus Aurelius, "he gave proof of his learning not by mere words or knowledge of philosophical doctrines but by his blameless character and temperate way of life."

And underneath this learning and character, he was still a *human* being.

We know that Marcus Aurelius was brought to tears like one, that he felt the same pain and losses and frustrations that everyone feels. We're told quite vividly by the *Historia Augusta* that Marcus wept when he was told that his favorite tutor had passed away. We know that he cried one day in court, when he was overseeing a case and the attorney mentioned the countless souls who perished in the plague still ravaging Rome.

We can imagine Marcus cried many other times. This was a man who was betrayed by one of his most trusted generals. This was a man who one day lost his wife of thirty-five years. This was a man who lost *eight* children, including all but one of his sons.

Marcus didn't weep because he was weak. He didn't weep because he was un-Stoic. He cried because he was human. Because these very painful experiences made him sad. "Neither philosophy nor empire," Antoninus said sympathetically as he let his son sob, "takes away natural feeling."

So Marcus Aurelius must have lost his temper on occasion, or he never would have had cause to write in his *Meditations*—which was never intended for publication—about the need to keep it under control. We know that he lusted, we know that he feared, we know that he fantasized about his rivals disappearing.

It was not *all* emotions he worked on domesticating, but the harmful ones, the ones that would make him betray what he believed. "Start praying like this and you'll see," he wrote to himself. "Not 'some way to sleep with her'—but a way to stop wanting to. Not 'some way to get rid of him'—but a way to stop trying. Not 'some way to save my child'—but a way to lose your fear."*

The wife of George Marshall, another great man of equal stature, in describing her husband would capture what made Marcus Aurelius so truly impressive:

> In many of the articles and interviews I have read about General Marshall the writers speak of his retiring nature and his modesty. . . . No, I do not think I would call my husband retiring or overly modest. I think he is well aware of his powers, but I also think this knowledge is tempered by a sense of humility and selflessness such as I have seen in few strong men.

If Marcus had naturally been perfect, there would be little to admire. That he wasn't is the whole point. He worked his way there, as we all can.

It should be noted that Marcus himself would not want us to be shamed by his example but be reminded of our own capacities. "Recognize

---

* For those times when he did fall short, Marcus had this advice: "When jarred, unavoidably, by circumstance, revert at once to yourself, and don't lose the rhythm more than you can help. You'll have a better grasp of harmony if you keep on going back to it."

that if it's humanly possible," he said both to us and to himself, "you can do it too."

Marcus Aurelius managed to not be corrupted by power, managed to not be afraid as he faced a terrible epidemic, managed to not be too angered by betrayal, nor utterly broken by unfathomable personal tragedy. What does that mean? It means *you can do the same.*

At the core of Marcus Aurelius's power as a philosopher and a philosopher king seems to be a pretty simple exercise that he must have read about in Seneca's writings and then in Epictetus's: the morning or evening review. "Every day and night keep thoughts like these at hand," Epictetus had said. "Write them, read them aloud, talk to yourself and others about them."

So much of what we know about Marcus Aurelius's philosophical thinking comes from the fact that for years he did that. He was constantly jotting down reminders and aphorisms of Stoic thinking to himself. Indeed, his only known work, *Meditations*, is filled with quotes from Chrysippus, allusions to themes from the writings of Panaetius and Zeno, stories about Socrates, poems from Aristophanes, exercises from Epictetus as well as all sorts of original interpretations of Stoic wisdom. The title of *Meditations*, which dates to 167 AD, translates from *ta eis heauton*, "to himself." This captures the essence of the book perfectly, for Marcus truly was writing for himself, as anyone who has read *Meditations* can easily feel.

How else can we understand notes that reference, without explanation, "the way [Antoninus Pius] accepted the customs agent's apology at Tusculum," or even more obliquely, speaking of moments of divine intervention, when he writes only, "the one at Caiteta." These were moments far too insignificant to have made the historical record but that influenced the author, the *man*, enough that he remembered them decades later and was still mulling them over.

Meditations is not a book for the reader, it was a book for the author. Yet this is what makes it such an impressive piece of writing, one of the great literary feats of all time. Somehow in writing exclusively to and for himself, Marcus Aurelius managed to produce a book that has not only survived through the centuries, but is still teaching and helping people today. As the philosopher Brand Blanshard would observe in 1984:

> Few care now about the marches and countermarches of the Roman commanders. What the centuries have clung to is a notebook of thoughts by a man whose real life was largely unknown who put down in the midnight dimness not the events of the day or the plans of the morrow, but something of far more permanent interest, the ideals and aspirations that a rare spirit lived by.

The opening pages of *Meditations* reveal that spirit quite well, for the book begins with a section entitled "Debts and Lessons." Across seventeen entries and some twenty-one hundred words (a full ten percent of the book), Marcus takes the time to acknowledge and codify the lessons he had learned from the important people in his life. In the privacy of these pages, he recognized his grandfather for his courtesy and serenity of temper; his father for manliness without ostentation; his mother for piety and generosity; his tutor for instilling a positive work ethic; the gods for surrounding him with good people. He even thanks—not to put too fine a point on it—Rusticus for teaching him "not to write treatises on abstract questions, or deliver moralizing little sermons, or compose imaginary descriptions of The Simple Life or The Man Who Lives Only for Others."

Why was he writing this if it would never be seen? If the people would never fully know what they meant to him? Marcus explains:

When you need encouragement, think of the qualities the people around you have: this one's energy, that one's modesty, another's generosity, and so on. Nothing is as encouraging as when virtues are visibly embodied in the people around us, when we're practically showered with them. It's good to keep this in mind.

What Marcus was using this writing for, then, is for the true intended purpose of Stoicism—for getting better, for preparing himself for what life had in store. In Book Two, he opens by noting that the people he will meet in the course of the upcoming day will be surly and rude and selfish and stupid. Was this to excuse himself from good behavior? Or to justify despair? No, Marcus wrote, "no one can implicate me in ugliness," nor could they hurt him or make him angry. He had to love people—*the* people. He had to be ready . . . and be good.

Indeed, one of the most common themes in Marcus's writings was his commitment to serving others, that notion of *sympatheia* and a duty to act for the common good, first advanced by Zeno but carried on by Chrysippus and Posidonius in the centuries since. The phrase "common good" appears more than eighty times in *Meditations*, which for a Stoic makes sense but is surprising considering how nearly all of his predecessors viewed the purpose of the state. Yet here we have Marcus writing, "Whenever you have trouble getting up in the morning, remind yourself that you've been made by nature for the purpose of working with others."

But he did have to remind himself of that regularly, as we all must, because it is so easy to forget.

Marcus used this private journal as a way to keep his ego in check. Fame, he wrote, was fleeting and empty. Applause and cheering were the clacking of tongues and the smacking of hands. What good was posthumous fame, he notes, when you'll be dead and gone? And for that matter, when people in the future will be just as annoying and wrong about things as they are now?

"Words once in common use now sound archaic," he wrote. "And the names of the famous dead as well: Camillus, Caeso, Volesus, Dentatus . . . Scipio and Cato . . . Augustus . . . Hadrian and Antoninus and . . . Everything fades so quickly, turns into legend and soon oblivion covers it." Alexander the Great and his mule driver, Marcus writes, both died and both ended up buried in the same cold ground. What good was fame or accomplishment? It didn't hold a candle to character.

At Aquincum, the Roman camp near present-day Budapest where Marcus Aurelius visited the Second Legion and is believed to have written parts of *Meditations*, archaeologists have uncovered a larger-than-life limestone statue of an emperor in a toga. At first glance it looks like the head has been broken off. But a closer inspection reveals that the head was designed to be replaceable. The statue was part of a shrine for the cult of the emperor, and they wanted to be able to swap the head out each time a new one took the throne.

Knowing that he was only a placeholder helped Marcus prevent his position from going to his head. He built few monuments to himself. He didn't mind criticism. He never abused his power.

Hadrian once got angry enough that he stabbed a secretary in the eye with a writing stylus. Of course, there were no consequences. Marcus could have taken advantage of this freedom to behave as he liked. Instead he kept his temper in check, refused to lash out at the people around him, even if they would have let him get away with it. "Why should we feel anger at the world," he writes in *Meditations*, cribbing a line from a lost Euripides play, "as if the world would notice."

It cannot be said, for all his dignity and poise, that Marcus was a perfect ruler. No leader is, nor would Marcus have expected he could be.

He must be faulted for persecutions of the Christians under his reign—a stain on both him and Rusticus. Yet even here, he was considered by Tertullian, an early Christian writer who lived through the last years of his rule, to be a protector of Christians. Although he made some minor improvements in the lives of slaves, he was—like all the Stoics—incapable of questioning the institution entirely. For all his talk of being a "citizen of the world," and his belief in a unity between all dwellers on this planet, he regarded large swaths of the world's population as "barbarians" and fought and killed many of them. And of course, for a successor, he ultimately chose—or was forced to choose, as only the second emperor since Augustus to have a male heir—to pass the throne to his son Commodus, who turned out to be a deranged and flawed man.*

It's unfair to compare Marcus only to his own writings, or to the impossibly high standards of his philosophy. Instead, he should also be looked at in the company of the other men (and women) who held supreme power, which Dio Cassius did well when he observed that "he ruled better than any others who had ever been in any position of power."

The rule is that sensitive, thoughtful men like Marcus Aurelius turn out to be poor leaders. To be a sovereign or an executive is to come face-to-face with the messiness of the world, the flaws and foibles of humanity. The reason there have been so few philosopher kings is not just a lack of opportunity—it's that philosophers often fall short of what the job requires. Marcus turned out to have the ivory shoulders, as well as the sharp mind, required for the job. "Don't go expecting Plato's Republic," he reminded himself. He had to take reality on reality's terms.

---

* There is not room here to discuss the complicated and disappointing life of Commodus, but if you have seen the movie *Gladiator*, you have a surprisingly accurate picture of the man. Why was Commodus the way he was? No one can say, but the loss of so many brothers and sisters must explain some of it, and certainly much of Marcus and Faustina's responsibility for it.

He had to make do with what was there. For an idealist and a lover of ideas, Marcus was also, like Abraham Lincoln, impressively pragmatic. "The cucumber is bitter?" he said rhetorically. "Then throw it out. There are brambles in the path? Then go around. That's all you need to know." Nothing better expressed his leadership style and his view of progress than this quote:

> You must build up your life action by action, and be content if each one achieves its goal as far as possible—and no one can keep you from this. But there will be some external obstacle! Perhaps, but no obstacle to acting with justice, self-control, and wisdom.
>
> But what if some other area of my action is thwarted?
>
> Well, gladly accept the obstacle for what it is and shift your attention to what is given, and another action will immediately take its place, one that better fits the life you are building.

This seems to be how he thought about the politicians he worked with as well. Instead of holding them to his standards or expecting the impossible—as many talented, brilliant leaders naturally do—he focused on their strengths and was tolerant of their weaknesses. Like Lincoln again, Marcus was not afraid of being disagreed with, and made use of common ground and common cause as best he could. "So long as a person did anything good," Dio Cassius writes, Marcus "would praise him and use him for the service in which he excelled, but to his other conduct he paid no attention; for he declared that it is impossible for one to create such men as one desires to have, and so it is fitting to employ those who are already in existence for whatever service each of them may be able to render to the State."

Ernest Renan, a nineteenth-century biographer of Marcus, puts it perfectly: "The consequence of austere philosophy might have produced stiffness and severity. But here it was that the rare goodness of the nature of Marcus Aurelius shone out in all its brilliancy. His severity was confined only to himself."

Musonius Rufus, some forty-odd years before Marcus was born, had been approached by a Syrian king. "Do not imagine," he had told the man,

> that it is more appropriate for anyone to study philosophy than for you, nor for any other reason than because you are a king. For the first duty of a king is to be able to protect and benefit his people, and a protector and benefactor must know what is good for a man and what is bad, what is helpful and what harmful, what advantageous and what disadvantageous, inasmuch as it is plain that those who ally themselves with evil come to harm, while those who cleave to good enjoy protection, and those who are deemed worthy of help and advantage enjoy benefits, while those who involve themselves in things disadvantageous and harmful suffer punishment.

Could Musonius have imagined—persecuted and abused by five consecutive Roman emperors—that his vision would one day take hold in such a man? That everything the Stoics had spoken of and dreamt about would come true so beautifully and yet so fleetingly? He had said it was impossible for anyone but a good man to be a good king, and Marcus, who had read Musonius, did his best to live up to this command.

Could Epictetus have imagined that his teachings would make their way to the first emperor who would, as Marcus did, make real steps toward improving the plight of Rome's slaves? Along with his stepfather,

Antoninus, he protected the rights of freed slaves and even made it possible for slaves to inherit property from their masters. We're told that Marcus forbade the capital punishment of slaves and made excessively cruel treatment of them a crime as well. Was it the story of Epictetus's broken leg that inspired him? Was it the Stoic virtue of justice that compelled him to care about the less fortunate? While it's disappointing that Marcus lacked the vision to do away with the institution entirely, it remains impressive anytime someone is able to see beyond or through the flawed thinking of their time and make, if only incrementally, the world better for their fellow human beings.

These would not have been easy decisions, nor uncontroversial ones, but he made them, as a Stoic must. Forget protests. Forget criticism and the agendas of the critics. Forget the hard work it takes to enact something new or pioneering. Do what is right.

Come what may.

It is obvious in retrospect that Marcus used the pages of his journal to calm himself, to quiet his active mind, to get to the place of *apatheia* (the absence of passions). The word *galene*—calmness or stillness— appears eight times in his writings. There are metaphors about rivers and the ocean, the stars and beautiful observations about nature. The process of sitting down, with a stylus and wax tablet or papyrus and ink, was deeply therapeutic for him. He would have loved to have spent *all* his time philosophizing, but that was not to be, so the few minutes he stole in his tent on campaign, or even in his seat in the Colosseum as the gladiators fought below, he savored as opportunities for reflection.

Also in these pages he was steeling himself against the blows that fate seemed to so regularly target him for. "Life is warfare and a journey far from home," he writes. It was literally true. Some twelve years of his life would be spent at the empire's northern border along the Danube River, fighting long, brutal wars. Dio Cassius describes the scene of

Marcus returning to Rome after one long absence. As he addressed the people, he made a reference to how long he'd been forced to be away. "Eight!" the people cried lovingly. "Eight!" as they held up four fingers on each hand. He had been gone for *eight years*. The weight of this hit in the moment, and so too must have the adoration of the crowd, even though Marcus often told himself how worthless this was. As a token of his gratitude and beneficence, he would distribute to them eight hundred sesterces apiece, the largest gift from the emperor to the people ever given. He did not stop there. On his return, he forgave countless debts owed to the emperor's private treasury, actually burning the documents in the Forum so they could not ever be recovered.

Marcus may have lived humbly, but no one could say he was not generous to others. In fact, his policies as emperor perfectly adhered to the principles he jotted down one day in his diary: "Be tolerant with others and strict with yourself."

How exhausting it must have been to be so self-disciplined. Yet there are no complaints in *Meditations*, no private lamentations or blame-shifting. When Marcus dreamt of escaping his burdens, thought of the beach or the mountains or time in his library with beloved books, he reminded himself that he didn't need a vacation to recover. He didn't need to travel to relax. "For nowhere can you find a more peaceful and less busy retreat than in your own soul," he wrote. "Treat yourself often to this retreat and be renewed."

As we said, Marcus's early years were defined by loss, and so were his later ones. There would be one blow after another. In 149, he lost newborn twin boys. In 151, he lost his firstborn daughter, Domitia Faustina. In 152, another son, Tiberius Aelius Antoninus, died in infancy. That same year, Marcus's sister Cornificia died. Shortly after, Marcus's mother, Domitia Lucilla, died. In 158, another son, whose name is unknown, died. In 161, he lost his adoptive father, Antoninus Pius. In 165, another son, Titus Aurelius Fulvus Antoninus (twin brother of Commodus), died. In 169, he lost his son Verus, a sweet boy, during what was supposed to be routine surgery, whom he had hoped would rule alongside Commodus, as he had ruled with his own brother. That same year he lost that brother—his co-emperor—Lucius Verus. He would lose his wife of thirty-five years not long after.

Of Marcus's boys, five died before he did. Three of his daughters as well. No parent should outlive their children. To lose eight of them? So young? It staggers the mind. "Unfair" does not even come close. It's grotesque.

How easily this could shatter a person, how easily and understandably it might cause them to toss away everything they ever believed, to hate a world that could be so cruel. Yet somehow we have Marcus Aurelius writing, after all these twists of fate, a note that captures the essence of leadership and the incredible resilience of the human spirit.

—It's unfortunate that this has happened.

No. It's fortunate that this has happened and I've remained unharmed by it—not shattered by the present or frightened of the future. It could have happened to anyone. But not everyone could have remained unharmed by it.

Marcus held Antoninus, his adoptive father, up as his example always. He was particularly inspired, he said, by "the way he handled the material comforts that fortune had supplied him in such abundance— without arrogance and without apology. If they were there, he took advantage of them. If not, he didn't miss them." "Accept it without arrogance," Marcus would write later in *Meditations* about the ups and downs, the blessings and curses of life, "and let it go with indifference."

Is there a better encapsulation of that idea of "preferred indifferents" that Zeno and Cleanthes and Chrysippus and Aristo had argued about all those years ago?

There is no theme that appears more in Marcus's writing than death. Perhaps it was his own health issues that made him so acutely aware of his mortality, but there were other sources. In his book *How to Think Like a Roman Emperor*, Donald Robertson tells us that the Romans believed the burning of incense might protect a family from falling ill. Since he did not flee Rome as many other wealthy citizens did during the plague, Marcus woke up to a surreal-smelling city—a mixture of the putrid smell of dead bodies and the sweet aroma of incense. As Robertson writes, "For over a decade the scent of smoke of incense [was] a reminder to Marcus that he was living under the shadow of death and that survival from one day to the next should never be taken for granted."

His writings reflect this insight, time and time again. "Think of yourself as dead," he writes. "You have lived your life. Now take what's left and live it properly." On another page he says, "You could leave life right now, let that determine what you do and say and think." The final two entries in *Meditations*, which may well have been written as he lay dying, pick up the theme again. What does it matter if you live for this long or that long? he asks. The curtain falls on every actor. "But I've only gotten three acts!" he says, giving voice to that part inside all of us that is scared to die.

> Yes. This will be a drama in three acts, the length fixed by the power that directed your creation, and now directs your dissolution. Neither was yours to determine. So make your exit with grace—the same grace shown to you.

To do this would be the final test of this philosopher king, as it was for each of the Stoics and every human being. We all die, we don't control that, but we do influence how we face that death, the courage and poise and compassion we bring to it.

We're told that Marcus was quite sick toward the end, far away from home on the Germanic battlefields, near modern-day Vienna. Worried about spreading whatever he had to his son, and also to avoid any complications about succession, Marcus bade him a tearful goodbye and sent him away to prepare to rule. Even with his own end moments away he was still teaching, still trying to be a philosopher, particularly to his friends, who were bereft with grief. "Why do you weep for me," Marcus asked them, "instead of thinking about the pestilence and about death which is the common lot of us all?" Then, with the dignity of a man who had practiced for this moment many times, he said, "If you now grant me leave to go, I bid you farewell and pass on before."

He would survive a day or so more. Perhaps it was in these last few moments, weak in body but still strong in will, that he jotted down the last words that appear in his *Meditations*—a reminder to himself about staying true to his philosophy:

So make your exit with grace—the same grace shown to you.

Finally, on March 17, 180, at age fifty-eight, he turned to his guard and said, "Go to the rising sun; I am already setting." Then he covered his head to go to sleep and never woke up.

Rome—and us, her descendants—would never see such greatness again.

CONCLUSION

A hundred years before Zeno, in what is now known as Pericles's "Funeral Oration," the great Athenian statesman set out to mourn the loss of so many thousands of his brave countrymen. As he struggled to find the words to express their sacrifice and heroism, he reminded the grieving people of Athens that the glory of the dead was not in their accomplishments or in the monuments that would be erected in their honor, but in the legacy of what they had done for their country. It was their memory, what they inspired, which was "woven into the lives of others." Many centuries later, Jackie Robinson would express the idea even more succinctly. "A life is not important," his tombstone reads, "except in the impact it has on other lives."

So it goes for the Stoics whose lives we have just detailed, men and women whose influence not only continues to this day, but shaped the lives of the other men and women in this book.

Zeno, driven by shipwreck to philosophy, and thus creating a school that has stood for nearly twenty-five hundred years . . .

Cleanthes, whose hard work and frugality quite literally supported Zeno and his studies . . .

Chrysippus, who cleaned up and codified so many of the early Stoic theories . . .

Cato, whose martyrdom did not save the Republic but inspired Seneca, Thrasea, and Agrippinus when they faced their own deaths, and eventually and most powerfully inspired the American revolutionaries to create their own republic in his image . . .

Porcia, who encouraged her husband to strike a blow against tyranny . . .

Rusticus, who passed that copy of Epictetus to Marcus Aurelius . . .

Musonius Rufus, who taught Epictetus in the first place . . .

Epictetus, whose worldview gave Toussaint Louverture and James Stockdale the strength they needed in their dank prison cells . . .

In some cases, their influence came directly through writing, but more often than not, their influence came by action. How they *lived*. What they *did*.

The Stoics had learned this from Socrates. Plutarch, who was the source for so much of the material in this book, observed that "Socrates did not set up desks for his students, sit in a teacher's chair, or reserve a prearranged time for lecturing and walking with his pupils." On the contrary. "He practiced philosophy while joking around," Plutarch said, "and drinking and serving on military campaigns and hanging around the marketplace with some of his students, and finally, even while under arrest and drinking the hemlock. He was the first to demonstrate that our lives are open to philosophy at all times and in every aspect, while experiencing every emotion, and in each and every activity."

Beautiful.

But more beautiful is the impact that example had on Marcus Aurelius, on Zeno, on Musonius Rufus, on Thrasea, and on Rutilius.

The Stoics too served on military campaigns. They hung out in the marketplace. They too, fairly or unfairly, faced arrest and were forced to commit suicide. In this, they proved they were philosophers. In those actions, those choices, they wrote their best work—sometimes in their own blood.

"There is no role so well suited to philosophy as the one you happen to be in right now," Marcus Aurelius would write. He probably meant the *role* of emperor, but the meaning can easily be extended: The role of parent. The role of spouse. The role of a person waiting in line. The role of a person who has just been given bad news. The role of a person who is rich. The role of a person sent into exile or delivered into bankruptcy. The role of a person who finds themselves enslaved, literally or otherwise.

All of this was philosophy. All of this was what made someone a Stoic.

How we do those jobs, how we play those roles, that's what matters. Epictetus, who actually was a slave before he was a philosopher, would tell his students to go out in the world and "eat like a human being, drink like a human being, dress up, marry, have children, get politically active—suffer abuse, bear with a headstrong brother, father, son, neighbor, or companion. Show us these things so we can see that you truly have learned from the philosophers."

By and large, the Stoics showed what they learned from the insights of Zeno, from the five hundred lines that Chrysippus wrote each day, from the some fifty books written by Cleanthes, from the lectures of Epictetus, and from the meditations that Marcus Aurelius penned. They showed what they learned from the example of Cato, from the effortless courage of Agrippinus, and from the cautionary tales of Seneca and Cicero and Diotimus.

Did many of the Stoics fall short? Absolutely. They were tempted by wealth and made embarrassing compromises as they groped for fame. They lost their temper. They lied. They eliminated rivals ... or looked the other way while someone else did. They were silent when they should have spoken up. They enforced laws that they ought to have questioned. They were not always happy; they did not always bear adversity with the dignity one would expect.

The history of Rome is a story of outsized ambition and drive, a tale of power and excess and often brutality. Most of Rome's leaders were monsters, memorable only because of their misdeeds. Even for all the Stoics' flaws, their restraint and goodness stand in stark relief to most of their contemporaries. "How monotonously alike all the great tyrants and conquerors have been," the great C. S. Lewis once observed, "how gloriously different the saints."

No one in this book managed, in every minute of their life, to live up to those lofty virtues of courage and justice and moderation and wisdom. Yet in their unique struggles and triumphs, they each managed to teach us something, proving, intentionally or not, why the principles they purported to believe were superior to the choices they actually made.

Most of all, the Stoics taught us by the fact that they *tried*. What matters is what *we* can learn from their successes and their failures in this lifelong pursuit.

"Show me someone sick and happy," Epictetus said, "in danger and happy, dying and happy, exiled and happy, disgraced and happy. Show me! By God, how much I'd like to see a Stoic. But since you can't show me someone that perfectly formed, at least show me someone actively forming themselves so, inclined in this way. . . . Show me!"

Ultimately, that is the message of this book and what has defined the stories we have told and the figures we have profiled.

We hope these pages contribute to the unbroken chain of influence that these Stoics' lives have had, an influence that remains active to this day. Indeed, one of the most difficult choices made here was the decision not to profile any so-called "modern Stoics" who are continuing to wrestle with, practice, and exemplify Stoic principles in their own lives.

Whether that's media titan Arianna Huffington, who carries a laminated note card of a Marcus Aurelius quote in her purse at all times, or General James Mattis, who has carried Marcus Aurelius's *Meditations* with him on military campaigns for decades, Stoicism is alive and well in the modern world—with all the same brilliance, boldness, and humanness. There are writers like Tim Ferriss who have helped popularize Stoicism to millions, and Laura Kennedy, whose thoughtful "Coping" column runs in *The Irish Times*, and Donald Robertson, who specializes in the treatment of anxiety and the use of cognitive behavioral therapy (CBT).

Chrysippus had been an elite athlete and a Stoic, while today Stoicism is a daily practice for stars in the NFL, the NBA, MLB, World Cup rugby and soccer. Michele Tafoya of *Sunday Night Football* is an active student of the philosophy, which would make Musonius Rufus smile. On the wall of the clubhouse of the Pittsburgh Pirates is a quote from Epictetus: "It's not things that upset us. It's our judgement about things." Zeno and Seneca and Cato and Cicero were Stoics who oversaw enormous fortunes and large business ventures, just as today Silicon Valley entrepreneurs like Kevin Rose and Wall Street billionaires like Thomas Kaplan maintain their own Stoic practices alongside their businesses. Right now in Washington, D.C., there are senators who get together each morning in the Capitol building and discuss Stoicism, just as their counterparts did in Rome thousands of years ago and the founding fathers did in 1776. May the spirit of Helvidius Priscus grow in that chamber.

As was true in the ancient world, there are also countless other Stoics with less glamorous occupations, who nevertheless experience trials and tribulations that they endure thanks to the wisdom these philosophers helped discover. They are parents. They are citizens. They are teachers. They are mortals with the same desires and fears, hopes and dreams as everyone who has ever lived.

Like you, like Seneca, like Epictetus, like Posidonius, they are trying to do the best they can. They are trying to be the best version of themselves they can be. They are reading and practicing, trying and failing, getting back up and trying again.

As we all must do.

And they will ultimately and inevitably—as all the Stoics in this book did—come to the end of their life at some point. Every one of us dies, the Stoics said, but too few of us actually live. Too many of us die before our time, living—unthinkingly—the kind of life that Seneca described as hardly being different than death.

The irony of this book is that while it is about the *lives* of the Stoics, in many cases, the most interesting and significant act in the lives of these men and women was their *death*.

To the Stoics, all of life was a preparation for death. As Cicero had said, to philosophize is to learn how to die. Seneca, even at the height of his powers, was preparing for the close of life. So was Cato. So was Thrasea. So was Zeno. That's how they were able to muster—in that terrifying or sad moment—courage and dignity, cleverness and compassion.

Whether a Stoic died at the hands of a tyrant or from laughing too hard at a good joke—as Chrysippus did—they were teaching us, they were applying what they had studied for so long in the most important of settings.

In a way, that is a fitting lesson to conclude with. Many of the Stoics fell short of their philosophy in life, but there are no Stoics in these pages who did not die well.

Except for Cicero, who wavered at the end, who compromised, who fled. And it should be noted—not smugly, but convincingly—that he was the one lover of Stoicism who could not truly commit, who prescribed the medicine but refused to take it himself.

As Epictetus wrote, "Is it possible to be free from error? Not by any means, but it is possible to be a person stretching to avoid error."

That's what Stoicism is. It's *stretching. Training.* To be better. To get better. To avoid one more mistake, to take one step closer toward that ideal. Not perfection, but progress—that's what each of these *lives* was about.

The only question that remains for us, the living heirs to this tradition: Are we doing that work?

Interested in learning
even more about Stoicism?

Visit

DailyStoic.com/email

to sign up for a daily email,

engage in discussion, get advice,

and more.

THE
DAILY STOIC

366 MEDITATIONS
ON WISDOM,
PERSEVERANCE, AND
THE ART OF LIVING

FEATURING NEW TRANSLATIONS OF
SENECA, EPICTETUS, AND MARCUS AURELIUS

RYAN HOLIDAY
#1 Bestselling Author of *THE OBSTACLE IS THE WAY*
and STEPHEN HANSELMAN

THE
DAILY STOIC
JOURNAL

366 DAYS OF WRITING
AND REFLECTION ON
THE ART OF LIVING

RYAN HOLIDAY
and STEPHEN HANSELMAN
Bestselling authors of *THE DAILY STOIC*

THE WAY,

THE ENEMY,

THE KEY

THE TIMELESS COLLECTION
BY #1 *NEW YORK TIMES* BESTSELLING AUTHOR

RYAN HOLIDAY

RYAN HOLIDAY

THE OBSTACLE IS THE WAY
The Timeless Art of Turning Trials into Triumph

RYAN HOLIDAY

EGO IS THE ENEMY

RYAN HOLIDAY

STILLNESS IS THE KEY

PORTFOLIO
PENGUIN

TIMELINE OF THE STOICS AND THE GRAECO-ROMAN WORLD

Boldface indicates either philosophers who were a universal influence on all Stoics afterward or a Stoic person/place/event.

BC

535–475   **Life of Heraclitus of Ephesus (influenced all the early Stoics)**

490   First Persian invasion of Greece and the Battle of Marathon

470   **Birth of Socrates outside the walls of Athens**

450s   **Completion of the Stoa Poikilē, the famous "painted porch" on the Athenian *agora***

430   Birth of Xenophon of Athens, student of Socrates

412   **Birth of Diogenes of Sinope, founder with Antisthenes and Crates of Thebes of the Cynic school**

399   Trial and execution of Socrates in Athens

387   Plato founds the Academy in Athens

384   Birth of Aristotle in Stagira, Chalkidiki

382   Birth of Antigonus the One-Eyed in Elimiotis, Macedonia

371   Birth of Theophrastus, successor to Aristotle, in Eresos, Lesbos

365   Birth of Crates of Thebes, Cynic student of Diogenes of Sinope

360   Birth of Stilpo of Megara

356   Birth of Alexander the Great in Pella, Macedonia

354   Death of Xenophon, whose book on Socrates would convert Zeno to philosophy

347   Aristotle establishes first school in Assos

343   Aristotle appointed tutor of the young Alexander the Great

336   Philip II of Macedon murdered; Alexander succeeds him

335   Aristotle founds the Lyceum in Athens

334   Birth of Zeno, founding scholarch (official head) of the Stoa, in Kition, Cyprus

333   Alexander liberates Cyprus from Persian rule

330   Birth of Cleanthes, the second scholarch of the Stoa, in Assos

323   Death of Alexander and start of the Wars of Succession

Death of Diogenes of Sinope in Corinth

323–322   Aristotle departs Athens for Chalcis, Euboea, where he dies in 322; Theophrastus succeeds him as head of the Lyceum

312   Zeno arrives in Athens following a shipwreck (following Persaeus's account "at age twenty-two")

Kition's last king, Pumathion, killed by Ptolemy I

306   Epicurus founds his school in Athens

Demetrius the Besieger takes Cyprus from Ptolemy I; declares his father, Antigonus the One-Eyed, king

Birth of Persaeus of Kition, student, roommate, and personal secretary to Zeno

Birth of Aristo of Chios

305–304   Demetrius besieges Rhodes

301   Death of Antigonus the One-Eyed at the Battle of Ipsus, Phrygia

Zeno begins teaching at the Stoa Poikilē

279   **Birth of Chrysippus, the third scholarch of the Stoa, in Soli, Cilicia**

Gauls invade Macedonia, desecrating the royal tombs, killing Karaunos; aborted invasion of Greece

278   Antigonus II Gonatas and Antiochus I reach treaty creating Europe/Asia division

276   Antigonus II reestablished as king of Macedonia

Zeno of Kition and Aratus of Soli invited to Antigonus's court in Pella

Ptolemy II defeated by Antiochus I in Syria

272   Victories by Ptolemy II in southern Anatolia

264   Arcesilaus succeeds as sixth head of the Academy, and is a primary skeptical opponent of the early Stoics

Antigonus II puts Athens under siege (until 262)

262   **Death of Zeno, the founding scholarch of Stoicism, in Athens; succeeded by Cleanthes**

261   Antigonus II defeats the navy of Ptolemy II at the Battle of Cos

256–253   Antigonus II restores Athenian autonomy, pulling his garrison out of Athens

245   Ptolemy III Euergetes appoints Eratosthenes, who studied with Zeno and Aristo, to head of the Library of Alexandria and as tutor to Ptolemy IV Philopator

243   **Death of Zeno's student and roommate Persaeus at battle with Aratus in Corinth**

239   Death of Antigonus II

Seleucus defeated by Antiochus Hierax, retreating to Cilicia

235   Sphaerus joins the court of Cleomenes, king of Sparta

230   Death of Cleanthes in Athens; succeeded by Chrysippus

Birth of Diogenes in Seleucia on the Tigris in Babylon; he would become the fifth scholarch of the Stoa

226   A great quake topples the Colossus of Rhodes

222   Cleomenes III defeated by Antigonus III Doson, escapes to Egypt

Death of Ptolemy III; accession of Ptolemy IV Philopator

Sphaerus follows Cleomenes to Alexandria by invitation of Philopator

214   Carneades, the great Academic skeptic, born in Cyrene (modern-day Libya)

206   Death of Chrysippus in Athens; Zeno of Tarsus succeeds him as fourth scholarch of the Stoa

185   Birth of Panaetius in Rhodes, who would become the seventh and last scholarch of the Stoa

168   Romans defeat Perseus of Macedon, last of the Antigonids, in the Third Macedonian War, occupying Greece and Macedon

Crates of Mallus, a Stoic teacher and head of the Library of Pergamum, is sent by the Attalid king (allies of Rome) on a mission to Rome

158   Birth of Publius Rutilius Rufus

155   Greek philosophy comes to Rome when Athens sends ambassadors from the major schools—Carneades (Academy head), Critolaus (Lyceum head), and Diogenes (Stoa head)—to appeal imposed fine

149–146   Scipio's siege of Carthage

144   Panaetius goes to Rome

142   Death of Diogenes of Babylon; succeeded by Antipater of Tarsus, sixth scholarch of the Stoa

140–138   Panaetius joins Scipio Aemilianus in his mission to the East

140   Archedemus of Tarsus founds a Stoic school in Babylon

138   Rutilius Rufus studies with Panaetius in Rome

135   Birth of Posidonius, the great polymath and disciple of Panaetius, in Apamea, Syria

133   Attalid dynasty cedes all territory to Rome

Death of Tiberius Gracchus and trial of Gaius Blossius, student and friend of Antipater of Tarsus

129   Death of Antipater of Tarsus; succeeded by Panaetius in Athens

Death of Scipio Aemilianus (Scipionic Circle)

Gaius Blossius commits suicide after participating in Aristonicus's failed utopian coup against Rome in Pergamum (132–129)

Death of Carneades, head of the Academy

110   Epicurean philosopher Philodemus born in Gadara, Syria

109   Death of Panaetius in Athens; end of scholarchy, rival teachers carry on Stoic teachings

106   Birth of Cicero

100   Diotimus forges letters of Epicurus

95   Birth of Cato the Younger

88–86   Beginning of First Mithridatic War; Sulla's siege of Athens, scattering of the major schools. Philo of Larissa becomes Cicero's teacher in Rome.

86   Cicero's first book, *De Inventione* (On Rhetorical Invention), completed

79   Cicero visits Rhodes, where he first studies with Posidonius

78   Cicero visits Rutilius Rufus in Smyrna; Rutilius dies not long after

74   Birth of Athenodorus Cananites near Tarsus, Cilicia, a Stoic teacher of Octavian

70   Birth of Porcia Cato

      Birth of Arius Didymus?

60   Stoic teacher Diodotus dies in Cicero's home, leaving him his estate

56   Cicero completes *De Oratore* (On Oratory)

55   Cicero "feasts on the library of Faustus Sulla" near his villa in Cumae, part of the war booty of Sulla's siege of Athens, containing the library of Aristotle among other works

54   Cicero begins *De Re Publica* (On the Republic); publishes in 51 BC

51   Death of Posidonius; Cicero begins *De Legibus* (On Laws)

46   Death of Cato by suicide in Utica, Carthage; Cicero and Brutus write eulogies; Cicero writes *Stoic Paradoxes*

45   Cicero writes *Consolation to Himself* and *Hortensius: An Exhortation to Philosophy* (now lost), *Academica*, and *On Moral Ends*

45–44   Cicero writes *Tusculan Disputations* and *On the Nature of the Gods*

44   Cicero writes *Cato Maior* (On Old Age), *On Divination*, *On Fate*, *On Reputation*, *Topica*, *Laelius* (On Friendship), and *On Duties* (his last book)

      Athenodorus Cananites comes to Rome with young Octavian

43   Death of Cicero by order of Mark Antony

40/35   Philodemus dies in Herculaneum, leaving his library at the Villa of Piso

31   Octavian defeats Mark Antony and Cleopatra at Actium

30   **Octavian enters Alexandria with Arius Didymus**

27   Octavian becomes Augustus, the first Roman emperor

c. 4   **Birth of Seneca in Corduba (modern Córdoba) in southern Spain**

AD

10   **Death of Arius Didymus**

c. 20   **Birth of Gaius Musonius Rufus in Volsinii, Etruria**

c. 35   **Birth of Euphrates of Tyre**

37   Death of Tiberius, succession of Caligula

       Birth of Nero

c. 40   **Birth of Dio Chrysostom in Prusa, Bithynia**

41   Death of Caligula; succeeded by Claudius

       Seneca exiled to Corsica by Claudius

49   **Seneca recalled from Corsica to tutor Nero**

50   **Cornutus begins teaching in Rome, students include Lucan and Persius**

c. 52   Saint Paul appears in court before Seneca's brother Gallio (Acts 18:12–17)

       Before or after this date, Paul gives his sermon on "Mars Hill" (Areopagus) in which he refers to Cleanthes's *Hymn to Zeus*

54   Death of Claudius; succeeded by Nero

55   **Birth of Epictetus in Hierapolis, Phrygia**

60–62   **Gaius Rubellius Plautus sent to exile in Syria by Nero, accompanied by Musonius Rufus**

61   Birth of Pliny the Younger in Como, Italy

62   Plautus executed in Syria by Nero's troops; Musonius Rufus returns to Rome

62–65   Seneca retreats from court life and begins his last flurry of writing, including his *Moral Letters* to Lucilius

64   Great Fire of Rome

65   **Seneca commits suicide under the order of Nero**

65–68   **Musonius Rufus banished by Nero to the island of Gyara**

66   **Death of Thrasea Paetus**

68–69   Nero commits suicide with the assistance of Epaphroditus; succeeded by Galba

        Musonius Rufus returns to Rome under Galba

69   Year of the Four Emperors; Vespasian consolidates power

71   Vespasian banishes all philosophers from Rome except for Musonius Rufus for a time

75   **Vespasian exiles and murders Helvidius Priscus; Musonius Rufus returns to Syria**

78   **Musonius Rufus returns to Rome with the support of Titus**

79   Death of Vespasian; succeeded by Titus

        Eruption of Vesuvius, witnessed by an eighteen-year-old Pliny the Younger

81   Death of Titus; succeeded by Domitian

        Pliny the Younger serves as staff officer to the Gallic Third Legion in Syria, writes about his time with Euphrates there later

85   **Epictetus, already studying with Musonius Rufus, is freed by Epaphroditus, Nero's personal secretary; starts his own school in Rome**

86   **Birth of Arrian, historian and Stoic student of Epictetus who recorded his teachings, in Nicomedia, Bithynia**

93   Domitian banishes philosophers from Rome, including Epictetus, who moves his school to Nicopolis

95   Domitian murders Epaphroditus for his role in Nero's death

96   Death of Domitian; succeeded by Nerva

98   Death of Nerva; succeeded by Trajan

100   Birth of Junius Rusticus, grandson of Arulenus Rusticus, and Stoic mentor of Marcus Aurelius

101   Death of Musonius Rufus?

107–11   Arrian attends Epictetus's lectures in Nicopolis and records them in what will become the *Discourses* and *Handbook*

112/3   Death of Pliny the Younger in Bithynia

117   Death of Trajan; succeeded by Hadrian

118   Euphrates of Tyre commits suicide by drinking hemlock, with Hadrian's blessing

120   Hierocles flourishes, composing his Circles around this time

121   Birth of Marcus Aurelius in Rome on April 26

135   Death of Epictetus

131–37   Arrian appointed governor of Cappadocia by Hadrian

138   Death of Hadrian; succeeded by Antoninus Pius, Marcus Aurelius's adoptive father

161   Death of Antoninus Pius; succeeded by Marcus Aurelius

165   Execution of Justin Martyr by judgment of Junius Rusticus

170   Death of Junius Rusticus

176   Marcus Aurelius reestablishes the four chairs of philosophy in Athens

180   Death of Marcus Aurelius in Vindabona on March 17

197   Tertullian writes positively in Carthage about Cleanthes's theology and Marcus Aurelius's being "a protector" of Christians in his *Apologetics*

c. 200   Sextus Empiricus and Alexander of Aphrodisias write polemics against Stoicism

Clement of Alexandria writes about Stoic philosophical positions in his *Stromata*

Diogenes Laërtius begins the studies that will produce his ***Lives of the Eminent Philosophers***

SOURCES CONSULTED
AND FURTHER READING

Primary Stoic Texts and Histories

Annas, Julia, ed. *Cicero: On Moral Ends*. Cambridge: Cambridge University Press, 2001. Contains a very helpful introduction and timeline of Cicero's writings.

Dyck, Andrew R. *A Commentary on Cicero, De Officiis*. Ann Arbor: University of Michigan Press, 1996.

Edelstein, Ludwig, and I. G. Kidd. *Posidonius*. Vol. 1, *The Fragments*. 2nd ed. Cambridge: Cambridge University Press, 1989.

Graver, Margaret. *Cicero on the Emotions: Tusculan Disputations 3 and 4*. Chicago: University of Chicago Press, 2002.

Graver, Margaret, and A. A. Long, trans. and commentary. *Letters on Ethics by Lucius Annaeus Seneca*. Chicago: University of Chicago Press, 2015.

Kidd, I. G. *Posidonius*. Vol. 2, *The Commentary*. Cambridge: Cambridge University Press, 1988.

———. *Posidonius*. Vol. 3, *The Translation of the Fragments*. Cambridge: Cambridge University Press, 1999.

Loeb Classical Library. Cambridge, MA: Harvard University Press. Includes important doxographical and historical source works such as Diogenes Laërtius, Plutarch, Tacitus, Suetonius, Dio Cassius, Athenaeus, Aulus Gellius, *Historia Augusta,* and others, along with Cicero and the many primary Stoic texts by Seneca, Epictetus, and Marcus Aurelius. www.loebclassics.com.

Long, A. A., trans. *How to Be Free: An Ancient Guide to the Stoic Life, Epictetus' Encheiridion and Selections from Discourses*. Princeton, NJ: Princeton University Press, 2018.

Long, A. A., and D. N. Sedley. *The Hellenistic Philosophers*. 2 vols. Cambridge: Cambridge University Press, 1987.

Lutz, Cora E. *Musonius Rufus: The Roman Socrates*. Yale Classical Studies, vol. 10. New Haven, CT: Yale University Press, 1947. This collection of Musonius's lectures and fragments was reissued without the Otto Hense Greek text under the title *That One Should Disdain Hardships: The Teachings of a Roman Stoic*, with an introduction by Gretchen Reydams-Schils. New Haven, CT: Yale University Press, 2020.

Mensch, Pamela, trans., and James Miller, ed. *Diogenes Laertius' Lives of the Eminent Philosophers*. Oxford: Oxford University Press, 2018. Not only a superb translation, but the collected essays are invaluable.

Pomeroy, A. *Arius Didymus: Epitome of Stoic Ethics*. Atlanta: Society of Biblical Literature, 1999.

Ramelli, I. *Hierocles the Stoic: Elements of Ethics, Fragments and Excerpts*. Atlanta: Society of Biblical Literature, 2009.

Thom, Johan C. *Cleanthes' Hymn to Zeus*. Studies and Texts in Antiquity and Christianity 33. Tübingen: Mohr Siebeck, 2005.

von Arnim, Hans. *Stoicorum Veterum Fragmenta*. Leipzig: Teubner, 1903–5. Reprinted in four volumes by Wipf & Stock, Eugene, OR.

Historical and Intellectual Background

Adams, G. W. *Marcus Aurelius in the Historia Augusta and Beyond*. New York: Lexington Books, 2013.

Algra, K., J. Barnes, J. Mansfeld, and M. Schofield, eds. *The Cambridge History of Hellenistic Philosophy*. Cambridge: Cambridge University Press, 1999.

Arena, Valentina. *Libertas and the Practice of Politics in the Late Roman Republic*. Cambridge: Cambridge University Press, 2012.

Astin, A. E. *Scipio Aemilianus*. Oxford: Oxford University Press, 1967.

Barnes, Jonathan. *Mantissa: Essays in Ancient Philosophy IV*. Edited by Maddalena Bonelli. Oxford: Clarendon Press, 2015.

Barrett, Anthony A. *Agrippina: Sex, Power, and Politics in the Early Empire*. New Haven, CT: Yale University Press, 1996.

Bartsch, Shadi, and Alessandro Schiesaro, eds. *The Cambridge Companion to Seneca*. Cambridge: Cambridge University Press, 2015.

Berthold, Richard M. *Rhodes in the Hellenistic Age*. Ithaca, NY: Cornell University Press, 2009.

Billows, Richard A. *Antigonos the One-Eyed and the Creation of the Hellenistic State*. Berkeley: University of California Press, 1990.

Birley, A. R. *Marcus Aurelius: A Biography*. London: Routledge, 2002.

Branham, R. Bract, and Marie-Odile Goulet-Cazé. *The Cynics: The Cynic Movement in Antiquity and Its Legacy*. Berkeley: University of California Press, 1996.

Davies, Malcolm. "The Hero at the Crossroads: Prodicus and the Choice of Heracles." *Prometheus* 39 (2013): 3–17.

Dawson, Doyne. *Cities of the Gods: Communist Utopias in Greek Thought.* Oxford: Oxford University Press, 1992.

Drinkwater, John F. *Nero: Emperor and Court.* Cambridge: Cambridge University Press, 2019.

Everitt, Anthony. *Cicero: The Life and Times of Rome's Greatest Politician.* New York: Random House, 2003.

Garland, R. *The Piraeus: From the Fifth to the First Century B.C.* London: Bristol Classical Press, 1987.

Gill, C. *The Structured Self in Hellenistic and Roman Thought.* Oxford: Oxford University Press, 2006.

Goodman, Rob, and Jimmy Soni. *Rome's Last Citizen: The Life and Legacy of Cato, Mortal Enemy of Caesar.* New York: Thomas Dunne, 2014.

Grant, Michael. *The Antonines: The Roman Empire in Transition.* London: Routledge, 1994.

Green, Peter. *Alexander to Actium: The Historical Evolution of the Hellenistic Age.* Berkeley: University of California Press, 1990.

Griffin, Miriam, and Jonathan Barnes, eds. *Philosophia Togata I: Essays on Philosophy and Roman Society.* Oxford: Clarendon Press, 1996.

Haskell, H. J. *This Was Cicero: Modern Politics in a Roman Toga.* New York: Alfred A. Knopf, 1942.

Laffranque, Marie. *Poseidonios D'Apamée.* Presses Universitaires de France, 1964.

Lavery, Gerard. "Cicero's Philarchia and Marius." *Greece & Rome* 18, no. 2 (1971): 133–42.

Millar, Fergus. *The Roman Near East: 31 BC–AD 337.* Cambridge, MA: Harvard University Press, 1993.

Mitchison, Naomi. *The Blood of the Martyrs.* Edinburgh: Canongate, 1988. First published 1939.

Morford, Mark. *The Roman Philosophers: From the Time of Cato the Censor to the Death of Marcus Aurelius.* London: Routledge, 2002.

Nussbaum, M. *The Therapy of Desire.* Princeton, NJ: Princeton University Press, 1994.

Quinn, Josephine C. *In Search of the Phoenicians.* Princeton, NJ: Princeton University Press, 2018.

Raven, James, ed. *Lost Libraries: The Destruction of Great Book Collections Since Antiquity.* London: Palgrave Macmillan, 2004. In particular, chapter 3, T. Keith Dix, "Aristotle's Peripatetic Library."

Rawson, Elizabeth. *Cicero: A Portrait.* London: Bristol Classical Press, 1994. Originally published 1975.

———. *Intellectual Life in the Late Roman Republic.* London: Duckworth, 2013. Originally published 1985.

Romm, James S. *Dying Every Day: Seneca at the Court of Nero.* New York: Alfred A. Knopf, 2014.

Sedley, David. "Philodemus and the Decentralisation of Philosophy." *Cronache Ercolanesi* 33 (2003): 31–41.

Smith, William, ed. *A Dictionary of Greek and Roman Biography and Mythology.* 3 vols. London: I. B. Tauris, 2007. Originially published 1849.

———. *A Dictionary of Greek and Roman Antiquities*. 2 vols. Cambridge: Cambridge University Press, 2013. Originally published 1842.

Striker, G. *Essays on Hellenistic Epistemology and Ethics*. Cambridge: Cambridge University Press, 1996.

Williams, Gareth D., and Katherina Volk. *Roman Reflections: Studies in Latin Philosophy*. Oxford: Oxford University Press, 2015.

Wilson, Emily. *The Greatest Empire: A Life of Seneca*. New York: Oxford University Press, 2014.

Woolmer, Mark. *A Short History of the Phoenicians*. London: I. B. Tauris, 2017.

Works on Stoicism

Bobzien, Susanne. *Determinism and Freedom in Stoic Philosophy*. Oxford: Clarendon Press, 2001.

Brennan, T. *The Stoic Life*. Oxford: Oxford University Press, 2005.

Brunt, P. A. *Studies in Stoicism*. Edited by Miriam Griffin and Alison Samuels. Oxford: Oxford University Press, 2013.

Colish, Marcia L. *The Stoic Tradition from Antiquity to the Early Middle Ages*. Vol. 1, *Stoicism in Classical Latin Literature*. Leiden: E. J. Brill, 1985.

———. *The Stoic Tradition from Antiquity to the Early Middle Ages*. Vol. 2, *Stoicism in Christian Latin Thought Through the Sixth Century*. Leiden: E. J. Brill, 1985.

Edelstein, Ludwig. *The Meaning of Stoicism*. Martin Classical Lectures, vol. XXI. Cambridge, MA: Harvard University Press, 1966.

Engberg-Pedersen, T. *Paul and the Stoics*. Louisville, KY: Westminster John Knox Press, 2000.

Erskine, Andrew. *The Hellenistic Stoa: Political Thought and Action*. Ithaca: Cornell University Press, 1990.

Gould, Josiah B. *The Philosophy of Chrysippus*. Albany: State University of New York Press, 1970.

Graver, Margaret. *Stoicism and Emotion*. Chicago: University of Chicago Press, 2007.

Hadot, P. *The Inner Citadel: The Meditations of Marcus Aurelius*. Translated by Michael Chase. Cambridge, MA: Harvard University Press, 1998.

Hahm, David E. "Posidonius' Theory of Historical Causation." In *Aufstieg und Niedergang der Romischen Welt*, II.36.3, pp. 1325–63. Berlin: De Gruyter, 1989.

———. "Diogenes Laertius VII: On the Stoics." In *Aufstieg und Niedergang der Romischen Welt*, II.36.6, pp. 4076–182, indices pp. 4404–11. Berlin: De Gruyter, 1992.

Ierodiakoou, Katerina. *Topics in Stoic Philosophy*. Oxford: Oxford University Press, 1999.

Inwood, B. *The Cambridge Companion to the Stoics*. Cambridge: Cambridge University Press, 2003.

Jackson-McCabe, Matt. "The Stoic Theory of Implanted Preconceptions." *Phronesis* 49, no. 4 (2004): 323–47.

Jedan, Christophe. *Stoic Virtues: Chrysippus and the Religious Character of Stoic Ethics*. London: Continuum, 2009.

Klein, Jacob. "The Stoic Argument from Oikeiōsis." *Oxford Studies in Ancient Philosophy* 50 (2016): 143–200.

Long, A. A. *Hellenistic Philosophy: Stoics, Epicureans, Skeptics.* 2nd ed. London: Duckworth, 1986.

———. *Problems in Stoicism.* London: Continuum, 2000.

———. *Stoic Studies.* Berkeley: University of California Press, 2001.

———. *From Epicurus to Epictetus: Studies in Hellenistic and Roman Philosophy.* Oxford: Oxford University Press, 2006.

———. *Greek Models of Mind and Self.* Cambridge, MA: Harvard University Press, 2015.

Long, A. G., ed. *Plato and the Stoics.* Cambridge: Cambridge University Press, 2013.

Meijer, P. A. *Stoic Theology: Proofs for the Existence of the Cosmic God and of the Traditional Gods.* Delft: Eburon, 2007.

Motto, Anna Lydia. *Seneca Sourcebook: Guide to the Thought of Lucius Annaeus Seneca.* Amsterdam: Adolf M. Hakkert, 1970.

Newman, Robert J. "Cotidie Meditare: Theory and Practice of the Meditation in Imperial Stoicism." In *Aufstieg und Niedergang der Romischen Welt,* II.36.3. Berlin: De Gruyter, 1989.

Obbink, Dirk, and Paul A. Vander Waerdt. "Diogenes of Babylon: The Stoic Sage in the City of Fools." *Greek, Roman, and Byzantine Studies* 32, no. 4 (1991): 355–96.

Papazian, Michael. "The Ontological Argument of Diogenes of Babylon." *Phronesis* 52, no. 2 (2007): 188–209.

Reydams-Schils, Gretchen. *The Roman Stoics: Self, Responsibility, and Affection.* Chicago: University of Chicago Press, 2005.

———. "Philosophy and Education in Stoicism of the Roman Imperial Era." *Oxford Review of Education* 36, no. 5 (2010): 561–74.

Robertson, Donald. *How to Think Like a Roman Emperor: The Stoic Philosophy of Marcus Aurelius.* New York: St. Martin's Press, 2019.

Sambursky, Samuel. *The Physics of the Stoics.* London: Routledge, 1959.

Sandbach, F. H. *The Stoics.* 2nd ed. London: Duckworth, 1994.

Scaltsas, Theodore, and Andrew S. Mason, eds. *The Philosophy of Epictetus.* Oxford: Oxford University Press, 2007.

Schofield, M. *The Stoic Idea of the City.* Chicago: University of Chicago Press, 1999.

Schofield, M., and G. Striker, eds. *The Norms of Nature.* Cambridge: Cambridge University Press, 1986.

Sellars, J. *Stoicism.* Berkeley and Durham: University of California Press and Acumen, UK, 2006.

———. "Stoic Cosmopolitanism and Zeno's 'Republic.'" *History of Political Thought* 28, no. 1 (2007): 1–29.

———. *The Art of Living: The Stoics on the Nature and Function of Philosophy.* London: Bloomsbury, 2013.

———. *Hellenistic Philosophy.* Oxford: Oxford University Press, 2018.

Sorabji, Richard. *Emotion and Peace of Mind: From Stoic Agitation to Christian Temptation.* Oxford: Oxford University Press, 2000.

Star, Christopher. *The Empire of the Self: Self-Command and Political Speech in Seneca and Petronius.* Baltimore: Johns Hopkins University Press, 2012.

Stephens, W. O. *Epictetus and Happiness as Freedom.* London: Continuum, 2007.

Valantasis, Richard. "Musonius Rufus and Roman Ascetical Theory." *Greek, Roman, and Byzantine Studies* 40 (2001).

Weiss, Robin. "The Stoics and the Practical: A Roman Reply to Aristotle." DePaul College of Liberal Arts and Social Sciences, Theses and Dissertations, Paper 143 (2013), http://via.library.depaul.edu/etd/143.

INDEX OF STOICS

Page numbers in **boldface** refer to dedicated chapters.